The Rise of Business Ethics

In 1973, Daniel Bell argued that corporations in post-industrial societies increasingly needed to behave in accord with widely accepted social norms, particularly in terms of ethical behaviour and social responsibility. Yet widespread criticism of business behaviour was not an invention of the 1960s and 1970s or a product of changing commercial norms. The key feature historically has been business scandal. Understandings of how the field of business ethics has emerged are undeveloped, however.

This book is the first attempt to explain the conditions which saw a focus develop on business ethics, especially in the 1960s and 1970s, and how the broader field developed to encompass related notions such as corporate governance, corporate social responsibility, ethical leadership, sustainable business and responsible management education.

The Rise of Business Ethics provides an introduction and analysis of the key developments in contemporary business ethics by examining them in terms of their diachronic development—the key thinkers, the key issues, the key institutions and how they each contributed to contemporary understandings of business ethics, governance and practice. Addressing the topic from a European as well as a North American perspective, *The Rise of Business Ethics* will be of interest to researchers, academics and students in the fields of business ethics, business and society, business history, organization studies and political economy.

Bernard Mees is an Associate Professor of Management at the University of Tasmania, Hobart, Australia.

Routledge Studies in Business Ethics

Business ethics is a site of contestation, both in theory and practice. For some it serves as a salve for the worst effects of capitalism, giving businesses the means to self-regulate away from entrenched tendencies of malfeasance and exploitation. For others business ethics is a more personal matter, concerning the way that individuals can effectively wade through the moral quagmires that characterise so many dimensions of business life. Business ethics has also been conceived of as a fig leaf designed to allow business-as-usual to continue while covering over the less savoury practices so as to create an appearance of righteousness.

Across these and other approaches, what remains critical is to ensure that the ethics of business is the subject of incisive questioning, critical research, and diverse theoretical development. It is through such scholarly inquiry that the increasingly powerful purview of corporations and business activity can be interrogated, understood and, ultimately, reformulated. This series contributes to that goal by publishing the latest research and thinking across the broad terrain that characterised business ethics.

The series welcomes contributions in areas including: corporate social responsibility; critical approaches to business ethics; ethics and corporate governance; ethics and diversity; feminist ethics; globalization and business ethics; philosophical traditions of business ethics; postcolonialism and the ethics of business; production and supply chain ethics; resistance, political activism and ethics; sustainability, environmentalism and climate change; the ethics of corporate misconduct; the politics of business ethics; and worker's rights.

Disturbing Business Ethics
Emmanuel Levinas and the Politics of Organization
Carl Rhodes

The Rise of Business Ethics
Bernard Mees

For more information about this series, please visit: www.routledge.com/ Routledge-Studies-in-Business-Ethics/book-series/SE0900

The Rise of Business Ethics

Bernard Mees

Routledge
Taylor & Francis Group

NEW YORK AND LONDON

First published 2020
by Routledge
52 Vanderbilt Avenue, New York, NY 10017

and by Routledge
2 Park Square, Milton Park, Abingdon, Oxon, OX14 4RN

Routledge is an imprint of the Taylor & Francis Group, an informa business

First issued in paperback 2021

Library of Congress Cataloging-in-Publication Data
A catalog record for this book has been requested

ISBN: 978-1-138-61407-9 (hbk)
ISBN: 978-1-03-208273-8 (pbk)
ISBN: 978-0-429-46422-5 (ebk)

Typeset in Sabon
by Apex CoVantage, LLC

Contents

Acknowledgments

The ideas presented in this book reflect a long intellectual process. Upon becoming responsible for teaching a course on business ethics in 2008, it quickly became apparent to me that the field lacked a proper history. As a historian of ideas who had somehow ended up in a business school, this struck me as representing a considerable opportunity. But I had never been very comfortable with ethics as it was taught in philosophy departments.

My first teachers in ethics at university were Robin Jackson and Chris Mackie, who introduced me to Socrates and Plato while I was an undergraduate student at the University of Melbourne. I also took courses with Tim Mehigan and Gerhard Schultz, which first exposed me to the German tradition. Brian Scarlett provided my first insight into Aquinas during my honours year and I know most of what I remember about Martin Luther and John Calvin from Charles Zika's subjects on the Reformation. I may have been the only person in the School of Management who had formally studied ethics as an undergraduate at the time I started fulltime as a lecturer at the Royal Melbourne Institute of Technology.

At RMIT, Eva Tsahuridu introduced me to the ethical decision-making literature and George Cairns revived my interest in prudence. Ben Reynolds helped me put together my thoughts on ethical leadership, and any number of colleagues gave me useful advice as I presented some of my preliminary ideas at conferences. Many of the students, tutors and other colleagues I have taught with at RMIT and the University of Tasmania have also influenced the development of this book. David Varley at Routledge approached me to write a monograph on the topic after I had contributed two chapters to Routledge Companions on the history of business ethics—the *Routledge Companion to Business History* and the *Routledge Companion to Business Ethics* (Mees 2017a, 2018).

Outside the confines of university life, my late brother Paul was the first person to introduce me to Jacques Maritain and Catholic social thought. I still use my father Tom's old copy of Plato's *Republic*, and I owe most of what I know about 1950s Catholicism to my mother Roma. It is the 100th anniversary this year of when my grandfathers Ben Mees and Reg Kelly returned home from the First World War after serving in the Royal Navy and the Australian Imperial Force respectively. But the person who has most influenced the writing of this book is my partner Katy.

Preface

Among the photographs I have inherited from my grandmother Dail is one of her Irish cousin, Mother Kevin O'Donnell. Mother Kevin's main accomplishment, if I remember correctly, was that she nursed Pope Pius XII when he was ill in Rome. Pius XII was one of the most popular of the popes, a key figure in that 1950s world, now long gone, that I have only experienced second hand. It was a time of "thick Catholicism" that I know especially through photos and memories of stories I learned from older generations of my family.

I did not expect to come across Pius XII while researching this book, but his 1949 address to Catholic employers occurred at a key moment in the history of business ethics. Despite coming from an Irish Catholic family, Catholic social teaching was not something I remembered from school. Liberation theology was all the rage when I was growing up, but I only knew what "subsidiarity" was because my eldest brother was a political Catholic of the Dorothy Day variety.

The Catholic tradition of business ethics was missing from most of the accounts I read while preparing to write this book, however. A range of studies of business ethics had been published in Europe in the 1920s and 1930s, but they were never referred to in English-language sources. French academics were teaching courses in business ethics well before their British counterparts were, and German-language considerations of the interest groups affected by business seemed to predate the American fascination with "stakeholder theory". Was this just another anti-Catholic thing, or was it most readily explained as due to the language barrier?

American business ethics also turned out to be substantially Catholic, however. The first textbook published on the topic in the 1950s was full of references to Jacques Maritain and St Thomas Aquinas, and a famous survey of *Harvard Business Review* readers in 1961 had been undertaken by a Jesuit doctoral student. Pius XII's 1949 address to Catholic employers was published in the French Canadian journal *Relations industrielles*, and many of the key Protestant expressions of social responsibility and business ethics seemed to reflect responses to Catholic initiatives. The intellectual genealogy of business ethics looked less and less like that explained in the standard accounts.

At university I had been taught the usual secular narrative: that the French Revolution had thrown off Catholic superstition and that Anglo-Saxon Protestantism was the only progressive force in world history other than Marxism. But where had the Society of St Vincent de Paul come from, the largest charity in Australia? I increasingly found that secular and Protestant scholarship was often blinkered. It reacted against Catholic tradition and did not understand it. As in many other Western countries, Catholics dominated the more conservative wing of the trade union movement in Australia, but this was a matter for sneering among most of my colleagues—unionists of this type were social conservatives who weren't really part of the Left. Yet not only did Catholic social doctrine support trade unionism, but in some countries trade unions had been established by Catholic priests in accord with papal doctrine.

The Protestant tradition of business ethics was harder to discern. There was much talk of Protestant notions of "stewardship", but this focus seemed to stem from the writings of John Wesley, and the Protestant work ethic extolled by Max Weber didn't really seem very Christian to me at all. At any rate, most of the early leaders of Protestantism seemed to loathe one another. There is a park in Switzerland I've visited that has statues of Luther, Calvin and Zwingli in it, three figures who no doubt would have tried to throttle each other if they had been given the chance. With such disagreement among key Protestant denominations, was it actually possible to talk about a "Protestant business ethics"?

The best intellectual history, however, is one that tries to found itself in a strong sense of biography. Kant's notion of moral imagination was borrowed into history by German scholars in the late nineteenth century and into the English tradition by R.G. Collingwood (1946). Trying to navigate the history of ideas through a closer understanding of the lives of figures who made key contributions to intellectual production is typically a more rewarding manner in which to understand its course. Getting to know all that you can about a figure such as Edgar Heermance is more useful than wondering about how other Congregationalist pastors (or other alumnae of the Yale Divinity School) viewed business ethics. In keeping with the common practice of intellectual history, I have attempted to remain as faithful to actual texts and the influences these texts actually cite than by allowing broader assumptions to dictate my narrative.

My previous book in intellectual history, *The Science of the Swastika* (2008), focuses mostly on Germany. But this time I have tried to bring in other European traditions whenever I can. I would have liked to spend more time reading about Scandinavian responses to unethical business practice and South American debates over social justice. The business world is increasingly monolingual, and witnessing so many European business ethicists claim that the history of the field in their country began in the 1980s when the first American-style conference was held reminds me how much each of these communities has forgotten about their own traditions. More should also be written about the development of business ethics in Asia and Africa as well as South America. But both business history and business ethics are often neglected in business schools. Deans want more staff who can teach entrepreneurship, leadership and strategy, not the history of business or business ethics, less so (presumably) an amalgam of the two. An academic field without much of a sense of its own history, however, is not much of a discipline at all—it is difficult to be critical and reflective if you lack historical perspective. We cannot know the future, but we can learn about the past, and most of us recognise that we receive our sense of ethics predominately from our parents, not in a manner ignorant of our intellectual upbringing.

1   Introduction

Business ethics, like business regulation, has largely evolved as a corrective reaction to perceived wrongdoing by businesses. It principally represents a form of self-regulation, but business ethics is not a concept restricted merely to commercial actors. More broadly taken, business ethics also reflects a significant tradition of external criticism (or moralising) by members of society not directly involved in commerce—including journalists, clerics, social theorists, public officials and other commentators. Whether it is described as *La morale des affaires* (as in French), *Wirtschaftsethik* (in German) or *ética degli affari* (in Italian), the concept has a recognisable genealogy that dates back to the nineteenth century. What constitutes business ethics exactly has long been a matter of dispute, with little agreement arising over where business ethics sits in relation to applied philosophy, political economy, industrial relations, economics or other related disciplinary concerns. Historically, business ethics has been influenced by intrusions from all of these intellectual traditions, but it is generally recognised to be a separate matter from each of these related fields of inquiry, each of which has a different and discrete origin, focus and historical identity.

Business ethics has also long been seen to be a part of business education, particularly at university level. But the emergence of business ethics as a field of research and study is a product of more widespread concern at insufficient focus on moral standards in commercial life. Business practice has always had to change as social norms develop, but the great expansion in size and scope of commercial enterprises since the beginning of the twentieth century has seen business ethics and a broader concern with the ethical behaviour of commercial actors develop remarkably, first in Europe and the United States, and then more broadly internationally. Previous studies of the history of business ethics have not typically been contextualised within the broader notion of a history of ideas, however, or in terms of the development of the Western intellectual tradition more generally. Secularisation has also been a key feature of the development of ethics in the West, and particularly so in business as specialists in a secular form of business ethics emerged first in American universities.

Over the course of the twentieth century, business ethics became increasingly divorced from its basis in religious tradition, not just in Western countries, but also internationally.

Yet the intellectual history of ethics is part of the broader history of ideas and has had a particularly important influence on it, especially in terms of the reception of the approach of the nineteenth-century German philosopher Friedrich Nietzsche. Nietzsche's *On the Genealogy of Morals* (1887) is subtitled "a polemic"; it is an attack on Christianity. Its main argument was that Christianity was created by a cabal of priests in order to imprison the powerless in a system of self-defeating resentment, a conspiracy theory of the worst kind. A superb stylist with a talent for coining aphorisms, Nietzsche had always proved profoundly good at causing offense. His claims that "all moral philosophy hitherto has been tedious" and "God is dead . . . who will wipe this blood off us?" did not win him many friends (Nietzsche 1882, 181; 1886, 173). By the time of his death in 1900, Nietzsche had alienated most of his previous supporters. Unable to find a position in the university system, his works barely sold out their lowly initial print runs.

In the twentieth century, however, Nietzsche was lionised, first by the Nazis (Whyte 2008) and later by left-wing university professors—most notably among the latter Michel Foucault (Foucault 1977). Foucault's *Archaeology of Knowledge* (1969) is the most important methodological work in intellectual history in living memory, and for Foucault, the key contribution of Nietzsche was his conception of genealogy. Morality, as Nietzsche claimed, was an ever-changing phenomenon, influenced by key historical developments—of ruptures as well as continuities. It was certainly not a product of uniform human advancement. Where traditional Christian morality was argued by the medieval philosopher St Thomas Aquinas to be the product of a universal ethical rationality (Aquinas 1952, I 79), Nietzsche argued that Christianity promoted a "slave morality" in opposition to the "masterly morality" that had typified earlier European society.

While Enlightenment thinkers generally acceded to the argument of Nicholas de Condorcet (1795) that morality, like science, was cumulatively progressing, Nietzsche did not accept this myth of moral progress. According to Nietzsche, ideas such as compassion had their origin in the resentment held by slaves of their masters. His ugly analysis of the history of morality was founded on the truism that ethical standards had changed (and, according to Nietzsche, not necessarily always for the better) since the times of Homer and the highest points reached by ancient Greek civilisation. Nietzsche criticised the rise of Christian ethics as well as the scientism of atheists, seeing the ultimate goal of human flourishing in the "supermen" of the arts—the Rembrandts, the Goethes and the Wagners. His vision of morality was a heroic cultural concern, not an ethics of altruism or social justice. Both fascinating and at the same time repulsive, Nietzsche's *Genealogy of Morals* remains a foundational contribution to the history of ideas.

More recent attempts to prove that moral standards have improved as advancements in science have continued are similarly dismissed by many modern critics. The British philosopher John Gray (2012) argues that history is not amenable to explanations founded in scientism any more than it is considered proper (any longer) to invoke the will of God as determining the course of history. Does modern Islamic terrorism really constitute an ethical improvement on the wave of political murders perpetrated by nineteenth-century anarchists? Does mass, on-demand abortion truly represent a moral advance on previous attempts to focus more profoundly on the rights of the unborn child? These remain matters of contest and debate, no matter one's political opinion. How would we judge objectively whether the current practice regarding issues of this nature truly represent moral progress?

Business ethics entails a concern similar to that promoted over a century ago by Nietzsche. Unlike in Nietzsche's approach, however, business ethics attempts to be practical, restrained and respectable—it does not yell at business, nor does it seek to act as an apology for it. Business ethics as a field of research and study is a product of more widespread concern with the moral standards of contemporary business life. The sound and light of business studies remains entrepreneurship, leadership and strategy—all themes that seem more Nietzschean than most contemporary business ethics discourse does. Business ethics has clearer links to sophisticated intellectual traditions than many other aspects of business scholarship, but it emphasises a kind of morality that was dismissed by Nietzsche as being inspired by the ethical deliberations of the resentful.

Business ethics is described by the editors of the *Routledge Companion to Business Ethics* as a discipline focused on "the morals of commercial and corporate conduct" (Heath et al. 2018, 1). But business ethics is mostly dismissed by critics of contemporary commercial life. Commercial practice has always had to change as social norms develop—the outlawing of slavery in the British Empire at the beginning of the nineteenth century was perhaps the most important break with long-standing norms of commercial practice ever witnessed in the West. It is the great expansion in size and scope of corporations since the beginning of the twentieth century, however, that has seen business ethics and a broader concern with the moral behaviour of large commercial enterprises develop so remarkably, first influentially in the United States, and then more broadly internationally. It might be thought, therefore, that a comprehensive survey of American corporate responsibility, such as that of Archie Carroll and colleagues (2012), might be able to serve as a handbook of the history of business ethics. Business ethics could be seen as a reflection of globalisation or its earlier reflection Fordism—a development of the spread of American business norms internationally via the medium of multinational corporations.

Yet the rise of business ethics is not just a reflection of criticism of corporate behaviour in the United States, but also, somewhat perversely, of the rise of the modern business school. Business schools were initially founded to meet the labour needs of managerial capitalism, and business ethics has largely developed most recently as a discourse institutionalised in business schools. Very few philosophers gave much consideration to questions of business morality before the later decades of the twentieth century—and what sustained ethical thought as has been excavated by historians of the ethics of business before Nietzsche's day has tended to be described as belonging to a tradition of "commercial ethics", separating it from the more recent concerns typical of business school education (Mees 2018). From this perspective, business ethics is typically seen as a distinctly American development that spread across the Atlantic to Europe during the late twentieth century and, under the influence of business schools, has become a key part of global business education.

A closer study of business history reveals that this Americanising narrative is unduly occlusive, however—it shuts out other traditions and influences. In 1973, the American sociologist Daniel Bell argued that businesses in post-industrial societies would face increasingly widespread calls to behave in accord with broadly accepted social norms (Bell 1973). Yet widespread criticism of business behaviour was not an invention of American society in the 1960s and 1970s or a product of increasing educational norms. The key feature historically has been business scandal and the reactions to it that emerged in Western countries since the late nineteenth century. As Aquinas adumbrated in the Middle Ages, all of the world's major religious and philosophical traditions include general prohibitions on thievery, dishonesty, exploitation and cruelty (Aquinas 1952, I, 79). It is also wrong to suppose that business ethics was originally a product of American business schools. But while morality is a universal human notion, the idea that university students should undertake studies in business ethics is not. It has been most strongly influenced by American developments, but business ethics is not merely a reflection of business pedagogy or economic globalisation. It has its own genealogy (in the Nietzschean sense), and it has clearly describable characteristics and developments that are not all to be accorded products of Americanisation.

The first considerations of business ethics date to the late nineteenth century and were often quite broadly focused. The Columbia University economist John B. Clark's article "Business Ethics, Past and Present" which appeared in *The New Englander* in 1879 was a study of competition, but a more specific focus on the morals of proper business practice is already evident in works such as the Philadelphian real estate conveyancer Charles Rhoads's 1882 pamphlet *Business Ethics in Relation to the*

Profession of the Religious Society of Friends (Abend 2014, 120–1). The first publications with similar titles in Continental European languages ranged from Paul Gaultier's article "La morale des affaires", a criticism of American business in the *Revue bleue* from 1904, to the use of the German description *Wirtschaftsethik* by the Austrian theologian Ignaz Seipel which appeared in the name of his professional doctorate (*Habilitations-schrift*) on early Christian moral thinking on economic matters (Seipel 1907). The German term *Wirtschaftsethik* literally means "economic ethics" and sometimes seems closer in meaning to political economy than to business ethics. But a recent handbook on *Wirtschaftsethik*, edited by the Technical University of Dresden business ethicist Michael S. Aßländer (2011), features entries on topics such as corporate social responsibility, ethics codes, whistleblowing and sustainability reporting, and the German Jesuit philosopher Oswald von Nell-Breuning's 1928 doctoral dissertation on the ethics of stock-market speculation first appeared in a monographic series of Studien zur Katholischen Sozial- und Wirtschafts-ethik (Studies on Catholic Social and Business Ethics). Banned from publishing by the Nazis from 1936 to 1945, Nell-Breuning was one of the leading figures in the Continental European tradition of attempting to reconcile modern business practice with the moral teachings of the Catholic Church (Nell-Breuning 1928; Hagedorn 2018).

Another of the drawbacks in contemporary accounts of business ethics has been the failure of most treatments to explain ethical understandings that are widely present (as opposed to lacking) today in the business world. For example, the earliest recorded instance of an ethical judgement that might still be characterised as an essential part of business morality appears in Samuel Noah Kramer's bestselling *History Begins at Sumer* (Kramer 1956). The ancient Sumerian text that Kramer labels "The Pickaxe and the Plow: Labor's first victory" preserves a disputation from the third millennium BC. It begins with a pickaxe challenging a plough to see which implement is superior. The plough states that it is "the faithful farmer of mankind . . . the great nobles walk by my side, All the lands are full of admiration". The pickaxe, retorts in turn, that it is used in many more industries than the plough is, and furthermore:

> You, whose accomplishments are meager
> (but) whose ways are proud,
> My working time is twelve months,
> (But) the time you are present (for work) is four months,
> (While) the time you disappear is eight months,
> You are absent twice the time you are present.

The response of the plough (if any) is not recorded. The pickaxe won its case not just by arguing its broader utility, but particularly by asserting that a pickaxe is morally better because it works much longer hours.

A more developed sense of the valuing of industriousness can be recognised in the Parable of the Talents, a passage recorded in the Gospel
of Matthew as one of the key lessons told by Jesus (Matthew 25:14–30).
The parables of the New Testament are often set in commercial environments, and the Parable of the Talents (along with the Parable of the
Good Samaritan) is one of the two best-known teachings of Jesus. A talent in Biblical times was a large sum of money—the modern metaphori-
cal meaning of the term in English (used in expressions such as "talent
management") derives from this passage:

> a man going on a journey . . . called his servants and entrusted to
> them his property. To one he gave five talents, to another two, to
> another one, to each according to his ability . . .
>
> after a long time the master of those servants came [back] and set-
> tled accounts with them. He who had received the five talents came
> forward, bringing five talents more. . . . And he who had the two tal-
> ents came forward, saying, "Master, you delivered to me two talents;
> here, I have made two talents more". . . .
>
> He who had received the one talent also came forward, saying,
> "Master, I knew you to be a hard man, reaping where you did not
> sow, and gathering where you scattered no seed, so I was afraid, and
> I went and hid your talent in the ground. Here, you have what is
> yours." But his master answered him, "You wicked and slothful ser-
> vant! . . . cast the worthless servant into the outer darkness."
>
> (Matthew 25:14–30)

In the traditional Christian valuation, not only should industriousness be
rewarded, individuals who waste the gifts God has bestowed on them are
condemned to be cast out into a place where "there will be weeping and
gnashing of teeth" (Matthew 25:30).

Other global religious traditions feature their own particular teachings
about business and morality. Buddhism, for example, includes *sammā-
ājīva*, "right livelihood", as one of the principles of *sīla*, or "ethical conduct", in its *ariyo aṭṭhaṅgiko maggo*, or "noble eightfold path". "Right
livelihood" is defined negatively as that which does not include "Business in weapons, business in human beings, business in meat, business
in intoxicants and business in poison" in the Pali tradition (Aṅguttara
Nikāya 5.177, Brown 2008). There is a great amount of traditional religious teaching concerning proper business practice internationally. But
with the contemporary commercial system having such obvious Western
foundations, it has usually been supposed that any genealogy of contemporary business ethics should be primarily sought in the Western tradition. In fact, it has long been accepted that it was a particularly Western
and Christian focus on the moral valuing of hard work that led to the
development of capitalism.

By the eighteenth century, the Biblical notion that hard work should be rewarded had developed to such a stage in many Western countries that any idleness could be seen as wasteful. Max Weber summed up this development in his *Protestant Ethic and the Spirit of Capitalism* (Weber 1904/5) by citing the American revolutionary and statesman Benjamin Franklin. Weber stressed the importance of Martin Luther's teaching that any business occupation could be seen as a vocation (or calling from God), based on Luther's (1518) interpretation of 1 Corinthians 7:17: "Only let each person lead the life that the Lord has assigned to him, and to which God has called him". But by the eighteenth century, the connection between work and Christian religious teaching had developed into a focus on industriousness and thrift. In a short essay addressed to "those that Would be Rich", Franklin summed up his understanding of hard work and saving in terms of small and substantial sums of money: of groats (i.e. fourpence), shillings and pounds (Franklin 1736, 56):

> He that spends a groat a day idly, spends idly above six pounds a year, which is the price [in interest] for the use of one hundred pounds [of credit]. . . .
> He that idly loses five shilling's worth of time, loses five shillings, and might as prudently throw five shillings into the sea.
> He that loses five shillings, not only loses that sum, but all the advantage that might be made by turning it in dealing, which by the time that a young man becomes old, will amount to a considerable amount of money.

Laziness and waste were not just immoral, they went against good business sense.

But the moral imagination of the Western businessman did not end with the extolling of hard work and saving by figures such as Franklin. Rather than deprecating it as representing a morality of slaves, Weber exalted Christianity by arguing that Luther's teaching was the source of the work ethic upon which capitalism was founded. A religiously informed valuing of work, particularly prevalent among Protestants, was essential to understanding the origins of modern industrial society.

By 1956, Weber's notion of a Protestant work ethic had become so dominant in American thought that a survey of American business ethics from that year led by the Harvard University sociologist Francis X. Sutton (Sutton et al. 1956) concluded that the valuing of hard work was the only moral principle broadly upheld in commercial life at the time. But there was little sense that moral philosophers were interested in the ethical reasoning of American businessmen during the 1950s. Instead, religious figures, business leaders and business school educators were the main proponents of business ethics in the immediate post-war period.

The first attempt to describe the changes that had occurred in business ethics since Franklin's day was by the American historian Morrell Heald. Heald's *Social Responsibilities of Business* (1970) was "a study of the ideas and activities through which American businessmen, in the course of the first sixty years of the twentieth century, have attempted to define and respond to the relationship of their firms to the surrounding community" (Heald 1970, x). A more recent publication in the same vein was produced by Carroll and colleagues in 2012 under the auspices of the Center for Ethical Business Cultures at St Thomas University in Minneapolis, Minnesota, funded by Harry Halloran, an energy industry executive and former Augustine seminary student. Carroll's team consisted mostly of business ethicists, and the resultant work is monumental—filled with pictures and a full 568 pages long, it is more a celebration of American business than an analytical history in the style of Heald's. It also treats business ethics only as an aside to the development of American corporate responsibility programmes, but in many ways it is only an extended and much-better-resourced form of Heald's earlier survey.

Another survey of American corporate social responsibility was published by William Frederick in 2006. Frederick's *Corporation, Be Good!* is an "eyewitness, I-was-there account" (Frederick 2006, 1) of the American development of corporate social responsibility since 1950. Frederick stresses that it was separate groups that advocated for social responsibility, business ethics and stakeholder management among American business school academics. But in 2014, the Uruguayan sociologist Gabriel Abend published a historical work, *The Moral Background*, that is more squarely focused on business ethics. It, again, concentrates only on American business, however, and is chronologically centred on the late nineteenth and early twentieth centuries. It describes two conceptual foundations of American business ethics—the image of the "Christian merchant" and "Standards of Practice". More analytical than the book of Carroll and colleagues or that of Frederick, it is articulated as a work of historical sociology and a contribution to the underdeveloped field of moral sociology.

For Europe, the only dedicated monographic treatment is Michael Marinetto's *Corporate Social Involvement* (1998), a comparative historical study of British and Italian "business engagement in social action concerned with the general well-being of society" (Marinetto 1998, viii). Oddly enough for a work focused on Italy, Marinetto (who is currently employed at Cardiff Business School in Wales) completely ignores the most significant body of thought concerning business ethics stemming from that country—that of Catholic social thought. A more searching contribution to European business ethics was produced by the American Catholic priest Joseph Gremillion as part of his doctorate in social studies from the Gregorian University in Rome. Gremillion's *Catholic Movement of Employers and Managers* (1961) is the only monographic study in

English of the Catholic tradition of business ethics, covering especially the early traditions of business ethics and social responsibility in France, the Low Countries and Italy. Gremillion was later associated with the University of Notre Dame in Indiana, and his work (partly) makes up for the notable lack of consideration of the Catholic tradition that is typical otherwise of the historiography.

With their focus on social ethics, however, none of these works could be considered a contribution to the intellectual history of ethics of a kind comparable to Alasdair MacIntyre's *Short History of Ethics* (1966) or Terence Irwin's more ambitious *The Development of Ethics* (2007–2009). Nor are wider considerations of the ethical claims made by businesses available. The Prudential Assurance Association, the forerunner of Prudential plc, was founded in London in 1848, for example, and adopted a seal with the image of Prudentia, the medieval personification of the ancient virtue of *phronēsis* that is essential to Aristotelian ethics. Aristotle was the most influential systematic ethical philosopher of classical antiquity, and his *Nichomachean Ethics* from the fourth century BC remains a key text studied in university ethics classes today (Annas 1993). Most of the traditions of morality that informed business undertakings in the nineteenth century, however, and what modern reflections they have, have largely fallen outside the scope of histories of business ethics (or even business history). Like the logo of Prudential plc that features a profile of Prudentia and her mirror (her snake reduced to an earring), they are typically not considered part of business ethics as it has usually been conceptualised in the historiography.

Yet not only is business ethics often seen in a socially and culturally etiolated manner, but even the intellectual developments that led to the production of a work such as Norman Bowie's *Business Ethics: A Kantian Perspective* (1999) have long remained genealogically obscure. Although a Protestant, the eighteenth-century German philosopher Immanuel Kant is the most significant figure in the history of modern Western philosophy, and his contribution to contemporary business ethics has been immense. In his *Groundwork of the Metaphysics of Morals* (1785), for example, Kant famously wrote that:

> where there is a good deal of trade a prudent merchant does not overcharge but keeps a fixed general price for everyone . . . but this is not nearly enough for us to believe that the merchant acted in this way from duty and basic principles of honesty; his advantage required it . . . the action was done neither from duty nor from immediate inclination but merely for purpose of self-interest.
>
> (Kant 1785, 11)

Kant and his focus on duty, however, does not figure in the works of figures such as Heald, Abend and Carroll and colleagues. Kant's ethics were subject to a revival in American business schools in the 1970s that lay outside the scope of most previous inquiries into the history of business ethics.

The other main Enlightenment contributor to modern moral philosophy was Jeremy Bentham. In his *Introduction to the Principles of Morals and Legislation* (1789), Bentham set out an alternative framework to that of Kant based on the notion of a "felicific calculus". Bentham claimed that the principal measure of what is good is what produces the most human pleasure. Developed further by John Stuart Mill (1863), Bentham's focus on pleasure stressed the utility of an action—its outcome rather than its means. Aristotle had defined "good" by means of a recourse to *eudaimonía* or "human flourishing", while Kant focused predominately on duty. Bentham and Mill instead stressed a calculus of outcomes, with the ends more important than the means.

In a posthumously published work compiled from his notes, Bentham (1834) had described his ethics as deontology (cf. Greek *deon*, "that which is binding, needful, right"), but the description was already being used in the nineteenth century as "a term well chosen, to describe a system of ethics founded on any other than Mr. Bentham's principle" (Whewell 1872, xxviii). Utilitarianism clearly came to influence many contributions to Protestant thought in the nineteenth century, but Kantian deontology seems not to have had any influence on business ethics until the 1970s. The introduction of Kantian thought into business ethics occurred in a manner quite unlike that in which utility or even notions such as prudence made their way into nineteenth-century business understandings. The manner in which Kantian deontology entered business ethics (and has since become so important) was one of the key signs of the secularisation of ethics during the twentieth century, as ideas entered the business tradition without first being mediated by religious influence. Secularisation has long been understood to be one of the key characteristics of contemporary Western thought, and it was the principal transformation that occurred in business ethics during the twentieth century.

Weber (1920) described secularisation in terms of "disenchantment", as part of a general move in Western societies away from traditional religious explanation towards scientific rationality. But the secularisation of business ethics occurred at a time when predictions of the general decline of religion had been largely abandoned by social scientists. As Peter Berger acknowledges, "The world today, with some exceptions . . . is as furiously religious as it ever was, and in some places more so than ever . . . 'secularization theory' is essentially mistaken" (Berger 1999, 2). The secularisation of business ethics has been institutional—promoted by the rise of business ethics in universities—not a reflection of declining numbers of churchgoers. Where the key ethical influences on businessmen were once largely religious, the teaching of business ethics in business schools has been the main medium for the transformation of business ethics internationally.

How this process occurred is the subject of the following chapters. Chapter 2 begins with a consideration of the rise of the modern corporate form and the influence of nineteenth-century reactions to capitalism on business ethics. The following chapter focuses on business philanthropy and the main Western religious traditions of early-twentieth-century business ethics, both Protestant and Catholic. Chapter 4 describes the rise of the social responsibility movement first in the United States and its spread to Europe in the 1970s, while Chapter 5 focuses on the emergence of the field of business ethics proper, both in the United States and in Europe. Chapter 6 explores the emergence of the idea of corporate governance and its internationalisation in the 1990s, while Chapter 7 concentrates on the rise of psychological theories of ethics and ethical leadership in business. The two final chapters outline the emergence of the notion of sustainability and the development of international bodies such as the United Nations Global Compact as well as a consideration of the influence of Critical Management Studies on business ethics in light of the Global Financial Crisis.

2 The Corporate Revolution

With its focus on commercial and corporate conduct, business ethics is most often connected with the behaviour of corporate executives and the staff they supervise. But the modern corporation, with its shareholders, employees and managers, is a product of the nineteenth century and the development of industrial capitalism. The corporate revolution of the early twentieth century began in Great Britain, and the genealogical origins of contemporary business ethics are largely to be sought in the period contemporary to the emergence of large, shareholder-owned businesses in much of the Western world. The emergence of the main discourses of contemporary business ethics, seen in the Nietzschean sense of a genealogy of morals, reflects a series of political, economic, religious and philosophical developments. These include the rise of the nineteenth-century workers' movement and its intellectual expression in Marxian thought, the emergence of Catholic social justice teaching (and its reflection in subsequent Protestant initiatives) and the eclipse of classical liberalism by social liberalism in most Western countries by the end of the nineteenth century.

As a development of the nineteenth century, the large commercial firm is the primary subject of business ethics. The modern legal structure of the corporation is also often seen to be a key concern in assessments of business behaviour, as it is a legal construct that evolved to facilitate commercial activity without including an explicit moral requirement. Corporations do not legally require a moral compass or conscience—an inner sense which distinguishes what is right from what is wrong. The 2004 film and book, *The Corporation*, by the American-Canadian legal scholar Joel Bakan characterised modern corporations as psychopaths—beings that are amoral because they lack any sense of conscience (Bakan 2003). But corporations of the type Bakan analysed were already a century old at the time and are still not called corporations today in the United Kingdom, the country that first developed the modern corporate form.

The Rise of the Modern Corporation

The modern corporate form is usually acknowledged to be one of the great developments of nineteenth-century capitalism. The "genius" of the modern corporation is often hailed by advocates of contemporary capitalism and is typically seen to be epitomised in its American legal and commercial expression. In 1982, the American law professor Daniel Fischel described the genius of the modern corporate form as enabling "individuals who have wealth but lack managerial ability to invest while simultaneously allowing professional managers who lack personal wealth to run enterprises" (Fischel 1982, 1275). But the legal form taken by most large businesses internationally nowadays was argued for by its first English proponents in terms of economic liberty, not managerial efficiency.

The modern corporation is an economic and legal expression of the political ideology of liberalism. Liberalism is so dominant in Western societies today that the idea is often confused with the politics of particular parties (e.g. the Democratic Party in the United States) or has otherwise been reconceptualised in a manner that obscures both its importance and ubiquity in contemporary political and economic life. But according to Gray:

> Liberalism . . . is the political theory of modernity. Its postulates are the most distinctive features of modern life—the autonomous individual with his concern for liberty and privacy, the growth of wealth and the steady stream of invention and innovation, the machinery of government which is at once indispensable to civil life and a standing threat to it—and its intellectual outlook is one that could have originated in its fullness only in the post-traditional society of Europe after the dissolution of medieval Christendom.
>
> (Gray 1986, 82)

The nineteenth century was the key period in the flourishing of liberalism, both economically and politically. It was a particularly important period in the development of business law, and the main economic power at the time was the British Empire. With its colonies in the Americas, Asia, Oceania and Africa, modern commercial norms were largely British norms, and these were economically liberal. But the development of the legal form taken by most large commercial enterprises today was a comparatively late nineteenth-century development, with its British origins dating the early years of the reign of the long-serving English monarch Queen Victoria.

At the time of Victoria's coronation in 1837, British commercial regulation was still in a state of development and flux. But after a series of liberalisations, by 1856 English company law had reached its classical "modern" form. The Vice-President of the Board of Trade, Robert Lowe, introduced the Joint Stock Companies Act of 1856 to the English Parliament with the rousing words "I am arguing in favour of human liberty—that people may be permitted to deal how and with whom they choose without the officious interference of the state" (Lowe 1856, 131). Since 1720 and the scandal concerning the speculative build-up in the value of the shares of the South Sea Company, restrictions had been introduced into English company law to make joint-stock companies more stable and to limit the potential for fraud. But Lowe argued that the English Parliament should not "throw the slightest obstacle" in the way that joint-stock companies were established; instead, Parliament should "arm the courts of justice to check extravagance or roguery in the management of companies" (Lowe 1856, 131). Before the 1840s, British businesses had been required to apply to the English Parliament to receive a Royal Charter of incorporation; with the 1856 companies act, a great liberalising of business law ensued.

As the English barrister John William Smith argued in his 1843 *Compendium of Mercantile Law*, however, British commercial regulation was already quite different in this manner from that which applied in Germany and France. According to Smith:

> The mercantile law of England is perhaps of all laws in the world the most completely the offspring of usage and convenience, the least shackled by legislative regulations. Thus, the performance of one of the most obvious parts of the duty of a merchant, and one which the laws of most other countries enforce by many and anxious provisions, viz. the keeping a correct account of his transactions, is left by us to be enforced solely by public opinion and by the dread of the reproach and loss of credit which would follow the detection of any gross irregularity. It is, perhaps, in consequence of this that we find such high and peculiar sentiments of commercial honour prevalent among English merchants.

The contrast could be seen especially in terms of how joint-stock companies were regulated. Enacted in 1807, the French Code de commerce set down the first national legal provisions for a joint-stock company (*Société anonyme*), but such bodies were strictly regulated until liberalisation occurred in 1867 (Lefebvre-Teillard 1981). Established in 1866, the first General German Commercial Code included only a provision for a joint-stock partnership with unlimited liability (*Kommanditgesellschaft*)—the modern German limited liability company (*Gesellschaft mit beschränkter Haftung; GmbH*) was introduced to the General German Commercial Code only as late as 1892 (Flume 2014). The French and German commercial codes have been particularly influential internationally, with, for example, the Commercial Code of Japan being modelled partly on the Code de commerce and the General German Commercial Code, while Chinese Company Law was inspired by both Japanese and English statutes (and hence reflects all three main European legal traditions) (Kirkby 1995; Flume 2014). But the limited liability joint-stock company laws of Germany and France were clearly only liberalised along English lines after the passing of the Joint Stock Companies Act of 1856.

The notion of a separate fictitious "corporate personality" can be dated much earlier, with corporations sole and corporations aggregate part of medieval English law (O'Hara 1988). A corporation was a fictitious group whose existence survived the individuals who at any one time might constitute its membership. By early modern times any number of groups could be called a corporation—most commonly a municipal borough or a guild. The traditional legal form of business was a partnership or a company in all parts of Europe, but with unlimited liability for the business's debts applied to at least one of its members. When legal provisions similar to the Joint Stock Companies Act 1856 were enacted in the United States, however, the commercial legal structures used by joint-stock businesses were called corporations rather than companies (Handlin and Handlin 1945). American states had been much more willing to grant commercial charters than had the English Parliament (Sylla and Wright 2013). But in the late nineteenth century, American corporations were liberalised on the model of the English limited liability company, much as were similar bodies formed in other Western countries at the time.

By the early 1900s the dominant business legal form had developed five basic characteristics: separate legal personality, limited liability, transferable joint stock, delegated management and investor ownership (Turner 2017). In 1843, an English common law case, *Foss v. Harbottle*, had established the principle that the company (rather than its shareholders) was the proper plaintiff for wrongs done to it, establishing the notion of corporate "personhood" in business law, and that the courts would not intervene in management decisions of the company, so that a shareholder could not complain of actions which had been confirmed by the majority of shareholders. English common law also developed the notion of what the "proper purpose" of a company was, *Hutton v. West Cork Rly Co.* establishing in 1883 that a company could act to benefit members of the public other than shareholders, but only if the benefit provided was indirectly in the shareholders' best interest. Many of these decisions were ratified again by American courts at a later date, but the basic principles of company law had been made clear by the end of the nineteenth century.

The first large public companies were also formed in the United Kingdom in the late nineteenth century. Railways especially required much capital to be raised, and as Peter Payne (1967) stressed, a number of British companies with capitalisations of over two million pounds had emerged by 1905. A merger movement in the 1890s had added to the number of large public companies, and by the end of the Victorian era, listed firms such as Imperial Tobacco, J & P Coats and Vickers already had huge market capitalisations and thousands of employees. In the United States, large monopolies had developed by the late nineteenth century, but many of these were constituted as trusts—hence the use of the term "anti-trust" still in America to describe legislation aimed at reducing corporate monopoly power.

But the notion of a corporate revolution is more clearly an American idea. In 1901, the investment banker John P. Morgan launched US Steel by bundling Andrew Carnegie's steel interests into a listed corporation. Morgan established the first of what would later become the Fortune 500 on the New York Stock Exchange (Warren 2001). In the late nineteenth century, most large American businesses were partnerships or were undertakings whose shares were "closely held" rather than publicly traded (Wells 2002). Morgan's listing of US Steel instituted the rise of shareholder capitalism in America, as vast impersonal corporations run by managers who had not founded the businesses themselves came to dominate the economic landscape of the rising economic power.

Over the course of the next three decades, and particularly after the outbreak of the First World War, American industry grew on such a scale that by the time of the Great Crash in 1929, US Steel had become one of scores of large, listed American industrial corporations. Many, including General Motors, DuPont and General Electric, remain famous names today. Millions of shares were changing hands annually on the New York Stock Exchange as American corporations expanded overseas and American models of industrial production were widely copied internationally. The new American system of production was first described as "Fordist" (after the Ford Motor Company) by the Italian Marxist Antonio Gramsci in his *Prison Notebooks* written during his incarceration in the 1930s (Gramsci 1948–51). But along with the scale of industrial production, another development of Fordist industrialism had occurred.

The rise of so many large listed corporations first became a matter of social concern in the United States in the 1920s. John M. Clark's *Social Control of Business* (1926) expressed the worry that many critics of the large American corporations of the day had: how could such large undertakings be controlled by society? Business had grown to such a size that it joined government and the churches as the key social institutions in American society. Unlike governments and churches, American corporations also had little claim to any kind of moral tradition. In fact, the opposite was often considered to be the case—the managerial staff that ran large American businesses seemed increasingly unaccountable even to the shareholders who legally owned the corporations. Corporate managers had been revealed engaging in practices such as stock-watering (issuing stock at values far lower than the market rate) and the issuance of "blank stock" whose voting rights could be determined by corporate directors. The managers of American corporations could use these powers to transfer control rights among different groups of shareholders—they could control the corporation (Wells 2002).

Reflecting on the growth in size of corporations and the declining rights of shareholders, in 1932 the American lawyer Adolf A. Berle, Jr, and the economist Gardner C. Means declared that a "corporate revolution" had occurred (Berle and Means 1932, vii). In 1927, Berle had approached his old army colleague Means to collaborate on a book that Berle had won a grant to write on the growing power of American corporations (Smith et al. 2019). As they described it in their landmark study:

> Corporations have ceased to be merely legal devices through which the private business transactions of individuals may be carried on. Though still much used for this purpose, the corporate form has acquired a larger significance. The corporation has, in fact, become both a method of property tenure and a means of organizing economic life. Grown to tremendous proportions, there may be said to have evolved a "corporate system"—as there once was a feudal system—which has attracted to itself a combination of attributes and powers, and has attained a degree of prominence entitling it to be dealt with as a major social institution.
>
> (Berle and Means 1932, 1)

In 1931, Berle had begun a debate with E. Merrick Dodd in the *Harvard Law Review* over the responsibilities that corporate managers and directors owed to their shareholders and other members of the public directly influenced by the corporation. Berle (1931, 1932) and Dodd (1932, 1935) set out the two positions still often assumed in legal debates over the social responsibility of business (Wells 2002). Dodd argued that a corporation's officers should be allowed to take into account the needs and interests of a firm's employees, customers and other claimants when making decisions that might affect the performance of the firm. But in a landmark 1919 legal case, *Dodge v. Ford Motor Co.*, the Michigan Supreme Court had held that Henry Ford was required to operate the Ford Motor Company in the best interests of its shareholders, rather than for the benefit of his employees or customers. Ford had been refusing to issue a special dividend, reducing the value of the Dodge brothers' stocks, telling shareholders he would employ the company's profits "to employ still more men, to spread the benefits of this industrial system to the greatest possible number, to help them build up their lives and their homes" (Ford quoted in *Dodge v. Ford Motor Co.*).

The court's ruling was widely held to uphold the principle of shareholder primacy in American corporations law. The Michigan Supreme Court had found that Ford held a right to judgement over how to run the company, as long as he did not try to run it for any other purpose than as a profit-making enterprise. Attacking Dodd's premise, Berle argued that the primary duty of corporate officers was to run the business in the best interests of shareholders. It was not until 1954 that Berle conceded his position to Dodd in light of the 1953 judgement *AP Smith Manufacturing Co v. Barlow*, where business judgement was held by the Supreme

Court of New Jersey also to include a clear right for managers to take into consideration the interests of claimants on the corporation other than just shareholders (Berle 1954, 137). American courts now upheld the principle decided in *Hutton v. West Cork Rly Co.* in 1883 as long as managers did not go to the same extreme as Henry Ford had and try to redefine the "proper purpose" of a business altogether.

Socialism, Marxism and the Nineteenth-Century Worker Movement

Yet as Britain had industrialised in the late eighteenth century, advocates of commercial liberalism such as the Scottish philosopher Adam Smith had emerged. Smith's *Wealth of Nations* (1776) was widely hailed as the key articulation of economic liberalism in the nineteenth century and still is today. Economic liberalism was the commercial basis on which the British Empire relied and was exported internationally. Britain had been the first country to industrialise, and over the course of the nineteenth century international business had become substantially British.

As the Hungarian historian Karl Polanyi argued in his *Great Transformation* (1944), however, economic liberalism replaced an earlier form of commercial organisation that was embedded in a different social, political and moral order from that championed by Smith:

> Under [the previous systems of] feudalism and the guild system land and labor formed part of the social organization itself. . . . The same was true of the organization of labor. Under the guild system, as under every other economic system in previous history, the motives and circumstances of productive activities were embedded in the general organization of society. . . . The change from regulated to self-regulating markets at the end of the eighteenth century represented a complete transformation in the structure of society.
>
> (Polanyi 1944, 56–7)

Smith argued that economic liberalism would lead to a more moral society as each person was left free to make their own commercial decisions. But in contrast, Polanyi contended that the adoption of economic liberalism had been unnatural and, if not checked, would have necessarily led to moral disintegration as an amoral system was imposed by commercial interests onto broader society. Polanyi described the imposition of market conditions on Western countries during the nineteenth century as a "social catastrophe" (Polanyi 1944, 76). The advocates of economic liberalism had not created the more moral society that Smith had presumed would arise, but, instead, a worse one.

By the middle of the nineteenth century it was clear that industrialisation and its attendant ideology of liberalism had begun to transform the

Western world in manners not anticipated by figures such as Smith. New mechanical technologies and the factory system that had first arisen in Britain resulted in the emergence of an urban working class as country-folk flooded into the cities and towns looking for employment. Factory work for adults and children was typically dangerous, unhealthy and lowly paid. Living conditions in the new, overcrowded urban slums were squalid and unsanitary. Society was characterised by obvious poverty and inequality. The prospects for the urban working classes and Western society seemed bleak.

The social catastrophe that Polanyi described first became apparent in Britain, France and Germany, and provoked significant moral, social and political reactions. The United States faced similar concerns as its economy recovered after the conclusion of the American Civil War (1861–65), but the most influential discussions of business ethics and political economy at the time were British and Western European. Italy was comparatively late to industrialise but also had a key role to play because the Papacy was situated in Rome, and Italian clerics were the most influential in developing a considered response to the social catastrophe in the Catholic countries. France and the southern and western parts of Germany were Catholic, unlike Britain and the United States which were predominately Protestant and economically liberal nations. Religious difference played a key role in how different countries responded to the social crisis of the nineteenth century.

Yet the first of the traditions of response to the crisis was socialism and the nineteenth-century worker movement. Its most important early British proponent was the Welsh factory owner Robert Owen, the founder of the modern cooperative movement. Worker cooperatives such as those established by Owen in England and later in the United States became models for more successful establishments in Italy, France and Germany. Owen saw his work specifically in terms of morality and particularly the approach to ethics of his contemporary Jeremy Bentham. Owen was one of the United Kingdom's great social reformers, and as his biographer George D.H. Cole notes, Owen based his system on his theory of education (Cole 1925).

Bentham had declared that the principle of utility was that which should guide legal and social reform. "*It is the greatest happiness of the greatest number that is the measure of right and wrong*", Bentham (1776, ii, italics in original) advocated emphatically, excoriating traditional morality and the Church of England. Owen agreed with Bentham on religion and framed his social reform agenda, his *New View of Society* (1813), in a rejection of established principles of work, morality and education. He supported the eight-hour-day movement and the campaign to eradicate child labour, but he also experimented with new forms of firm management and ownership in his search for a "new moral world".

Owen's movement of reform was reflected in several other nineteenth-century social movements. From friendly societies to life insurance mutuals, nineteenth-century England was characterised by all kinds of experimental social and commercial relationships. Not all were designated socialist at the time, and none was as radical as those proposed on the European Continent. But a range of alternatives to organising commercial production in the form of joint-stock companies and partnerships were developed at the time—and similar arrangements influenced by British innovators such as Owen were established in Western Europe and North America as industrialisation spread internationally.

In France, Henri de Saint-Simon had been the first thinker to distinguish the emergent industrial society from that of the preceding agricultural age (Saint-Simon 1821). Inspired by advances in the physical sciences, he founded a movement of Saint-Simonianism that investigated social reform in the light of industrialisation. In his *Critique of Pure Reason* (1781), the great German philosopher Kant had influentially claimed:

> Our age is the genuine age of **criticism**, to which everything must submit. **Religion** through its **holiness** and **legislation** through its **majesty** commonly seek to exempt themselves from it. But in this way they excite a just suspicion against themselves, and cannot lay claim to that unfeigned respect that reason grants only to that which has been able to withstand its free and public examination.
>
> (Kant 1781, 100–1, n.*, emphasis in original)

Kant saw reason as a reforming rather than usurping social and political principle. But for Saint-Simon, science and industry would completely overthrow the moral and temporal role of the churches. Industrialists would control the new society, while scientists would replace priests as moral guides—the new society envisaged by the Saint-Simonians would be morally as well as industrially "scientific". In his later years, however, Saint-Simon retreated from his earlier scientism to promote a "new Christianity" in which society would be reformed through adopting a religion that was predominately concerned with improving the conditions of the poorest classes (Saint-Simon 1825).

An even more radical nineteenth-century French reformer was Pierre-Joseph Proudhon. Proudhon is perhaps most famous for his assertion "property is theft" and his founding of the anarchist movement (Proudhon 1840). An advocate of principles he described as "industrial democracy" and "mutualism", Proudhon's rambling journalism was both as witty (e.g. his *Manual of the Stock Exchange Speculator*) as it was radical (Proudhon 1853; Prichard 2013). His idea of industrial democracy would be widely embraced by trade unions, and his notion of mutualism would underpin twentieth-century ideas of labour-management cooperation. Proudhon was also an early supporter of the German radical Karl Marx.

Marx would later denounce Proudhon in his *Poverty of Philosophy* (1847), and with his co-author Friedrich Engels come to overshadow

Owen, Saint-Simon and Proudhon. His fiery *Communist Manifesto* (written with Engels) was composed for the newly formed Communist League just in time for the year of liberal revolutions that swept the European capitals in 1848. Unlike his early writings (most of which were released only after his death), the works published by Marx during his lifetime were much more systematic and influential than those of any other nineteenth-century would-be socialist reformer.

From the perspective of ethics, however, Marx has always been difficult to locate. Of Jewish ancestry, he was raised as a Lutheran and was a member of the "Left Hegelians"—German thinkers influenced by the Protestant philosopher Georg W.F. Hegel and his notion that history had a purpose. Hegel wrote widely on morality, justice, the ethical order and what he called the "doctrine of duties", particularly in his *Elements of the Philosophy of Right* (Hegel 1820). But it was Hegel's *Lectures on the Philosophy of History* (1837) that had the greatest influence on Marx. Hegel argued that history was progressive and bound by reason, and the Left Hegelians saw this purpose as being commensurate with promoting freedom and belittling Christianity.

Marx saw the industrial system as being the greatest impediment to human freedom. His fellow Hegelian David Strauss (1835) criticised the reliability of the accounts of the life of Christ preserved in the Gospels, while Ludwig Feuerbach (1841) argued that Christians project their moral fantasies onto the world. Designated Left Hegelians especially for their criticisms of Christianity, Marx became the most famous of the Hegelian radicals by turning the main focus of his social critique instead onto the political economy. In his *Critique of Hegel's Philosophy of Right* (1844), Marx argued "The criticism of religion ends in the doctrine that man is the supreme being for man; thus it ends with the categorical imperative to overthrow all relations in which man is a debased, enslaved, neglected, contemptible being" (Marx 1844, 137). Marx's great 1867 work *Capital* is subtitled a "critique of political economy" and sought to upend the moral basis of the commercial society that philosophers of capitalism had accorded the industrial system. Where Smith had argued that a society characterised by freely entered commercial relationships was morally superior to one where government tried to control the economy, Marx argued that capitalism was inherently immoral and wrong.

Marx's main criticism of capitalism (a designation he first popularised) was that it was unjust. But in his *Critique of the Gotha Programme* (1875), Marx went further still. Apart from setting out the principles of the Marxian doctrine "From each according to his ability, to each according to his needs", Marx declared "*every right*" to be a "*right of inequality*" (1875, 26–7, italics in original). Morality, for Marx, was an abstract ideology used by the entitled to justify their entitlement. Moral postulates were ideological, and ideology was determined by capitalist relations (Green 1983; Schwartz 2001).

Liberalism, Socialism and Catholic Social Thought

By rejecting both religion and morality, Marxian thought made little immediate contribution to business ethics other than a reactive, oppositional one. In response to the challenge of the Saint-Simonians in France, however, a new development in Catholic thinking emerged at the time, beginning with the foundation of charities such as the St Vincent de Paul Society, established by Frédéric Ozanam in 1833. Missions to the poor became characteristic of the period, with religious orders such as the Sisters of Mercy (founded in 1831) and the Sisters of the Good Shepherd (from 1835) being mirrored later in Protestant countries by institutions such as the Salvation Army (established in 1865). Traditions of mutual finance also developed on the Continent, most famously in the form of Friedrich Wilhelm Raffeisen's movement of cooperative banks (Kaltenborn 2018). Where Marx and other radicals increasingly came to promote violent revolution, Christian forms of socialism developed, with the apogee of the nineteenth-century Christian social movement coming with the adoption of a formal tradition of social justice teaching by the Catholic Church. Catholic social justice teaching has its official foundation in the 1891 Papal encyclical *Rerum novarum* [*On New Things*], the key Catholic summation of "The Rights and Duties of Capital and Labour".

Officially authored by Pope Leo XIII, *Rerum novarum* was drafted originally by the Jesuit theologian Matteo Liberatore and the Dominican Cardinal Tomasso M. Zigliari, two of the key figures in the Thomist revival in Italy. As the Church had been increasingly deprived of any temporal role over the course of the eighteenth and nineteenth centuries, Catholic thinkers had begun to reformulate the role of the Church in a manner more reflective of the political settlement in an increasingly secular Europe. Rather than embracing the ethics of Enlightenment thinkers such as Bentham or Kant, Catholic philosophers returned to St Thomas Aquinas's thirteenth-century *Summa Theologica*. The *Summa* included a rearticulation of ancient Greek ethics as it was encapsulated in Aristotle's *Nicomachean Ethics*. Where Aristotle had extolled especially prudence, justice, fortitude and temperance, the four key moral virtues of the ancient Greek tradition, St Thomas had added three more: faith, hope and love. The Thomist revival was a revival of the ancient Greek ethical tradition as much as it was a Christian one (Hennesey 1978; Rafferty 2014).

In the neo-Thomist tradition, the Catholic Church is a public guarantor of moral behaviour, and *Rerum novarum* recognised (among other matters) the role of trade unions in mitigating the worst effects of industrial capitalism. *Rerum novarum* was particularly focused on the philosophical virtue of justice and sought to stake out a middle ground between revolutionary socialism ("working on the poor man's envy of the rich"; Leo XIII 1891, 4) and a society ruled by "men of greed, who use human beings as mere instruments for money-making" (Leo XIII 1891, 42).

Rerum novarum attacked the secularisation of law and commerce that had occurred under economic liberalism:

> working men have been surrendered, isolated and helpless, to the hardheartedness of employers and the greed of unchecked competition . . . the hiring of labor and the conduct of trade are concentrated in the hands of comparatively few; so that a small number of very rich men have been able to lay upon the teeming masses of the laboring poor a yoke little better than that of slavery itself.
>
> (Leo XIII 1891, 3)

But the Church did not want to see Europe surrender to socialism either:

> Socialists . . . hold that by . . . transferring property from private individuals to the community, the present mischievous state of things will be set to rights, inasmuch as each citizen will then get his fair share of whatever there is to enjoy. But their contentions are so clearly powerless to end the controversy that were they carried into effect the working man himself would be among the first to suffer.
>
> (Leo XIII 1891, 4)

The emerging neo-Thomist notion of social justice can be seen in *Rerum novarum*, marrying the cardinal virtue of justice with the theological virtue of love. A formal notion of social justice, however, was not officially adopted into Catholic social teaching until the 1930s.

Yet social justice was a concept different from that held traditionally by liberals. The concept owes its origin to the period of the Italian Risorgimento and was first used by the Jesuit philosopher Luigi Taparelli d'Azeglio in his *Saggio teoretico di dritto naturale appoggiato sul fatto* [*Theoretical Treatise on Natural Law Resting on Facts*] (1841–43) which appeared during the debates over the beginnings of efforts to unify Italy into a single state. Taparelli's aim was to develop a Catholic theory of society that would be an alternative to the liberal theories of British philosophers such as Smith. Taparelli saw liberalism as a tyranny brought about by the Protestant Reformation, which exalted private judgement over the divine authority of the Catholic Church (Burke 2011; Behr 2019).

The liberal conception of justice is based on the principle of equality before the law as it was described most famously by the English political philosopher John Locke (1690). Liberals argued that all individuals should enjoy the same formal status, rights and entitlements in society and "not to be subject to the inconstant, uncertain, unknown, arbitrary Will of another Man" (Locke 1690, iv 22). Taparelli argued, against Locke, however, that such a notion was dangerous. Like many conservatives, he was shocked by the brutality of the French Revolution of 1789 which appealed to fraternity, liberty and equality, but treated kings, aristocrats and clergy so murderously. Social justice occurred for Taparelli when the natural inequalities in society were properly recognised and accepted—for example, that which exists between a father and his son: "Justice demands that the son render to the father an equivalent of the existence he has received from him" (Taparelli trans. Burke 2011, 38).

In contrast, "classical" or "old" liberals accepted inequality, but only after everyone had been allowed equality of opportunity. Formulated during the early years of liberalism, the principle of equality of opportunity required that every person should have the same chance to succeed or fail economically. But this principle did not mean social equality or equal rewards as such an outcome would be contrary to the complementary liberal principle of meritocracy. Since the foundational *Wealth of Nations* of Smith (1776), classical liberals had typically embraced the notion that because of differences between individuals' levels of ability and their willingness to work hard and take risks, unequal outcomes could be just. Liberals argued that society should be structured in a manner that provided incentives for people to maximise the individual talents they had, not to achieve equality of outcomes (Fry and Mees 2017).

Following Locke, liberals had traditionally placed great emphasis on individual rights, including the rights to life, liberty and private property. Locke was also an influential figure in developing the key principles of the liberal state: state power should be based on the consent of the people; it should be constitutional and based on formal, legal rules; individual rights must be guaranteed; and power should be fragmented (Locke 1690). Where Marx rejected rights altogether, Taparelli promoted social justice on the basis that inherited inequality was preordained by God and that liberalism promoted behaviours contrary to the natural basis of society in the family.

Yet with the social crisis of the nineteenth century, two different strands had begun to emerge in liberalism. Classical liberals maintained their commitment to small government, the market system and free trade (Robbins 1965). In their view, the role of the state should remain extremely limited, essentially to ensuring national security, personal security and law and order, and a system of justice including enforcement of contracts. They believed that state intervention would violate individual property rights and freedom of contract, which would destroy individual initiative (Coats 1971). Voluntary contractual exchanges driven by self-interest and private profits would maximise economic efficiency and national wealth. As Smith had famously written:

> As every individual, therefore, endeavours as much as he can, both to employ his capital in the support of domestic industry, and so to direct that industry that its produce may be of the greatest value;

every individual necessarily labours to render the annual revenue of the society as great as he can.

(Smith 1776, iv, 2, 9)

At a time of increasing concern with the ill-effects of industrial capitalism, an alternative approach to that of Smith was adopted by a group of "new" or "social" liberals. British social liberals such as the philosophers John S. Mill (1859) and Thomas H. Green (1884) maintained their commitment to most of the key principles of liberalism, including individualism and personal liberty, but modified their views on what the appropriate government response should be to achieve those ends, given the "social catastrophe" of urban conditions in the new industrial era. Rather than merely advocating negative freedom from government, they concluded that the state had an obligation to intervene to ensure positive freedom— that the state should act to enable the disadvantaged to have the freedom and genuine capacity to take opportunities to improve their lives.

A third approach was taken up by religious critics of liberalism. With the adoption of the term by neo-Thomist writers, social justice came increasingly to be seen as a solution to the most harmful effects of *laissez-faire* capitalism. As Leo Shields put it in his 1941 doctoral dissertation on social justice:

> The complete revolution in political ideology of which the French Revolution was the most evident sign consisted chiefly in individualizing people's social outlook. . . . The common good disappeared and its place was taken by such constructions as the utilitarian "greatest good of the greatest number". Belief in responsibility to the social group disappeared. . . . It was not long until desperate conditions of poverty and inequality had brought forth criticism in the name of justice.
>
> (Shields 1941, 5)

The solution, Shields continued, many saw as lying "in the duties of the individual to his society. . . . It was out of [this] trend that the current concept of social justice developed" (Shields 1941, 5–6). In Catholic countries such as Italy, conservative governments acted to develop legal frameworks that protected unions and restricted businesses in line with Catholic social teaching.

In Britain and the United States, the social liberal strand of political thought generally prevailed and held sway for the next century or so. Thus, under the influence of social liberalism, governments embarked on reforms to reduce the inequalities and perceived social injustices of capitalism: public education, welfare, and protection for the poor, paid for by taxes on businesses and the wealthy. Social liberalism also saw the advent of laws which regulated the terms of employment and legalised trade unions. Social liberalism and Catholic social thought promoted similar aims as Western societies acted to overcome the nineteenth-century social crisis.

But the main cause of criticism among clerical writers was the decline in community and sense of social obligation they saw epitomised in contemporary business. A group of social liberal critics in the United Kingdom even came to see their dissatisfaction with *laissez-faire* capitalism in terms of a new interpretation of the Gospels, developing a Protestant form of Christian socialism. Similar criticism arose in the United States at the time, particularly in terms of what would become known as the Social Gospel (Evans 2017). The most famous Christian socialist in Britain, however, the historian Richard H. Tawney, even criticised Weber's Protestant work ethic thesis. Instead, Tawney argued that the tenets of Luther that Weber had focused on represented an adaptation of religion to the rise of capitalism, not its cause (Tawney 1926). In his *Acquisitive Society*, Tawney had already criticised what he saw as a perversion of Christianity in the self-serving advocacy of business (Tawney 1921). He found it difficult to reconcile the message of the Gospels with the public utterings of the loudest beneficiaries of capitalism.

An ethical concern that nineteenth-century liberalism had in common with neo-Thomism, however, was a focus on thrift and prudence. As one of the cardinal virtues, in fact as the leading virtue of Aristotelean ethical thought, prudence was hailed as the key enabler of ethical thinking by Aquinas. But since the seventeenth century, the concept of prudence had been "eroded" in secular philosophical discourse in almost the opposite manner to which it had developed in commercial and neo-Thomist thought (Hariman 2003). Adam Smith had been the last major philosopher in the Enlightenment tradition to focus on it (Viganò 2017).

For Smith, prudence was essential to business practice. In his *Theory of Moral Sentiments*, Smith separated prudence into two types—inferior and superior—and he defined inferior prudence as "The care of the health, of the fortune, of the rank and reputation of the individual, the objects upon which his comfort and happiness in this life are supposed principally to depend" (Smith 1759, vi, 1, 5). The prudent man's frugality, parsimony and industry (or hard work) were a sacrifice of the enjoyment of immediate pleasures for the likelihood of greater pleasure in the future. The desire for present enjoyment might be stronger than the desire to prepare for pleasure in the future, but the virtue of prudence curbed the desire for immediate enjoyment (Smith 1759, vi, 1, 11). In fact, in his *Wealth of Nations*, frugality, parsimony and industry were all considered essential to building a successful business:

> Parsimony, and not industry, is the immediate cause of the increase of capital. Industry, indeed, provides the subject which parsimony

accumulates. But whatever industry might acquire, if parsimony did not save and store up, the capital would never be the greater. Parsimony, by increasing the fund which is destined for the maintenance of productive hands, tends to increase the number of those hands whose labour adds to the value of the subject upon which it is bestowed. . . . By what a frugal man annually saves, he not only affords maintenance to an additional number of productive hands, for that or the ensuing year, but, like the founder of a public workhouse, he establishes as it were a perpetual fund for the maintenance of an equal number in all times to come.

(Smith 1776, ii, 3, 16)

Throughout the nineteenth century, businessmen stressed the importance of prudence and hard work in running their firms. In his speech that introduced the English Joint Stock Companies Act in 1856, Lowe even spoke of a limited liability company as being an expression of "prudence and caution": "Its shareholders seem to say, 'we have entered into a partnership, but it is impossible to tell what may happen, and since the company may fail, we will not risk all we possess in the undertaking'" (Lowe 1856, 130). Popular nineteenth-century works regularly described prudence as a key virtue of business. Edwin Freedley's bestselling *Practical Treatise on Business* (1853) included prudence as one of the six essential habits of business (after industry, arrangement and calculation) and James Platt's even more successful *Business* (1875) advised the reader that "Prudence is essential to success" (Platt 1875, 128). Prudence remains a requirement of contemporary accounting practice and fiduciary law as a throwback to an earlier time when the term was still in common usage. But prudence was considered a key principle of nineteenth-century business, just as it was in neo-Thomist philosophy.

Yet considerations of the moral bases of capitalism or even the critiques of industrial society produced in Europe often seemed absent from American writings on business and management. As the economy of the United States surely grew to outstrip that of the British Empire in the new century, advances in American industrial management became particularly noted internationally. The first widely read book on business management, Frederick W. Taylor's *Principles of Scientific Management*, was hailed internationally upon its release in 1911, unusually for a book by an American writer at the time. The book summarised Taylor's efficiency principles and influenced contemporary European writers. It inspired his French contemporary, the mining engineer Henri Fayol, to release his *General and Industrial Management* (1916) and led to the adoption of similar efficiency movements in Germany, Russia, China and Japan (Wren and Bedeian 2009).

Unlike in the works of Fayol, however, there is no mention of ethics in Taylor's *Principles*. The only morality in Taylor's system was the principle of efficiency. Taylor's foreword takes US president Theodore Roosevelt's 1908 call for national efficiency as its point of departure. The first business ethics courses were already being offered in American universities in Taylor's day, but questions of morality seemed to have little or no place in scientific management. The American press had long bemoaned the "robber barons" of the Victorian era (Josephson 1934). But other than evidencing a broad dislike of laziness and waste, considerations of most matters of commercial morality were often strangely absent from the writings of the pioneers of industrial management in America.

That is not to say that American businessmen or consultants like Taylor had no interest in morality at all. Many Americans had engaged with the notion that business had moral responsibilities beyond profit-making in the nineteenth century, but their focus was typically framed in different manners from those advocated by European social critics, clerics and similar writers. A similar sense of social catastrophe engaged many American intellectuals and industrialists as the nineteenth century ended and a newly dominant liberal economy began clearly to outstrip that of the British. Different discourses of business ethics emerged in the United States from those that had arisen earlier in Europe, reflecting different religious, social and moral traditions and concerns.

3 Religion and Philanthropy

The corporate revolution occurred in the United States at the time that particular criticism had emerged of business, and two key figures in American industry had set up the world's two largest philanthropic organisations. The two richest men in America, Andrew Carnegie and John D. Rockefeller, Sr., created a new form of business philanthropy at the same time that the first university business schools were being established and the earliest business ethics programmes were emerging. Business philanthropy was crucially influenced by religious practice and was important in the later development of business ethics as key institutional and intellectual linkages emerged between business philanthropy programmes and efforts to develop better understandings of the proper role of business in society. But the key feature of business ethics in its first American articulation was the establishment of a series of ethics codes by commercial associations in light of the 1914 establishment of the Federal Trade Commission by the administration of President Woodrow Wilson.

Pope Leo XIII's *Rerum novarum* had also set in train the development of a movement of Catholic employers and an intellectual tradition of investigating the morality of commercial practices in Europe. Business ethics became an issue of concern for both Catholic and Protestant employers and moralists, particularly in terms of industrial welfare and employment relations. In the shadow of the Russian Revolution and the rise of Nazism in Germany, Christian employers and their clerical advisors established an emphasis on business ethics in response to the challenge of communism. By the end of the Second World War, a consensus had emerged that business had a key role to play in ensuring social harmony and a commitment to a lasting peace. A new sense of social responsibility developed at the time of what was known in political circles as the "post-war settlement".

Scientific Philanthropy

Marx and Engels began the *Communist Manifesto* with the warning "A spectre is haunting Europe—the spectre of communism" and ended it with the rallying cry "Working Men of All Countries, Unite!" (Marx and

Engels 1848). Rather than accede to Marxian claims that workers needed to be freed from the chains of wage labour, the typical response of the nineteenth-century entrepreneur had been to engage in employer paternalism or philanthropy. In keeping with the dominant political ideology of the age, the response was one of liberal voluntarism. Industrialists had created the factories which drew farm labourers to the cities as well as the urban poverty and social dislocation the emergence of the factory system conterminously engendered. Some employers took actions to ameliorate or resolve the worst of the negative effects of industrialisation.

Rather than join the radicals like Owen or Engels, many of the entrepreneurs of the nineteenth century engaged in activities that were described at the time as philanthropy. A range of responses emerged, from employer paternalism and industrial welfarism to engaging in "mutual gains" strategies and recognising early forms of organised labour (Shepherd and Toms 2019). Many of these employer responses have been traditionally associated with reflections of religious affiliation, perhaps most famously in England, with members of the Society of Friends and a form of Quaker paternalism (Child 1964; Rowlinson and Hassard 1993). Victorian employers such as Jeremiah Colman, George Cadbury, Joseph Rowntree and Titus Salt are often hailed as "enlightened entrepreneurs", pioneers of ethical business practice from an earlier age (Bradley 2007). The welfarist approach of such nineteenth-century employers included creating better housing for workers, organising education and providing sums of money to the new charities, whereas mutual gains approaches sought to address worker grievances and ensure less turbulence in labour markets. Many of these responses are criticised by social scientists today in light of the more profound changes to Victorian society demanded by figures such as Proudhon and Marx. But the origin of modern business ethics is most obviously to be sought among these earlier employer responses to the social and industrial problems of the age.

Hugh Cunningham (2016) has argued that the history of Western philanthropy must be seen as multi-layered. The earliest stratum he dates to ancient Greece, the second to the early Christian period and the third to the Middle Ages. The fourth is the "associated philanthropy" of the early modern era, that in the form of charity schools and workhouses lasted into the second half of the nineteenth century. The fifth of Cunningham's stages begins in the late eighteenth century with the revival of the Greek term *philanthropia* or "love of men" and the establishment in 1780 of the Société philanthropique de Paris in France. The benefactors in this form of philanthropy sought to achieve social improvement by providing their cities with public parks, art galleries, museums, concert halls and libraries. This type of philanthropy evolved into a form that was characterised by the Victorian feminist Josephine Butler as "large and comprehensive measures, organizations and systems planned by men and sanctioned by Parliament" (Butler 1869, xxxvii).

Cunningham's sixth historical type is global missionary philanthropy, a religious movement that sought to bring the benefits of Christianity and Western civilisation to the "heathen" nations. Cunningham's seventh stratum is philanthropy as a "gap filler", as Butler's masculine philanthropy was increasingly replaced by government action as Western parliaments began to take early steps on the road to establishing welfare states. The eighth stage, however, is Cunningham's "big philanthropic foundations", an American invention of the early twentieth century associated particularly with Andrew Carnegie and John D. Rockefeller, Sr.

As Benjamin Soskis (2010, 3) argues, American society found the emergence of large-scale philanthropy "both inspiring and alarming". The America of the Gilded Age (1870–1900) saw a "charity boom" dismissed by later critics as an attempt by business elites at "social control". As the country's cities filled up with foreign-born labour, wealth became particularly associated with figures such as Carnegie and Rockefeller. Despite the claims of its proponents to the contrary, however, "big philanthropy" has long been seen by its critics in Marxist terms—as a way for American industrial elites to maintain their privileged position and see off socialist revolution.

A Scotsman by birth, Andrew Carnegie sat somewhat outside the overtly religious environment that has always characterised American public life. Emigrating to Pittsburgh in 1848, Carnegie moved from working on the Pennsylvania Railroad into the iron industry at the end of the Civil War and returned to observant Presbyterianism only later in his life. His heroes included John Bright, one of the leaders of the movement to repeal the Corn Laws in the United Kingdom, and the Social Darwinist Herbert Spencer who had written only dismissively about philanthropy (Soskis 2010).

By 1900, Carnegie Steel was producing more of the metal than the whole of Great Britain—when he bought the Carnegie Company for $480 million, John P. Morgan called Carnegie the richest man in the world. But Carnegie had already decided before he married in 1887 that most of his fortune would go to charitable and educational purposes. His prenuptial agreement made it clear that the bulk of his estate would eventually go to philanthropy. "The man who dies rich dies disgraced" he said, giving away $350 million by the time he died in 1919 (Nasaw 2006, 350).

The idea that Carnegie was exercising social control is difficult to reconcile with what he explained in his writings. Carnegie had made his philosophy clear in works such as *Triumphant Democracy* (1886) and *The Gospel of Wealth* (1889), and clearly saw his role as that of a steward of American society—as a "trustee for the poor". As Soskis (2010) argues, American philanthropy grew out of a tradition of small-scale giving that was described by the French diplomat Alexis de Tocqueville in 1840 in the following terms: "small favors are done constantly. Few men are prepared to sacrifice themselves, but all are willing to lend a helping hand" (de Tocqueville 1840, 668). David Rothman (1971) points to the emergence of a kind of benevolent exceptionalism in the United States where even modest levels of poverty triggered an exaggerated response among nineteenth-century Americans. Neighbourly generosity was extended in scale and type as millions of migrants passed through Ellis Island and poor relief became a particular focus of public policy.

Nineteenth-century radicals already saw charity as both hindering social reform and demeaning to the recipient, while at the other end of the political spectrum, the Social Darwinist Spencer had dismissed charitable works as encouraging the lazy "to evade the harsh but salutary discipline of nature" (Spencer 1893, 383). American Catholics emphasised their commitment to the immediate relief of suffering; Protestants argued from utility and the need to weed out the deserving from the underserving poor (Soskis 2010, 34). Carnegie followed a different course again, as a proponent of a new "scientific" charity that was distinctly Protestant and American. But it was one that dates to the 1880s, and it was not a form of philanthropy that Carnegie originally developed.

The formation of the American Social Science Associations in 1865 was followed by the establishment of an independent National Conference of Charities and Correction in 1879 to promote scientific charity. Centred in the cities of the American North and Midwest, advocates of the scientific charity movement were clear about the threat posed by radical socialism to American society. "Charity has a twofold character", explained Charles Trusdell, the Methodist minister and director of the Chicago Relief and Aid Society. "It is the practical expression of sympathy with the afflicted, and the price that society pays for its own safety" (McCarthy 1982, 68). "Big philanthropy" was founded on the principles promoted by the American scientific charity movement in the 1880s.

As Elizabeth Harmon (2017) demonstrates, however, American "big philanthropy" also developed from an earlier tradition of public-private partnership between business and governments. The Carnegie Corporation of New York (1911) and the Rockefeller Foundation (1913) were established only after a century or more of experimentation with legal and financial arrangements, with an earlier tradition of public trusts that operated as public-private partnerships later superseded by private foundations that operated autonomously from business and government. Rather than mere contributors to the public, the biggest philanthropists— Rockefeller and Carnegie—came to see themselves as trustees for the national interest, and the nature and scale of their charitable foundations reflected this vision. Their notions of both stewardship and trusteeship would come to influence American understandings of the proper role of corporations and business ethics for much of the twentieth century.

But rather than Carnegie, it was John D. Rockefeller, Sr., who would prove most influential to business ethics. In 1855, the high-school dropout had begun his business career as a commission merchant in Cleveland,

Ohio. He began investing in oil refineries at the end of the Civil War and by 1870, his Standard Oil Company controlled 10 percent of the nation's petroleum refining capacity. Using strong-arm, anti-competitive tactics and slashing prices to undercut competitors, the Standard Oil Trust controlled 90 percent of American refined oil by 1882, and Rockefeller had developed a reputation as the leading robber baron in the country (Josephson 1934; Chernow 1998).

But Rockefeller had begun giving to charity well before he became involved in the kerosene business. A Baptist, Rockefeller had been making donations to charities all his working life. His approach to philanthropy first fell afoul of American public opinion in the 1890s, however, when it was revealed that he was giving money to religious institutions— as if they were being asked somehow to condone the behaviour of his monopoly kerosene producer. Rockefeller's main early critics were often Protestant pastors who claimed he was using his religious bequests in order to inflate his reputation and hence his profits. Rockefeller's solution was to stop giving money to religious foundations and instead form the country's first professional corporate-giving programme (Soskis 2010).

In 1891, Rockefeller hired the former Baptist minister Frederick Gates to be his philanthropic agent. Gates went through Rockefeller's charitable interests, reformed the pre-existing ad hoc structures Rockefeller had set up and developed formal philanthropic principles. Instead of responding to the many requests for funds the oil tycoon received each year, most of Rockefeller's philanthropy would subsequently go to medical charities as part of what he described in his autobiography as an "attempt to cure evils at their source" (Rockefeller 1909, 117). The Rockefeller Foundation was merely the last of the many charitable institutions he founded upon Gates's advice, including the Rockefeller Institute for Medical Research (1901) and the Rockefeller Sanitary Commission (1909). By the turn of the century, Rockefeller's sense of public stewardship and his range of charitable interests had been transformed into a professional enterprise of scientific giving under the leadership of Gates.

Ethics Codes and Business Education

The sense of stewardship that informed "big philanthropy" was a distinctly Christian expression. In medieval times, stewards were household servants, and their duty of stewardship originally referred to a requirement that they supply their lords with food and drink. But as it was used in the nineteenth century, the description "stewardship" was largely a Christian concept that emerged from the Biblical understanding that humans were given stewardship over the world by God. Abend (2014, 334–41) traces the use of the concept in American English to the works of John Calvin and the Puritan theologian Richard Baxter's interpretation of the Parable of the Talents (Baxter 1682, 34). Stewardship was also a key theme in the sermons of John Wesley, the co-founder of Methodism, particularly his *The Good Steward* (1768), and the American Congregationalist minister Leonard Bacon's sermon *The Christian Doctrine of Stewardship in Respect to Property* (1832). Stewardship had become a key duty of Protestant businessmen by the nineteenth century. They were stewards of the public good, not just their business undertakings.

The duty of stewardship assumed in "big philanthropy" also extended to educational bequests. Carnegie was particularly fond of establishing libraries, but the United States has also long had one of the most remarkable levels of public giving to universities as well. Historically, this philanthropic record has included bequests to business schools, and unlike in the United Kingdom where universities were also often funded by industrialists (Sanderson 1972), many of the oldest business schools in America as well as some of the oldest teaching arrangements for business ethics were directly funded by philanthropic bequests. None of the early American business schools was established by "big philanthropy", however, not even that at the university that bears Carnegie's name still today.

In 1881, the University of Pennsylvania established a business school, funded by a bequest of $100,000 from the Quaker industrialist Joseph Wharton. Business colleges of various forms had existed in America since at least the 1820s, but the Wharton School was the first to be established at a recognised university (Heald 1970, 71; Khurana 2007, 88). In 1898, the Universities of Chicago and California at Berkeley followed suit, establishing their business schools; and by 1908, Harvard had opened its doors to its first Master of Business Administration (MBA) enrolments. By the end of the First World War, over 10,000 students were enrolled in business schools at American universities. The practice of business management was rapidly professionalising, as undergraduate and graduate business students studied a mix of liberal arts and specialist business units.

Among these early business courses, some universities had begun offering specialist ethics units as early as the first decade of the twentieth century. The plan of the Wharton School had stressed that the

> general tendency of instruction . . . should be such as to inculcate and impress upon students . . . the immorality and practical expediency of seeking to acquire wealth by winning it from another rather than by earning it through some sort of service to one's fellow-men.
>
> (James 1891, 33)

The idea that business had a higher duty than moneymaking, that of service to society, was already a common theme in business education at the time of the foundation of the first business schools in American universities (Abend 2013, 2014).

Yet many of the lectures and other forms of instruction offered at the time bear little relationship to the kind of business ethics promoted today.

In 1879, the American economist John B. Clark had written about "Business ethics, past and present", describing how commercial laws and informal standards of business behaviour had developed to his day. In 1902, Colonel Harris Weinstock endowed the Barbara Weinstock Lectureship on the Morals of Trade at the College of Commerce at the University of California, and as he reflected in the preface to the first published Weinstock lecture, "Education has done splendid service in raising commercial standards. As a rule, the high-toned business man is enlightened, and, as a rule, the dishonest, unscrupulous man in business is ignorant" (Shaw 1904, v). A devout Jew, Weinstock evidently saw class snobbery as a key feature of American business ethics.

The early institutionalisation of business ethics in the United States was fitful, however, and the early lectures and materials such as those presented in the Weinstock lectures seem unfocused and merely moralising to the present-day reader. Yet most of the early business school curricula had a strong liberal arts component where students could be expected to learn about social issues more broadly. As Abend (2013, 2014) notes, for example, upon becoming dean of the College of Commerce at the University of Chicago, Leon C. Marshall developed a curriculum design for business students that required them to study English, modern languages, physics, mathematics and history and civics in first year, followed by history, psychology, philosophy, geography, sociology and economics in second year, and specialise in vocational courses only in third year. "However important it may be to turn out business men who can make money", Marshall claimed, "the most important task of all is to aid in promoting the progress and welfare of our society" (Marshall 1913, 101).

The key influence in the early development of American business ethics education was the code of conduct movement that had begun before the United States entered the First World War. In 1915, the delegates to the Sixth Annual Convention of the International Association of Rotary Clubs adopted a resolution that formalised a code of ethics for Rotary members. The general Rotary code included eleven principles, and specialist codes for Rotarians in individual professions were proclaimed over the next few years (including those for accountants, druggists, pharmacists, physicians, seed traders and shoe wholesalers, among many others). The 1915 general code read:

> My business standards shall have in them a note of sympathy for our common humanity. My business dealings, ambitions and relations shall always cause me to take into consideration my highest duties as a member of society. In every position in business life, in every responsibility that comes before me, my chief thought shall be to fill that responsibility and discharge that duty so when I have ended each of them, I shall have lifted the level of human ideals and

achievements a little higher than I found it. In view of this I hold that fundamental in a code of trade ethics for International Rotary are the following principles:

First: To consider my vocation worthy, and as affording me distinct opportunity to serve society.

Second: To improve myself, increase my efficiency and enlarge my service, and by doing so attest my faith in the fundamental principle of Rotary, that he profits most who serves best.

Third: To realize that I am a business man and ambitious to succeed; but that I am first an ethical man and wish no success that is not founded on the highest justice and morality.

Fourth: To hold that the exchange of my goods, my service and my ideas for profit is legitimate and ethical, provided that all parties in the exchange are benefited thereby.

Fifth: To use my best endeavors to elevate the standards of the vocation in which I am engaged, and so to conduct my affairs that others in my vocation may find it wise, profitable and conducive to happiness to emulate my example.

Sixth: To conduct my business in such a manner that I may give a perfect service equal to or even better than my competitor, and when in doubt to give added service beyond the strict measure of debt or obligation.

Seventh: To understand that one of the greatest assets of a professional or of a business man is his friends and that any advantage gained by reason of friendship is eminently ethical and proper.

Eighth: To hold that true friends demand nothing of one another and that any abuse of the confidence of friendship for profit is foreign to the spirit of Rotary, and in violation of its code of ethics.

Ninth: To consider no personal success legitimate or ethical which is secured by taking unfair advantage of certain opportunities in the social order that are absolutely denied others, nor will I take advantage of opportunities to achieve material success that others will not take because of the questionable morality involved.

Tenth: To be not more obligated to a Brother Rotarian than I am to every other man in human society; because the genius of Rotary is not in its competition, but in its coöperation; for provincialism can never have a place in an institution like Rotary, and Rotarians assert that human rights are not confined to Rotary clubs, but are as deep and as broad as the race itself; and for these high purposes does Rotary exist to educate all men and all institutions.

Eleventh: Finally, believing in the universality of the Golden Rule, "All things whatsoever ye would that men should do unto you, do ye even so unto them," we contend that society best holds together when equal opportunity is accorded all men in the natural resources of this planet.

(Rotary 1918, 620–1)

The next years saw a flurry of ethics codes appear in America. By 1924, over 300 separate ethics codes had been adopted covering all sorts of trades, and by 1925, 750 member organisations had signed up to "Principles of conduct" proposed by the US Chamber of Commerce. The Chamber of Commerce code had been prepared by a Committee on Business Ethics headed by Edwin B. Parker, and its "Fifteen Commandments of Business" went further than the Rotarian code in setting out duties such as "equitable consideration is due in business alike to capital, management, employees and the public", "representation of goods and services should be truthfully made and scrupulously fulfilled" and "waste in any form—of capital, labor, services, materials, or natural resources—is intolerable" (Parker 1924; Abend 2014, 183–90).

The immediate cause of the plethora of codes was a reaction to reform of the federal law concerning unfair competition, particularly monopolies abusing their position in the market. Rockefeller's Standard Oil Trust had been the most egregious abuser, but it had been broken up by the federal government in 1911 even though the Rockefellers had hired public relations consultants after the pioneering investigative journalist Ida Tarbell's 19-part exposure of the company's history of market abuse had appeared in *McClure's Magazine* in 1902–1903 (Tarbell 1904; Leccese 2017). And in 1914, the Federal Trade Commission Act had established a regulator of interstate trade, bringing to an end a period of anti-trust reforms aimed at eliminating all forms of unfair competition (Winerman 2003). The commercial codes also had an unexpected side effect. The ethics codes produced at the time were brought together by the Congregationalist pastor (and Rotarian) Edgar L. Heermance in a book published in 1924. Two years later Heermance subsequently produced the first analytical survey of business ethics in America.

The Yale economist Arthur T. Hadley (1907, 33–96) had earlier separated "the ethics of trade" from "the ethics of corporate management", but a similar distinction is not made clear in later works such as Heermance's 1926 *Ethics of Business*. As Heermance noted in his introductory chapter, a substantial change had occurred in public attitudes to business ethics since the early 1900s. The commercial codes witnessed that practices such as misleading advertising and improper accounting were considered key issues at the time (Heermance 1924, 1926). Keeping prices as low as possible for consumers was also flouted as a key moral concern of business in the decade that saw many of the first formal business ethics lectureships established at American universities (Filene 1922).

Earlier works such as the first Weinstock lecture at the University of California (Shaw 1904) and Edward D. Page's *Trade Morals* (1914) had been published before the United States had entered the First World War (Abend 2013). But the first survey of American business education, prepared for the Wharton School in 1929–30, noted that moral questions were only rarely addressed specifically in business school curricula at the time (Bossard and Dewhurst 1931, 409–10). Several business ethics professors produced similar studies to Heermance's pioneering 1926 work, most notably the philosopher Carl Taeusch, who after publishing a book on *Professional and Business Ethics* in 1926 (which included analyses of the ethics codes of lawyers, engineers, teachers and doctors as well as those of business, unions and farmers' associations) had been appointed the Harvard Business School's first (assistant) professor of business ethics (Abend 2014, 279–81). Other works on the topic from the time include the textbook *Business Ethics* (1926) produced by James Melvin Lee, the director of the journalism department at New York University; and *The Fundamentals of Business Ethics* (1926) by Everett William (Willie) Lord, the dean of the College of Business Administration at Boston University. A later textbook, *Business Ethics* (1937) by Frank Chapman Sharp and Phillip D. Fox, developed on a course that the German-educated philosopher Sharp had been teaching at the University of Wisconsin since 1913. Chester Barnard's *Functions of the Executive* (1938) also contained a whole chapter on moral leadership (originally presented as a lecture at Harvard), arguing that firms that developed reputations for immoral conduct would not survive. But both Taeusch and Sharp had left their teaching posts by the time that the William A. Vawter Foundation in Chicago offered a prize in 1936 for the best business ethics study of the year. The entries proved so disappointing, however, that the competition was never repeated (Abend 2013, 185–9).

After producing a second monograph on business ethics in 1931, Taeusch had left Harvard in 1935 to become an official in the US Department of Agriculture. Sharp had retired at age seventy from his position in the philosophy faculty at the University of Wisconsin in 1936, but Taeusch's experience at Harvard had not been as happy. In an article that appeared after he had left his university post, Taeusch put the paucity of academic writings on business ethics at the time down to the unwillingness of businessmen to read widely and the "snobbish attitude of many research workers toward anything which savored of business or economics" (Taeusch 1935, 81). He pointed to the appearance of business codes as key to the emergence of business ethics, but that "Many of these standards are stated in such vague terms as to be meaningless, some are easily recognized as camouflage or apologetics clouded with sentiment, and many of them flatly contradict one another" (Taeusch 1935, 89). Rather than follow the model of Weber, Taeusch had decided to adopt a case study approach to his work in business ethics while at Harvard (Taeusch 1932). But as he continued despondently:

> Even when challenged recently by government to write its own codes, business found itself unable to present an adequate or convincing basis for asserting generally acceptable social principles or rules of sound economic conduct, both of which are essential to ethical standards of behavior; and there was a deplorable lack of such imaginative and concrete suggestion as might have supplanted the deficiency of recorded or accepted practice. . . . The ideal of business self-regulation, so dear to the heart of the advocate of *laissez-faire*, or of functional pluralism, and an essential part of any system of business ethics, has failed.
>
> (Taeusch 1935, 94–5)

American business ethics had hit a dead end and was not to emerge again in the United States, at least overtly under the label of "ethics", until twenty years had passed.

Yet as Taeusch noted, similar ideas had already emerged at the time in Europe, although without the same emphasis on institutionalisation as occurred in the United States. Early European writings on commercial ethics from the early twentieth century include the economist Gustav Cohn's 1900 study of the development of debates over the "ethical character of the national economy" in light of Marxism and the emergence of Christian socialism. In 1907, the German neo-Kantian philosopher Franz Staudiger published a book on the *Wirtschaftliche Grundlagen der Moral* [*Economic Foundations of Morals*] as a critique of Marxism, as the moral basis of capitalist society became a key concern of conservative reaction. But the first dedicated study of business ethics in Germany was Benno Jaroslaw's *Ideal und Geschäft* [*Ideal and Business*] (1912). Jaroslaw was a businessman himself, and while his book was well received in the German sociological tradition by figures such as Ferdinand Tönnies (who discusses Jaroslaw's book at some length in his 1931 *Einführung in die Soziologie*), the issue of business and morality at the time never seemed to escape the bounds of Christian social teaching and conservative defences of the capitalist political order.

Between defences of the existing political system and criticisms of the lack of a formal ethical justification for Marxian thought, morality also informed the development of the emerging discipline of sociology. In France, Émile Durkheim focused expressly on morality, explaining that the key purpose of social solidarity was moral. As he emphasised in *The Division of Labour in Society*, "social solidarity is a *completely* moral phenomenon" (Durkheim 1893, 64, italics in original). James Dingley (1997) has stressed, however, that Elton Mayo, the major interpreter of

Durkheim in American management theory, understood social solidarity mainly in political terms. Mayo employed Durkheimian solidarity as a solution to what he saw as the pathology of trade unionism.

It is perhaps one of the great ironies of the Hawthorne studies, undertaken at Western Electric's Hawthorne plant outside Chicago from 1924 to 1932, that while they were so strongly focused on "management and morale" (Roethlisberger 1942), they did not seem to focus at all on morality. The term *morale* was borrowed from French military language in the sense of "good conduct", but only in terms of conduct that supported the achievement of group objectives. In their focus on how managers can maintain morale in employees, Mayo and his followers seemed unwilling to engage explicitly with the moral aspect of what they were doing. By making workplaces more humane, investigating and hoping to resolve what he called the *Human Problems of an Industrial Civilisation* (1933), Mayo avoided any direct reflection on the ethics of managerial manipulation.

As Griffin and colleagues (2002) have argued, Mayo's experience of labour unions in Australia before he arrived in the United States was wholly negative. According to Mayo, good conduct in the workplace was conduct that accorded with business objectives, and a manager's principal role was to educate his workforce. Labour unions, for Mayo, were pathological social actors. Workers overcome by reverie became prey to the evil schemes of labour union leaders. Chris Nyland (1998) has argued that, in contrast, Frederick Taylor saw unions as potential partners, in recognition of the possibility of mutual gains. Indeed, by the 1930s, Taylorists had become supporters of various forms of industrial democracy. Mayo's approach was to claim that only managers had the ability to make appropriate decisions and to deny any autonomy to their workforces (Bruce and Nyland 2011).

Early Social Responsibility

Instead of becoming employee focused, American business ethics remained predominately an outward-looking concern. Protestant advocates of good employee relations were supported by figures such as John D. Rockefeller, Jr. (1917), but few American employers seemed to accept that labour relations should be viewed in terms of business morals. In 1913, Rockefeller had hired vigilantes in an attempt to break up a strike at the Colorado Fuel & Iron Corp., and the resultant 1914 massacre of striking miners at Ludlow had only blackened the Rockefeller name further (Hallahan 2002). Rockefeller's belated conversion to employer paternalism seemed more to reflect an attempt to rescue the family name than it did a heartfelt engagement with business ethics.

Yet the end of the Second World War saw a renewed engagement of American business with ethics. Western European countries responded to the defeat of Nazism and the Soviet occupation of Eastern Europe by engaging with the labour movements in their respective countries in terms of a formal settlement of differences. In Italy and West Germany, new Christian Democratic Parties were established that embraced the Catholic Church's advocation of the role of trade unions in establishing social order. Similar policies were pursued in Britain as formal plans emerged to reconcile the interests of industry and the labour movement as rebuilding the devastated European economies took precedence over other concerns. Union influence grew and many industries were nationalised as a post-war settlement developed between capital and labour.

The role taken by European businesses during this settlement was typically seen at the time as a political as well as a moral duty. And in a 1948 study of the *Responsibilities of Business Leadership* based on speeches made at the Eighteenth Annual Conference of the Harvard Business School Alumni Association (Merrill ed. 1948), American business was also claimed to have a moral role in the rebuilding of post-war Europe. Yet this sense of ethical commitment did not extend to coming to an accommodation with socialism on the western side of the Atlantic. Instead, a different reflection of business ethics emerged in America during the immediate post-war era, the most famous contribution to which remains Howard R. Bowen's *Social Responsibilities of the Businessman* (1953). As Acquier and colleagues (2011) maintain, Bowen is widely acknowledged as the "founding father of the academic conception and study of corporate social responsibility" (Acquier et al. 2011, 607). American notions of business responsibility have been traced back by Abend (2014) to at least the Victorian period, but Bowen's book laid the foundation for the broader field of what today is known as CSR.

The development of CSR, however, represented a bifurcation in American business ethics. As Frederick (2006) notes, two distinct traditions emerged in discussions of ethical behaviour in business in the United States. In the 1950s and 1960s, the social responsibility of business tended to be stressed by Protestant writers, while Catholics focused instead on what they called business ethics. The United States was a majority Protestant country at the time—in fact, it has long been the largest Protestant nation in the world. Yet Catholic initiatives such as *Rerum novarum* usually predated similar Protestant responses. The idea that businesses had broader social responsibilities than duties to their shareholders was widely accepted in Europe in the 1930s, but the American discourse of corporate social responsibility developed in a manner largely isolated from European concerns.

Earlier figures than Bowen have been claimed to be harbingers of corporate social responsibility. Carroll and colleagues (2012), for example, date American debates over "social responsibility and the corporate economy" to the turn of the twentieth century—to the later years of the dominance of the "robber barons" (Josephson 1934)—while Abend

(2014) associates such early expressions of American business ethics with the nineteenth-century model of the Christian merchant. There is little notion of social responsibility in the writings of figures such as Carnegie or Rockefeller, however. Not only did they not run corporations, Carnegie's writings speak only of his responsibility to manage his business successfully (Carnegie 1889, 56), and in his biography John D. Rockefeller, Sr., restricts his discussion of commercial responsibility to managers needing to look after their shareholders (Rockefeller 1909, 66). It was the association with the new managerial class and the corporate revolution first described by Berle and Means in 1932 that is more properly to be associated with the emergence of a sustained discourse of corporate responsibility and hence CSR.

The essential difference between the responsibility felt by a figure such as Carnegie or Rockefeller and Bowen's notion of a social responsibility was not merely a matter of the legal structure their businesses were constituted as (Carnegie Steel was a partnership and Standard Oil was a trust), but instead it reflected the distinction made so critically by Berle and Means (1932) between the ownership and control of corporations. Carnegie and Rockefeller may have seen themselves as stewards of the public interest, but they both held unambiguous property as well as control rights over the firms they founded. With the corporate revolution, whatever social responsibility a business had was a matter for the managers of a corporation—CSR reflected the emergence of professional managers and the attendant ideology of what has become known as "managerialism". It represented a different sense of business obligation from that which had developed into "big philanthropy" and emerged separately from the Catholic neo-Thomist tradition.

Yet it is not often recognised that Bowen had been asked to write the *Social Responsibilities of the Businessman* by a committee of the Federal Council of Churches of Christ and that CSR in this way can be seen ultimately as a reaction to Catholic social thought. Bowen's book contains a chapter on Protestant (and not Catholic) ethics and appeared as part of the council's series on the Ethics and Economics of Society. It also included a response to Bowen's survey (which was begun with the support of a 1949 Rockefeller Foundation grant) by the Federal Council of Churches' F. Ernest Johnson, a leading Congregationalist religious studies educator. The *Social Responsibilities of the Businessman* is qualitatively different from previous studies and expressions of American business ethics by being so institutionally religious.

While post-war sociologists such as C. Wright Mills (1951) pursued a much more radical project than had Mayo, business ethics remained separate from the mainstream of American social science. Both Heermance and Lord had been Protestant ministers, and the Federal Council of Churches of Christ was an ecumenical Protestant organisation. But Catholic social teaching had been a more important influence on business ethics in Europe as *Rerum novarum* had inspired thinkers such as Nell-Breuning to further explore aspects of business and its relationship with religion. Catholic social thought was also propagated by Catholic employers' associations and, from the 1930s, especially through the means of the Union internationale des associations patronales catholiques or UNIAPAC, headquartered in Brussels, Belgium.

UNIAPAC was formed in 1931 as a union of the various national Catholic employers' associations that had emerged since the formation of the Algemene Katholieke Werkgebers Verenigung (General Catholic Employers Association) in the Netherlands in 1913. Similar associations were founded in Belgium and then France in 1921 and 1926 respectively, and earlier traditions of Catholic employer groups reached back into the nineteenth century. But it was in the relationship between the French industrialist Léon Harmel and Pope Leo XIII that the origins of the European movement of Catholic employers were sought by Gremillion in his 1961 history of UNIAPAC.

Harmel was a contemporary of Carnegie and Rockefeller whose family owned a woollen mill in Val-des-Bois, near Reims in the department of Marne, France (Coffey 2003). A third-generation industrialist, Harmel was famous in his day for his paternalistic work practices, offering employees the opportunity of factory housing and paying them what he called a "family wage"—"proportionate to his work and as sufficient as possible to support his needs and those of his family" (Harmel 1889, 76). Harmel's workers were entitled to the receipt of a pension on retirement, access to a credit union and a life insurance mutual. They also had access to a range of sports, artistic, musical and drama clubs established by the Harmel family business. Moreover, Harmel was a supporter of factory works councils and of developing a social partnership with his employees. The first of his two books, *Manuel d'une corporation chrétienne* [*Manual of a Christian Corporation*] (1877), outlined his approach to factory management and caught the attention of Pope Leo XIII (Coffey 2003).

It is clear that *Rerum novarum* was influenced by Harmel's approach to industrial management and that Harmel was instrumental in the establishment in 1884 of the Patrons du Nord, France's first Catholic employers' association (Gremillion 1961, 24–37; Coffey 2003). The movement of Catholic employers began in France and the Low Countries in reflection of the establishment of Catholic labour unions and Catholic agricultural associations, but especially of Harmel's *Manuel d'une corporation chrétienne* and the development of Catholic social doctrine.

Harmel's first group, the Confrérie de Notre-Dame de l'Usine (Fraternity of Our Lady of the Factory) that he founded in 1875, is perhaps best seen in light of the long-standing European tradition of business fraternities that reaches back into the Middle Ages. But in 1931, Pope Pius XI published his encyclical *Quadragesimo anno* on the fortieth anniversary of the appearance of *Rerum novarum*. The leaders of the Catholic employ-ers' associations took the occasion to form an international union, and over the coming years more branches would be formed, including in Brit-ain, South America, the Belgian Congo and French Indo-China. By the end of the 1950s, UNIAPAC had over 20,000 members—and manag-ers from all over Western Europe attended UNIAPAC's conferences on Catholic social doctrine and the responsibilities of employers. Harmel had described his work as charity, but after the publication of *Rerum novarum* his legacy would be promoted principally in terms of social justice. Where charity had become scientific under American "big philan-thropy", employer welfarism had developed into a matter of justice in the Catholic tradition.

Unlike *Rerum novarum* which had been an all-Italian production, Pius XI's encyclical was drafted by Nell-Breuning, the leading Jesuit business ethicist of the day. A full-blown form of Catholic business ethics had emerged, promoted and debated in works written in all the major Western European languages. UNIAPAC never developed an American affiliate, but it was under the influence of UNIAPAC and Catholic social thought that the first department of industrial relations was formed at the Univer-sity of Montréal in the 1930s and that Catholic priests would become so important in establishing the trade union movement in Quebec. *Rerum novarum* argued for the importance of workers being able to join labour unions and advised Catholic employers to put aside whatever hostil-ity they may have to the worker movement in order to promote social order and social justice. In 1949, Pius XII addressed a UNIAPAC meet-ing in Rome where he supported recent German developments towards establishing a "community of work" in terms of employee profit-sharing and for the first time indicated Papal approval of the push to establish co-determination arrangements in listed firms (Pius XII 1949; Gremil-lion 1961). Along with the writings of figures such as Nell-Breuning, the Catholic employers' movement was critical to establishing what would later be styled "Rhineland capitalism" or the European model of "social market capitalism".

The dominant form of Christianity in the United States was Protestant-ism, however—in fact, many Americans at the time were hostile to the Catholic Church in reflection of the founding of many of the original American colonies by English Calvinists. Yet North American Protestants had formed their own traditions of social policy and Christian ethics, particularly over the course of the nineteenth century. One of the key figures in the development of mainline Protestant social policy was Wal-ter Rauschenbusch, a theologian and Baptist pastor who taught at the Rochester Theological Seminary. His *Christianity and the Social Crisis* (1907) was an examination of the ills of industrial capitalism and what Christians should do about it. Rauschenbusch criticised the Catholic Church for "keep[ing] alive the despotic spirit of decadence of Roman civilization" (i.e. for not being sufficiently democratic) and mentioned Catholic social thought only in terms of it attempting to "quarantine the Catholic workingmen in organizations of their own and to keep them immune from the bacillus of socialism" (Rauschenbusch 1907, 192, 320). But it is clear that the key Protestant contributions to business ethics were usually proposed much later than, and often in reaction to, earlier statements by Catholic writers.

The Federal Council of Churches had first met in Philadelphia in 1908 as a national body representing thirty-one Protestant denominations and 17 million American Christians. In light of a report from its Committee on Church and Modern Industry, the council had adopted a "Social Creed of the Churches". The main purpose of the creed was to establish a united Protestant body in light of the development of ecumenicalism and what would later become known as the Social Gospel (Piper 1969; Evans 2017). The Social Gospel was an American and Canadian movement to apply Christian ethics to social problems that was particularly supported by mainline Protestant clergy, and in its focus on industrial conditions and the importance of workers' rights it represented the main North American Protestant equivalent of Catholic social thought.

Rather than being expressed in terms of a lengthy encyclical, the "Social Creed of the Churches" (as it was recorded and at least co-authored by the Methodist minister Harry F. Ward) featured a short list of beliefs concerning industrial conditions:

The Federal Council of Churches of Christ in America stands:

> For equal rights and complete justice for all men in all stations of life.
>
> For the abolition of child-labor.
>
> For such regulation of the conditions of toil for women as shall safeguard the physical and moral health of the community.
>
> For the suppression of the "Sweating System."
>
> For the gradual and reasonable reduction of the hours of labor to the lowest practical point, and for that degree of leisure for all which is a condition of the highest human life.
>
> For a release from employment one day in seven.
>
> For the right of all men to the opportunity for self-maintenance, a right ever to be wisely and strongly safe-guarded against encroachments of every kind.
>
> For the right of workers to some protection against the hardships often resulting from the swift crisis of industrial change.
>
> For a living wage as a minimum in every industry, and for the highest wage that each industry can afford.
>
> For the protection of the worker from dangerous machinery, occupational disease, injuries and mortality.

> For suitable provision for the old age of the workers and for those incapacitated by injury.
> For the principle of conciliation and arbitration in industrial dissensions.
> For the abatement of poverty.
> For the most equitable division of the products of industry that can ultimately be devised.
>
> (Ward 1914, 6)

Abolition of child labour and the eradication of sweatshop conditions were key issues for the Social Gospel movement. But by the 1930s, the influential Protestant thinker Reinhold Niebuhr, a Calvinist theologian at the Union Theological Seminary in New York, had come to advocate less idealistic ambitions, adopting a Christian realism that accepted that society was not perfectible by moralists or social scientists. Niebuhr's *Moral Man and Immoral Society* (1932) criticised American social liberals, dismissing their belief that individual self-interest could be fulfilled in a collective good as a "utopian illusion". Niebuhr argued that calls for justice arose naturally out of individual morality: "Individual men . . . are endowed by nature with a measure of sympathy and consideration for their kind", but that politics often brings out the worst in people (Niebuhr 1932, xi). "In every human group there is less reason to guide and check impulse . . . less ability to comprehend the needs of others and therefore more unrestrained egoism than the individuals, who comprise the group, reveal in their personal relationships" (Niebuhr 1932, xi–xii). Niebuhr's warnings regarding "collective ego" were seen by many subsequently as realised by the rise of Nazism and the violence and oppression particularly associated with the Soviet form of equalitarian social idealism inspired by Marx. Niebuhr quoted the Russian revolutionary Leon Trotsky's dismissal of middle-class morality: "we were never concerned with the Kantian priestly and vegetarian-Quaker prattle about the 'sacredness of human life'" (Niebuhr 1932, 177). Niebuhr was also critical of parliamentary socialism as it existed in Western Europe, but his main criticism was of social radicalism:

> An adequate political morality . . . must recognise that human society will probably never escape social conflict. . . . It will try to save society from being involved in endless cycles of futile conflict . . . by keeping it to a minimum. . . . The danger arises from the ease with which any social group, engaged in social conflict, may justify itself by professing to be fighting for freedom and equality.
>
> (Niebuhr 1932, 234–6)

Niebuhr inspired a new generation of American Protestants sympathetic to socialism to focus their energies on less radical approaches to social reform, particularly within the Democratic Party.

Over the course of the 1920s, the Federal Council of Churches had become especially tied to the Democratic Party and the American labour movement. As such, the council included an Industrial Relations Division that conducted industrial conferences, gave lectures in colleges and seminaries, mediated in labour disputes and encouraged research into social issues. The council had merged with other ecumenical groups in 1950 to become the National Council of Churches, but it was the largest mainline Protestant body in America at the time it commissioned Bowen to write the *Social Responsibility of Businessmen*. In 1949, however, popular fear of communist espionage had led to the development of McCarthyism, an anti-communist movement that affected Bowen personally.

Before the 1950 merger with seven smaller ecumenical groups, the Federal Council of Churches' Industrial Relations Division had been renamed the Department of Church and Economic Life, and it had just released a report in 1947 which advocated that "Property represents a trusteeship under God, and should be held subject to the needs of the community", as well as that "Christians must be actuated more largely by a service motive than by a profit motive" (Federal Council of Churches 1947, 14–15; Gunn 2009, 124–5). Moreover, the council had been involved in the 1948 creation of the World Council of Churches (whose founding had been financially supported by John D. Rockefeller, Jr.) and its inaugural Amsterdam assembly had featured the promotion of a statement that rejected both communism and capitalism: "The Christian churches should reject the ideologies of both communism and *laissez-faire* capitalism. . . . It is the responsibility of Christians to seek new creative solutions which never allow either justice or freedom to destroy each other" (Visser 'T Hooft ed. 1949, 80; Duff 1956).

Bowen's book, however, was published three years after he had been forced to resign as dean of the College of Commerce and Business Administration at the University of Illinois for allegedly being anti-business by colleagues who had not supported his attempts to modernise the school (Solberg and Tomlinson 1997). A Keynesian welfare economist, Bowen's reforms had been associated by his enemies with communist sympathies—unlike many of the economists at Illinois, Bowen was a Democrat and his 1948 book *Toward Social Economy* was institutionalist rather than economically liberal. Bowen subsequently became professor of economics at Williams College in Massachusetts, where he served as a consultant on the $100,000 "Ethics and Economic Life" grant from the Rockefeller Foundation to the Federal Council of Churches. His *Social Responsibility of Business* was very much written in the hope that "new creative solutions" to the problems of industrial society might emerge in post-war American economic life.

By the 1950s, both Catholic and Protestant discourses of business ethics and the proper role of business in society had emerged. And as the United States was the leading economic power of the day, discussions of the relationship of Christian moral thought to business practice in America would be particularly innovative and influential. Key ideas concerning stewardship and trusteeship had arisen in American business circles in the nineteenth century, and these were partnered in the new century by invocations of ideals of service and reform. Coming from the country with the largest affiliation to Protestantism, the writings of American Christians were also read in Europe, but the Catholic tradition, serving a much larger number of adherents, was more influential internationally. The notion that businesses had social responsibilities would increasingly become a topic of mainstream business thought, first in the United States, and then later in Europe. But the main currents regarding the social responsibility of business would be secular rather than religious as the development of American notions of CSR spread internationally in the 1960s and 1970s.

4 The Social Responsibilities of Business

The first major expression of business ethics to appear at the end of the Second World War was the social responsibility of business movement, or what by the late 1960s were being called corporate social responsibilities (Walton 1967). The notion that businesses had social responsibilities beyond those legally owed to their owners, employees and other parties they become involved with had previously been articulated most obviously in nineteenth-century philanthropic programmes. But figures such as Léon Harmel saw industrial welfarism also as an expression of charity, and with the emergence of Catholic social thought and Protestant forms of Christian socialism, industrial welfarism was increasingly described in terms of justice—as an ethical and political obligation. As discourses concerning business ethics continued to mature after the First World War, however, American discussions regarding the social responsibility of business had begun to assume a new character.

As the idea of social responsibility developed in the United States, it was increasingly adopted by transnational corporations, and a distinctively American style of corporate social responsibility spread internationally. By the 1970s, the notion that corporations had social responsibilities above and beyond maximising shareholder value had become commonplace in both the United States and Europe, and the idea was increasingly expressed in terms of developments that had first arisen in America. The philanthropic practices of business had been normalised and led to the development of the idea that corporations had responsibilities to the broader community beyond those established by law as American notions such as "social audit" began to be taken up in Western Europe. A postwar consensus had emerged in Europe that accepted the role of unions in establishing social order and a broadening acceptance that business had wider duties than just providing benefits to the owners and employees of firms. The expansion of state-sponsored social welfare programmes in Western Europe had led to the establishment of universal retirement pensions, and many countries had followed the German lead and established mandatory forms of industrial democracy, including works councils and co-determination. Few of these social policies were seen in terms of ethics any longer, however, as they were increasingly achieved through political processes and hence were mandated by law. American-style corporate social responsibility was distinguished from European developments by representing a voluntary activity not mandated by legislation.

The 1960s also saw an increasing secularisation of ethics, a development that had begun in university philosophy departments. Left-wing political movements also developed more clearly into secular middle-class expressions as ideas generated by academics disaffected by capitalism became important in campus protest movements. The key development in the United States, however, was the emergence of the anti-corporate movement, particularly in the form of "Nader's Raiders", a series of organisations and forums that sprang up around the American lawyer Ralph Nader, the author of a bestselling exposé of the American automobile industry. By the 1970s, corporate social responsibility had become a major issue of debate in American society, with protest groups, conferences and political inquiries being formed to investigate the sources and nature of corporate malfeasance and scandal. Where previous scandals had seen limited reaction, a sustained programme of reform began to develop in the 1970s as CSR and business ethics were first popularised and then spread internationally as discourses of corporate behavioural reform.

From Employer Paternalism to General Welfare

Ralph Nader's bestselling critique of the US automobile industry, *Unsafe At Any Speed* (1965), made him a household name. The previous year the young Harvard law graduate had accepted a position on the staff of Democratic Senator Patrick Moynihan, where he studied automobile safety in Washington, D.C. By 1968 Nader had appeared on the cover of *Newsweek* as he assembled a group of young lawyers to investigate other matters of consumer protection. Their report on the US Federal Trade Commission was published in 1969 as what the press dubbed "Nader's Raiders" became the most famous expression of the burgeoning anti-corporate movement of the day (Cox et al. 1970; Marcello 2004). Nader and his followers were criticising the way that US businesses treated their customers—the lack of responsibility they showed to society. As Nader argued in *Unsafe At Any Speed*:

> In 1964, automobiles killed 47,700 people and injured over four million. . . . But the dead and injured consumers of automobiles do not interfere with production and sales . . . when it comes to passenger safety . . . the so-called automotive safety engineer devotes himself to the defense of the automobile created by his colleagues in the styling and marketing departments.
>
> (Nader 1965, 129–30)

In 1978, Patrick E. Murphy, an assistant professor of marketing at Marquette University, Milwaukee, argued that the history of the adoption of social responsibilities by American businesses beyond the legislated minimum could be classified into four eras: a philanthropic era up until the 1950s; an "awareness" era until the late 1960s; an "issue" era up until 1973; and then a "responsiveness" era after 1974. Murphy's characterisation of the period up to the Second World War is inconsistent, however, with the historian Morrell Heald's 1970 study of the social responsibilities of American business since 1900. Heald points to a much earlier acceptance of the need for corporate managers to accommodate claimants on American businesses other than just owners and employees.

Instead, Heald (1970) traces the beginnings of the movement for American business to accept broader social responsibilities to the period before the Second World War and the time of developments such as the Community Chest movement. Founded in 1913 in Cleveland, Ohio, by the Federation for Charity and Philanthropy, over 1,000 Community Chest organisations had emerged by 1948. Heald dates the "enlargement" of business responsibility to the period after the 1914 establishment of the Federal Trade Commission (Heald 1970, 95–111). Advocates of the idea that business had a duty to serve the public were a characteristic of the 1920s and the Berle/Dodd debate of the early 1930s was another expression of the widening of understandings concerning the social role of business that occurred between the two World Wars. Heald describes the period from 1945 to 1960 in terms of "new horizons of corporate responsibility", the time of a further enlargement of the notion that businesses owed broader duties to society than increasing profitability and making goods and services more affordable to the public (Heald 1970, 207–42). Most of the earlier expressions of American business practice studied by Heald were obviously forms of philanthropy, however, and not as particular to the United States (or even North America) as were foundations like those of Carnegie and Rockefeller.

According to the first person to produce a study focused specifically on the social responsibilities of business, what has been known since the 1980s as CSR was an especially important post-war phenomenon. As Bowen wrote in 1953:

> We are entering an era when private business will be judged solely in terms of its demonstrable contribution to the general welfare—The acceptance of obligations to workers, consumers, and the general public is a condition for the survival of the free enterprise system.
>
> (Bowen 1953, 52)

By the "survival of the free enterprise system", Bowen was clearly referring to the challenge of socialism, which in the 1950s was often linked with Soviet communism, but in Western countries typically meant instead the prospect of nationalisation of key industries by governments. The spectre of Marxism was often referred to obliquely by writers such as Bowen at the time, even though Bowen himself had cause to resent the wilder excesses of McCarthyism. But it was clear to his audience what a reference to the survival of capitalism meant in the 1950s.

Most early accounts of the origin of business social responsibility have tended to support Bowen's account of its roots lying in the 1950s. There had been publications on the social responsibilities of American business in the late 1940s (e.g. Merrill ed. 1948; David 1949; Dempsey 1949; Davis 1957), but looking back on the origins of calls for American businesses to meet responsibilities other than economic ones, Keith Davis reflected in 1975:

> Beginning in the 1950s, the public's mood shifted sharply toward social concerns, and this mood was reflected in extensive social demands made on institutions. Since business interacts extensively with all of society, perhaps more of these demands were made on business than on any other institution. By sticking strictly to its economic role in the past, business had left the social side of its activities largely untended and was unprepared to deal effectively with social issues.

Davis had become one of the leading academic commentators on the social role of business at the time. A professor of management at Arizona State University, Davis had published a well-received management textbook on human relations in 1957, and since then he had written widely on business social responsibility. In 1960 he had famously proposed what he would later call the "iron law of responsibility": "social responsibilities of businessmen need to be commensurate with their social power" (Davis 1960, 71; Davis and Blomstrom 1966, 180). Citing a series of studies from the 1950s, beginning his list with Bowen's, but including other works from Clarence Randall's *A Creed for Free Enterprise* (1952) to Benjamin Selekman's *A Moral Philosophy for Business* (1959), Davis also advised that "the avoidance of social responsibility leads to gradual erosion of social power".

In 1973, Davis set out the cases for and against the assumption of social responsibilities by business. On the positive side, Davis argued that adopting social responsibilities served the long-run interests of business. It improved the public image of business, and its adoption might mean less requirement for regulation. Businesses, he maintained, could be well-suited to help society—they had the power and opportunity to do so. But there were well-known objections to this view. Businesses should be focused primarily on shareholder value, social responsibility programmes were costly and reduced profits, and businesses should not be held responsible for matters outside their area of expertise (Davis 1973).

In 1975, however, Davis argued that the debate over the social responsibility of business had reached a level of "some maturity". Davis proposed five principles, following from his iron law, that he called guidelines of the "social responsibility mode". The five guidelines were:

1. Social responsibility arises from social power.
2. Business shall operate as a two-way open system with open receipt of inputs from society and open disclosure of its operations to the public.
3. Social costs as well as benefits of an activity, product, or service shall be thoroughly calculated and considered in order to decide whether to proceed with it.
4. Social costs of each activity, product, or service shall be priced into it so that the consumer (user) pays for the effects of his consumption on society.
5. Beyond social costs business institutions as citizens have responsibilities for social involvement in areas of their competence where major social needs exist.

The notion of social costs Davis saw in terms of what Bowen (1953, 155–6) had called social audit. Bowen's notion had been further developed in the early 1970s (Bauer and Fenn 1972; Corson and Steiner 1975), but had often been labelled in different manners. In 1962 Theodore Kreps had called for measurement of the "Social performance of business" and in 1975 S. Prakash Sethi similarly called for the measurement of "Corporate Social Performance" (Sethi 1975). But like the expression "Corporate Social Responsibility", a range of different descriptions were being used for the idea of trying to measure and report on the contribution that businesses made more generally to society at the time.

Other commentators from Davis's day sought to describe the change in sentiment in more specific terms. In 1960, Frederick had traced the calls for business to recognise a new form of social responsibility to a collapse in confidence in economic liberalism, in the theory of *laissez-faire*. Pointing to the work of the economist John Maynard Keynes and "the growth of the largescale corporation, with its tendency to divorce legal ownership from actual control of operations", Frederick claimed:

> Under the *laissez-faire* philosophy, there had been a social theory by which private interests could be harmonized with the interests of society at large. This meant that there was no need to be concerned deliberately with the social responsibility of private businessmen; it would be produced automatically.
>
> (Frederick 1960, 55)

Frederick pointed to "five major currents of thought about business responsibility in American society" that had developed since 1950. They included "the idea that corporate managers should voluntarily act as trustees of the public interest" (with Frederick's footnote referring to Berle and Means's 1932 study) and that "Christian ethical principles of conduct" should be applied to the "problems of business enterprise". The post-war period had seen a revival in churchgoing and calls for greater application of Christian moral standards to business in periodicals such as the *Harvard Business Review* (Ohmann 1955; Campbell 1957; Johnson 1957). Frederick also pointed to J. Kenneth Galbraith's (1952) argument that "the answer to concentrated business power is more power" and that a "countervailing power" to business needed to be built up elsewhere in society. The social pessimism inherent in the works of figures from George Orwell to C. Wright Mills were a fourth current identified by Frederick. The last major current he identified was in the calls of people such as Clarence Randall, the former chairman of the Inland Steel Company, to reform the "capitalist ethic" in his *A Creed for Free Enterprise* (1952).

Frederick (2006) would also point to the importance of the 1951 *Harvard Business Review* article on "management's responsibility in a complex world" by Frank Abrams, the CEO of Standard Oil of New Jersey. But the emergence of calls for business to assume social responsibilities must also be seen in light of the success that large American corporations had in developing their image in the years before the Second World War as benevolent giants. From dangerous threats to society, by the end of the war, American corporations had managed to establish for themselves a positive image in wider society. As it has been traced by historians such as Louis Galambos (1975) and Roland Marchand (1998), from the 1920s American big business had begun to pursue public relations programmes aimed at establishing social and moral legitimacy in the minds of the American public. The successful promulgation of this "fable" (as Marchand described it), evidenced particularly by Galambos's statistical surveys, continued on through the challenge of the Depression years and into the Second World War as the mood among the US public shifted from toleration of big business to a palpable, widespread and carefully crafted sense of trust. By the 1950s, however, thirty years of public relations campaigns that painted American corporations as key social institutions had led to the expectation of action.

The growing interest in the social role and responsibilities of business that had emerged over the course of the 1950s eventually saw the founding of specialist journals such as *Business & Society*. Supported by the College of Business Administration of Roosevelt University in Chicago, in its 1960 "declaration of independence", the editors of *Business & Society* claimed the publications in the journal would "attempt to examine the total fabric wherein the contributions of the humanities, the sciences and the arts are inextricably interwoven with the concerns of modern management" (Editors 1960, 3). According to its anonymous editorial, the journal was deliberately aimed at bridging the gap between "business" and "culture", between "Philistines" and "dilettantes" (Editors 1960, 3). But the inspiration for the foundation of *Business & Society* does not seem to have been the 1960 articles of Davis and Frederick, or even the books written by Bowen and other advocates of reform in business behaviour. It was instead a response to concerns like those explored most prominently at the time in 1959's Gordon and Howell report.

In 1956, the Ford Foundation (established in 1936 by Edsel and his father Henry Ford) had commissioned a pair of economists, Robert Gordon and James Howell, to investigate the adequacy of university and college business education in the United States. Among the recommendations that appeared in their 1959 report was an increase in the general education content of undergraduate business education to more than 50 percent—i.e. a larger liberal-arts component in business administration programmes. The Gordon and Howell report also argued that all business faculty members should engage in research and scholarship in order to lift the general standards of business education. The number of degrees in business granted by US post-secondary institutions had grown from 1,576 in 1920 to 50,090 in 1958—one in seven degrees being awarded by American universities and colleges were now in business (a number second only to education). Gordon and Howell especially advocated increasing the breadth of the business curriculum in terms of developing a sense of social responsibility in students:

> The business manager, particularly in the larger firm, possesses great power for good or harm, and public opinion demands that this power be exercised with responsibility . . . business education must be concerned not only with competence but also with responsibility, not only with skills but also have an obligation to do what they can to develop a "sense of social responsibility" and a high standard of business ethics in their graduates.
>
> (Gordon and Howell 1959, 15, 111)

A similar report released the same year had been funded by the Carnegie Corporation. Led by the economist Frank C. Pierson, the Pierson report focused more on the technical skills required for a business education. Nonetheless Pierson and his colleagues recognised the growing call for American business students to be taught about ethics and social responsibility:

> One of the most important influences shaping the work of business schools is the increasing attention being given to the social responsibilities of business enterprises. Formal standards embodied in law and government regulations are but one aspect of this development. Even more pervasive are the informal rules and obligations which

the community expects business to meet, whether they involve deal-ings at a national, state, or local levels. No one would argue that there is a clear and precise code of conduct applicable to business in its relations with representatives of government, unions, suppliers, stockholders, rival firms, and the like, but the norms within which employers operate are nonetheless real.

(Pierson et al. 1959, 92)

Soon after the appearance of the Gordon and Howell, and Pierson reports, Richard Eells and Clarence Walton produced the landmark textbook *Conceptual Foundations of Business* (1961). In 1956, Eells, as manager of public relations research at General Electric, had published *Corpora-tion Giving in a Free Society* in order to encourage a more widespread uptake of business philanthropy (including a call for reform of taxation arrangements to encourage more corporate charity). His next work, *The Meaning of Modern Business* (1960) analysed American business corpo-rations from the perspective of political economy in order to promote what he called the "metrocorporation"—i.e. one that was fully respon-sive to the needs of modern American society. His 1961 book with Wal-ton, the associate dean of the Graduate School of Business at Columbia University, however, was more ambitious still. Walton had undertaken his doctoral studies in history at the Catholic University of America before becoming involved with business administration, and the textbook he produced in 1961 with Eells (who was still an employee of General Elec-tric at the time) reflected the results of a faculty taskforce established in 1958 to revise the curriculum of the graduate school at Columbia Univer-sity. It was envisaged that the new business curriculum would include a course on "the major ideas and institutions that make an important part of the environment within which business transactions take place" (Eells and Walton 1961, v). Produced after the new unit had run over four successive semesters, *The Conceptual Foundations of Business* sought to provide a detailed historical survey of the political, legal and economic background of contemporary Western commercial practice in line with the Gordon and Howell report's emphasis on exposing business students to aspects of society and social responsibility of the kind that they might be expected to experience in a liberal arts degree.

Eells and Walton's book may have been too ambitious, but it was soon followed by other textbooks on the subject. James McGuire called his 1963 survey of the type *Business and Society*, and Davis produced his own in 1966 (in collaboration with Robert L. Bromstrom) entitled *Busi-ness and its Environment*. Courses of study on business and society began to become more common in American business schools, and in 1971 the Academy of Management (which had been founded in 1936) formed its Social Issues in Management division. Key members of the division (such as Bill Frederick) used their position to lobby the American Assembly of

Collegiate Schools of Business (AACSB), the accrediting association for American business schools, to include the social, legal, and political environment of business, as well as business ethics, in its curriculum guidelines. In a 1973 survey of business and society units undertaken by the Viatorian academic Thomas F. McMahon (1975a, 1975b), an associate professor of socio-legal studies at Loyola University of Chicago, almost 40 percent of the 550 graduate and undergraduate business programs surveyed included a course dedicated to socio-ethical issues, while a third more covered business and society topics in other subjects. McMahon was sponsored to undertake his survey by the University of Virginia's Centre for the Study of Applied Ethics and the Colgate Darden Graduate School of Business in conjunction with Loyola. It found that George Steiner's *Business and Society* (1971) and *Issues in Business and Society* (1973) were the most popular textbooks in use at the time while the most widely studied problems covered in the units surveyed were "prejudice and unfairness regarding employees", "dishonest advertising" and "pricing policies (collusion, discrimination)" (McMahon 1975a, 1975b).

By now, however, figures such as Nader and his consumer-advocate "raiders" had inspired the emergence of a new horizon in the history of corporate social responsibility in America. Influenced by the social unrest occasioned by the civil rights protests of the 1960s and the period of the Vietnam War, an impatience had grown among many Americans with the refusal of business to change to meet their social expectations. The key point of contention was the under-representation of ethnic minorities (particularly African Americans) in American business at the time, but also concerns with misleading advertising and issues of product safety. The criticism of business corroded the high respect that many American businesses had won by the 1940s and saw the emergence of widespread distrust in corporate America.

The 1960s are remembered across the Western world as a time of student radicalism, idealism and hope. In the United States, the politics of the period was especially characterised by the rise of the New Left, a description hailing originally from France. In 1960, C. Wright Mills wrote "A Letter to the New Left" that appeared in the English *New Left Review*. A radical Weberian rather than a Marxian sociologist, Mills called for the development of more "structural criticism and reportage and theories of society, which at some point or another are focussed politically as demands and programmes". Reacting to the claims of an "end to ideology" promoted most pointedly by Daniel Bell (1960), Mills dismissed Stalinism and Soviet movements such as "socialist realism". He instead observed:

> For socialists of almost all varieties, the historic agency has been the working class—and later the peasantry . . . [but] in both cases, the historic agency (in the advanced capitalist countries) has either

collapsed or become most ambiguous: so far as structural change is concerned, these don't seem to be at once available and effective as our agency any more. . . . It is with this problem of agency in mind that I have been studying, for several years now, the cultural apparatus, the intellectuals—as a possible, immediate, radical agency of change. . . . The Age of Complacency is ending. . . . We are beginning to move again.

(Mills 1960, 21)

Mills's letter provided an inspiration for a new kind of politics to emerge on university campuses (Geary 2009). But with Mills's untimely death in 1962, it was left to other left-wing intellectuals to lead the push to transform "the cultural apparatus, the intellectuals" into a "radical agency of change". The figure who became most widely associated with the new politics in both the United States and Europe was instead a Jewish refugee from Nazi Germany. Herbert Marcuse, a former student of the philosopher Martin Heidegger and member of the Institute for Social Research in Frankfurt, became more widely known as the "Father of the New Left".

Marcuse was always uncomfortable with the title, and unlike Mills, his books rarely touched on key issues of business management. Where Mills's *Power Elite* (1956) was a study of corporate executives, senior military and government officials, Marcuse's *One-Dimensional Man* (1964) was a general critique of Western industrial society (Kellner 1984; Frey 2004). Marcuse tried to reconcile Marxian thought with Freudian psychoanalysis in a manner typical of members of the Frankfurt School, complaining that consumerism and the Western system of political economy made even liberal democracies such as the United States "oppressive". But as Marcuse reflected in 1969 in an interview with the German news magazine *Der Spiegel*:

It is true that a large degree of coincidence has arisen between my ideas and the experiences which students drew independently from their practice and from their thinking. I am very happy about this harmony. I do not know how far it goes. But there is no paternal or patriarchal relationship. . . . I would very much like to be the father of the New Left, if this father role did not include an authority which is more or less readily accepted by the children. This very authoritarian-paternalistic position is repugnant to me.

(Marcuse 1969, 36–7)

Marcuse agreed with Mills:

The working class has itself changed in the conditions of late capitalist society . . . new sections of the population,—the technical intelligentsia—can become radical potentials, and that to the extent

to which they become aware of the contradiction between the decid-
ing role of the technical intelligentsia in the production process and
its lack of power in relation to all vital general social questions.

(Marcuse 1969, 42)

Marcuse had become especially associated with student protests because
he joined in with them. He distinguished his activist position from that
adopted by his other former Frankfurt School colleagues:

It was in connection with the founding of a College for Problems
of the Oppressed Racial and National Minorities in San Diego—the
Lumumba-Zapata College—which was to be directed by Negroes
and Mexicans. To win their demands, they occupied, together with
leftist white students, the offices of the University treasurer. During
the demonstration in which I took part, a door was broken down.
That was the only act of violence which occurred and I immediately
declared that I was ready to pay for the replacement of the door. I
would not call this participation in any radical practice. But that is
what I mean by taking of position which is more than the theoretical
taking of position.

(Marcuse 1969, 38–9)

Marcuse belonged to a tradition of intellectuals inspired by Marx that
are designated *Marxisant* in French—they were influenced by Marx
rather than being intellectually orthodox Marxists. Like other proponents of Frankfurt School "critical theory" (which takes its name from
the critiques of Kant), Marcuse had argued in *One-Dimensional Man*
that modern society had created an oppressive machine:

Today political power asserts itself through its power over the machine
process and over the technical organization of the apparatus. . . . The
brute fact that the machine's physical (only physical?) power surpasses
that of the individual, and of any particular group of individuals,
makes the machine the most effective political instrument in any society whose basic organization is that of the machine process. But the
political trend may be reversed; essentially the power of the machine
is only the stored-up and projected power of man. To the extent to
which the work world is conceived of as a machine and mechanized
accordingly, it becomes the potential basis of a new freedom for man.

(Marcuse 1964, 5–6)

This machine of work oppressed individuals through the imposition of
false or imposed needs:

We may distinguish both true and false needs. "False" are those which
are superimposed upon the individual by particular social interests

in his repression. . . . No matter how much such needs may have become the individual's own, reproduced and fortified by the conditions of his existence; no matter how much he identifies himself with them and finds himself in their satisfaction, they continue to be what they were from the beginning—products of a society whose dominant interest demands repression. . . . Most of the prevailing needs to relax, to have fun, to behave and consume in accordance with the advertisements, to love and hate what others love and hate, belong to this category of false needs.

(Marcuse 1964, 7)

But rather than specifying what true needs are, Marcuse concedes, "In the last analysis, the question of what are true and false needs must be answered by the individuals themselves" (Marcuse 1964, 8). Individuals were oppressed by a system in which they were encouraged to oppress themselves through their inability to control their desire to consume the bounty made widely available to them by the Fordist system of production.

Figures such as Marcuse stood outside mainstream discourses concerning consumerism and the moral role of corporations in society. The fruits of Western prosperity had been inverted by thinkers like Marcuse into instruments of oppression—a problem of affluence not experienced by earlier, poorer generations. But radical university professors and radical students demanding significant social change represented the leftmost extreme of the spectrum of public opinion in which the more moderate criticisms of American business advanced by figures such as Nader had to be understood.

Yet by the end of the 1960s, CSR was becoming an increasingly mainstream concern. In 1971, the leading American business-led public policy advocate, the Committee for Economic Development, published a statement on the social responsibilities of business corporations. The statement reflected a project that began in 1966 under the leadership of the former Atomic Energy Commission chairman David E. Lilienthal that originally focused on defining the economic objectives which a socially responsible business might be expected to have, and how meeting these objectives might be evaluated. After 1967, however, Lilienthal's team gradually began to focus more surely on the social problems that large corporations might be able to help resolve. Lilienthal later left the chairmanship of the group, replaced by glass-making executive Raymon Mulford, as the Committee for Economic Development became more focused on how American businesses could do more to meet social needs. Supported financially by the John D. Rockefeller III Fund, the Committee for Economic Development's statement, released in 1971, proved a major rebuttal to the University of Chicago economist Milton Friedman, who in 1970 had published a stinging rebuke of advocates of business social responsibility in what is now a famous article that originally appeared in the *New York Times Magazine*.

Friedman's article "The social responsibility of business is to increase its profits" contained very little new from what readers of his 1962 book *Capitalism and Freedom* would have expected—it was substantially just a reworked section on "the social responsibility of business and labour" from his earlier work (Friedman 1962, 133–6). Yet the background to the 1970 article was different from that which had prompted Friedman to publish *Capitalism and Freedom* eight years earlier. Friedman's 1962 book was a collection of speeches he had first given in the 1950s, since revised by his wife Rose, that defended *laissez-faire* capitalism in a similar manner as had the Austrian economist Friedrich Hayek in his *Road to Serfdom* (1944). In 1962, Friedman had called "the acceptance by corporate officials of a social responsibility other than to make as much money for stockholders as possible" a "fundamentally subversive doctrine" (Friedman 1962, 133). Yet Friedman's *New York Times* article was printed as a comment on "Campaign GM"—a group of activists led by the Naderite civil rights lawyer John C. Esposito who had bought shares in General Motors and had demanded at the corporation's stockholders' meeting in May that year that General Motors name three new directors to represent the public interest and establish a committee to analyse the corporation's consumer safety and pollution records. The proposition was overwhelmingly rejected by shareholders, but General Motors management responded by forming a public-policy committee. In response, Friedman described the drive for businesses to adopt social responsibilities as "pure and unadulterated socialism", adding that "Businessmen who talk in this way are unwitting puppets of the intellectual forces that have been undermining society" (Friedman 1970, 33).

The Committee for Economic Development disagreed. The committee's statement instead proposed a three-concentric-circles model of social responsibility for businesses that comprised an inner, an intermediate and an outer circle. The inner circle represented the basic responsibility business had for its economic function, providing products, services, jobs and economic growth. The intermediate circle focused on responsibilities businesses had to act in a manner alert to society's changing social values and priorities, including environmental conservation, relationships with employees and meeting the expectations of consumers for information, fair treatment and protection from harm. The outer circle referred to newly emerging responsibilities that business should be involved in to help address broader problems in society, such as urban decay and poverty.

As the report's authors acknowledged:

> By operating efficiently, business concerns have been able to provide people with both the means and the leisure to enjoy a better life. Moreover, the competitive marketplace has served as an effective means of bringing about an efficient allocation of a major part of the country's resources to ever-changing public requirements. . . .

[But] there is now a pervasive feeling in the country that the social order somehow has gotten out of balance, and that greater affluence amid a deteriorating environment and community life does not make much sense.

The case for businesses to accept social responsibilities was gaining broader acceptance. In 1969 the commercial news magazine *Business Week* presented its first awards for business citizenship in recognition of contributions made by American industry toward the solution of the country's environmental and social problems. Over the course of the 1970s, corporate social responsibility would increasingly become normalised, not only in the United States, but now also in Europe.

George A. Goyder (1951, 1961), the managing director of British International Paper Ltd, was the first Englishman to write specifically on the subject of business responsibility. As Michael Marinetto (1999) explains, Goyder had been influenced by the Christian Frontier Council which had been set up in 1939 by the Scottish missionary Joseph H. Oldham to promote Christian ethics in business. But by the end of the 1960s, social responsibility debates had more clearly spread from the United States to Great Britain, where in 1967 a Foundation for Business Responsibilities had been founded in London. It was a charity operated by Aims of Industry, an advocacy group that had been formed in 1942 to oppose the threat of nationalisation (Wilson 1951). Over the next few years the foundation would publish a series of works, including Michael Ivens's *Industry and Values* (1970) and Kenneth Corman's *Business Responsibilities* (1972). By 1973, even the Confederation of British Industry had caught the social responsibility bug, publishing a report on "The Responsibilities of the British Public Company" (produced by a committee chaired by Harold Watkinson), and in 1976 a Corporate Responsibility Centre was set up in London by the corporate affairs consultant Jan Dauman while he was undertaking a doctorate on business social responsibility programmes at Brunel University (Dauman 1981). Dauman noted that only Michael Beesley at the London Graduate School of Business Studies (Beesley 1974; cf. Beesley and Evans 1978) and Keith McMillan at the Administrative Staff College at Henley-on-Thames (Kempner et al. 1974) had been actively researching the area otherwise (Dauman 1981, 3), although works such as Simon Webley's 1974 survey conducted on behalf of the Public Relations Consultants Association (Webley 1974) were also being undertaken at the time.

Dauman had come to the United Kingdom in 1969 to work at IBM as an assistant to John Hargreaves, IBM UK's director of public affairs. In 1975 Dauman published a book, *Business Survival and Social Change*, with Hargreaves (Hargreaves and Dauman 1975)—Dauman had worked on social projects, dealing with matters including refugees, art, urban problems, youth and the handicapped, including helping the National

Westminster Bank which had established a social policy committee on its board in 1973 (Marinetto 1998). Dauman advocated corporate social responsibility as part of a "new social contract" where unions, consumer advocates and governments were all expecting more from British public companies. His 1981 dissertation set out a series of corporate social programmes he had studied in the United States and his plans and accomplishments in British industry over the course of the 1970s.

The key moment in the development of British understandings of the social responsibilities of industry, however, is argued by Daniel Kinderman (2012) to have been a 1977 lecture given by Charles C. Pocock, the managing director of the Anglo-Dutch petroleum giant Royal Dutch/ Shell and chair of the London Graduate School of Business Studies. Kinderman argues that Pocock's Ashridge Lecture "More Jobs: A Small Cure for a Big Problem" was "seminal" to the early development of CSR in the United Kingdom.

The focus of Pocock's talk was resolving the issue of "structural unemployment". He did not think it could be eradicated by "well-meaning social legislation, in which the theme of job protection is uppermost" (Pocock 1978, 5). Pocock pointed instead to the role of small business in job creation and the negative effect of fair wages clauses and the collective bargaining provisions of the British Employment Protection Act 1975 (Pocock 1978, 9). "It may be unfair", Pocock mused in his advocation of labour market deregulation, "but it is less unfair than nothing" (Pocock 1978, 8). Pocock was calling for the dissolution of the European post-war settlement in the United Kingdom.

Tellingly, however, Pocock went further to say "Industry cannot just opt out of society's problems, particularly those that press on the local community where it operates" (Pocock 1978, 5). He pointed especially to training programmes where businesses cooperated with local schools. Pocock argued for a break with the post-war dialogue of social partnership between business and unions, replacing it with a partnership between business and local communities. In 1980, a conference was duly held at the Civil Service Staff College in Sunningdale Park on "Corporate Community Involvement". The conference, sponsored by the British Government's Department of the Environment, brought leading industry figures in Britain together with advocates of CSR from the United States (Department of the Environment 1980). The Sunningdale conference eventually led to the formation of Business in the Community, a charity established in 1981 under the auspices of the Prince of Wales. Royal Dutch/Shell provided administrative support for the charity, as did the Department of the Environment. Business in the Community was founded the same year that the long series of privatisations of British government businesses began under the Conservative government of Margaret Thatcher, and it is consequently linked by Kinderman (2012) with the Conservative Party's economic reform agenda, decried by its critics as "neo-liberalism".

By the 1970s, the American discourse of corporate social responsibility had also spread to the European Continent, when the first German studies specifically focused on the social responsibilities of business appeared. Klaus T. Schroder's pioneering 1978 theoretical treatise on the *Soziale Verantwortung in der Führung der Unternehmung* [*Social Responsibility of the Directorship of Business*] was the first German monographic study, followed by Hans Böhm's *Gesellschaftlich verantwortliche Unternehmensführung* [*Socially Responsible Business Directorship*] (1979) and Joachim K. Weitzig's *Gesellschaftsorientierte Unternehmenspolitik und Unternehmensverfassung* [*Society-Oriented Business Policy and Business Structure*] (1979). West Germany had been built up after the Second World War as a bulwark against communism, and the creation of its "social market economy" had included granting senior management of the largest German firms a level of power and influence peculiar to the Federal Republic. But as Gunther H. Roth argued in 1979, since 1937 the German Corporations Code had required that management boards recognise a duty to the "common welfare of the people". Although the Nazi corporations law had been repealed in West Germany, the principle was still recognised in both the Federal Republic and Austria. Special provisions as to how this duty might be upheld had never been enacted, but a tradition of "social accounting" had begun in Germany in 1972 when the power generator STEAG (and later BASF, Shell and BP) began to publish a "balance sheet" of the business's expenditures on public and social matters (Böhm 1977, 271, n. 12; Roth 1979).

The idea of corporate social responsibility had now become an international concern, but the limits of what was meant by responsibility still was not clear. In 1979, however, Archie Carroll proposed an influential four-part definition of CSR that separated business responsibilities into four categories: economic, legal, ethical and discretionary. Carroll described ethical responsibilities as "additional behaviours and activities that are not necessarily codified into law but nevertheless are expected of business by society's members" (Carroll 1979, 500). Yet Carroll distinguished discretionary (or voluntary) responsibilities from ethical concerns:

> societal expectations do exist for businesses to assume social roles over and above those described thus far. These roles are purely voluntary, and the decision to assume them is guided only by a business's desire to engage in social roles not mandated, not required by law, and not even generally expected of businesses in an ethical sense. Examples of voluntary activities might be making philanthropic contributions, conducting in-house programs for drug abusers, training the hardcore unemployed, or providing day-care centers for working mothers.
>
> (Carroll 1979, 500)

Increasingly, corporate social responsibility would be distinguished from business ethics because it was voluntary and not necessarily expected of corporations by the public. Philanthropy and other expressions of corporate charity went over and above the ethical standards demanded by corporate critics such as Nader. The social responsibilities of business no longer included treating consumers honestly or employees decently, but belonged in another category of business activity altogether. The business and society issues described in the 1975 survey led by McMahon had included prejudice, dishonest advertising and collusion in pricing, and a similar concern with relationships with employees, customers and the environment was included in the Committee for Economic Development's three-circles model. But these were no longer matters of business social responsibility in Carroll's account. Social responsibility had begun to be seen as a quite different matter than it had been when it was conceptualised by advocates of employer paternalism or even figures such as Berle and Dodd. Philanthropy and charitable community work had been hived off from general standards of ethical behaviour into a redefined category of corporate volunteerism.

Yet as Frederick (2006) notes, by the 1970s CSR had begun to be seen as having failed. In 1979 the Committee for Economic Development had retracted its earlier support for CSR, declaring that "Preference should be given to the use of markets and market incentives in working toward the nation's social and economic goals" (CED 1979; Frederick 1981). Even Bowen had begun to despair about the prospects of CSR, stating pessimistically in 1978 "I have come to the view . . . that corporate power is so potent and so pervasive that voluntary social responsibility cannot be relied upon as a significant form of control over business" (Bowen 1978, 128–9). It increasingly looked as if the American post-war social responsibility movement had failed. As more scandals engulfed American business in the late 1970s, a renewed focus on business ethics emerged, particularly in terms of applied philosophy and business education.

5 Business Philosophy

If the promise of corporate social responsibility had seemed to wane at the end of the 1970s, such was not the case with business ethics. One of the key issues stressed in Richard Eells's first work on business ethics had been that businessmen needed to develop a personal philosophy. By the 1970s, pioneers such as Eells were joined by a range of philosophy professors and other university-trained business philosophers. The first annual conferences on business ethics were held as a new emphasis on morality become apparent under the administration of Jimmy Carter. Foreign bribery was outlawed as Kantian approaches to business ethics were developed and debated. A pronounced revival in business ethics education emerged as earlier ambivalence about the usefulness of applied ethics was overcome and the theologically based ethics of earlier generations was replaced by a secularised normative canon. Business ethics became more established as a discipline as business education grew in popularity and new international networks of business ethicists emerged. By the 1980s, business ethics had finally become a fully fledged academic field. The first institutes for business ethics were also established at this time, and by the 1980s the teaching of dedicated business ethics courses had spread also now to European universities.

Yet Eells's book appeared at a time when business ethics was dominated by clerical contributions, particularly those produced by Catholic scholars. The first business ethics conferences in the United States also predated the entry of secular philosophers into the field. When American business ethics had been revived after the departure of philosophers such as Taeusch from academic life, it was the Catholic tradition that had most characterised publications in business ethics in the United States. A similar early Catholic concern with the ethics of business practice was also evident in Europe, where most of the publications on business ethics from the 1920s through to the 1960s were written from a religious perspective. Established in a manner independent of Catholic social thought, the new business ethics of the 1970s served to secularise what had previously been a field typified by religiously influenced sentiment.

Neo-Thomist Business Ethics

In 1976, a major scandal concerning the American defence contractor Lockheed burst onto the pages of the international press. The scandal hit hardest in Japan, where the former Prime Minister Kakuei Tanaka and over a dozen Japanese officials had been accused of taking bribes to ensure All Nippon Airways had bought planes from Lockheed. Questionable payments of up to $25 million from 1968 through 1975 had been made by Lockheed to foreign officials according to the US Securities and Exchange Commission (Clinard and Yeager 1980). Other corporate scandals revealed by the commission included the discovery that the International Telephone and Telegraph Company (ITT) had sought to engage the Central Intelligence Agency in a 1970 plan to manipulate the outcome of the Chilean presidential election (Solomon and Linville 1976). Over 500 cases of questionable and illegal conduct were uncovered from 1974 to 1976 as public confidence in American business collapsed. Bribery of foreign officials was outlawed with the passing of the Foreign Corrupt Practices Act 1977 as the Carter administration took concerted action to reform US business practice.

The sense of public disgust was widespread and shared by public officials on both sides of the political divide. Fred T. Allen, of postage meter manufacturer Pitney Bowes, reflected in the *Wall Street Journal* that "This is an appalling situation. We, who have devoted our lives to the growth and profitability of large corporations, are thought of, collectively, as little more than manicured hoodlums" (Allen 1975). Other businessmen reacted defensively, with Charles Bowen, the chairman of leading management consulting firm Booz, Allen and Hamilton complaining of "a bunch of pipsqueak moralists running around trying to apply U.S. puritanical standards to other countries" (New York Times 1976). William E. Simon, the Republican-appointed Secretary of the Treasury, spoke for many, however, when he addressed the matter in terms of corporate ethics:

> There are overwhelming moral grounds for a strong business ethic. History teaches us that no free society or free economy can long survive without an ethical base. It is only through a shared moral foundation— a set of binding ground rules for fair conduct—that free associations, be they social, diplomatic, or commercial, can flourish and endure. Far from being a luxury, a sound business ethic is essential to the preservation of free enterprise. The real question facing the American business community today is not whether it can "afford" strong ethical standards, but how much longer it can go on without them.
>
> (Simon 1976, 405–6)

The first major study of American corporate crime duly appeared in 1980 written by the sociologists Marshall Clinard and Peter Yeager. Over the course of the late 1970s, sociological and criminological focus was brought to bear on the widespread corporate wrongdoings that flooded American newspapers at the time (Schrager and Short 1978). The Watergate scandal, which had led to the resignation of President Nixon in 1974 (and had encouraged the Securities and Exchange Commission to investigate corporate bribery), suggested to many that the country was facing an unprecedented ethical crisis. Earlier works on business and society and the moral role of corporations in America were quickly forgotten as business ethics was reborn in a new philosophised guise. The widening sense of national distress concerning business standards at the time led to the foundation of the first national centre for business ethics and a new series of business ethics conferences in the United States.

American business first responded through recourse to another wave of ethics codes. In 1976, the Securities and Exchange Commission advocated that corporations create or renew their ethics guidelines, and the two leading business lobby groups, the Business Roundtable and the Conference Board, joined the call for American businesses to improve their conduct through a renewed focus on ethics codes. With the passing of the Foreign Corrupt Practices Act, the interest in ethics codes quickly subsided. But analysing a selection of 119 codes collected by the Business Roundtable and the Conference Board, Cressey and Moore (1983) found that 43 percent of the codes had either been drafted or revised in 1976 and almost two-thirds had been written or revised between 1975 and 1977.

Just as the flurry in production (and renewal) of ethics codes in the 1920s had seen an equivalent interest from business schools, the scandals of the 1970s provoked a reaction among American academics. But this time the reaction came from scholars working in philosophy departments—and in much greater numbers. Much of the intellectual production that emerged at the time ignored the longer-standing tradition of theological or Christian ethics that had especially characterised discussions in the 1950s and 1960s. Academic philosophy had changed since the 1930s when Taeusch had abandoned business ethics; it had become substantially secularised as American philosophy departments had become increasingly separated from religious studies. But in light of the new series of scandals that had emerged in the American press, a new range of enterprising philosophy professors set about re-establishing the business ethics field.

One of the key issues stressed in Eells's *The Meaning of Modern Business* (Eells 1960) is that the modern corporation lacked a philosophy. The Church and the State had well-developed institutional philosophies, but not contemporary American business. Eells pointed to the 1956 study led by Francis X. Sutton that found a "basic stability, indeed almost a stubborn intellectual conservatism" in US business focused on assertions of individualism and simplistic *laissez-faire* assumptions (Sutton et al. 1956, 385). American businessmen in the 1940s, as Eells characterised the findings of Sutton and colleagues, thought of themselves as rational, cold and practical and had little interest in anything apart from a "fundamental conviction that certain economic laws govern the affairs of men". The typical American corporate executive thought that "his pursuit of profit automatically served the welfare of society and was indeed the prerequisite of economic efficiency" (Eells 1960, 22).

In 1958, the industrial engineer Ralph C. Davis of Ohio State University set out his personal philosophy of management in the *Journal of Insurance*. Rather than being slavishly focused on economic efficiency, it included concepts such as "Belief that values constituting customer satisfaction are primary objectives of management. Profits are necessary but collateral objectives". Davis also advocated for "Belief in private property, free competition, and opposition to forces weakening the free market system" and "Belief in high ethical standards as a basis for sound business relations" (Davis 1958, 1–2). But a more explicitly philosophical take on business had already appeared by that date in terms of the 1956 textbook on business ethics by the University of Notre Dame associate professor of philosophy Herbert Johnston.

Johnston was a Canadian Catholic who had studied at the University of Toronto under the renowned neo-Thomist philosopher Jacques Maritain, one of the key advocates of the creation of the United Nations' Declaration of Human Rights of 1948. As Johnston explained in the foreword to the first edition of his *Business Ethics*, he had been teaching a subject on the "moral dimension of business situations" since 1950. "The need for moral training as an integral part of business education has been frequently and forcefully stated, and has come to be pretty well recognized" Johnston explained. "Either a separate course in business ethics or at least a definite number of class periods set aside for this subject should prove a practical means of approach" (Johnston 1956, v).

Explaining why a course in general ethics for business students would be unsuitable, Johnston asserted "you could drive a heavy tank through the gap between the conclusions reached in general ethics and the ordinary student's application of these conclusions . . . to the moral problems that he meets in the business world" (Johnston 1956, vi). Johnston adopted the case method for his textbook, arguing that "it involves the student personally in the work of the course" (Johnston 1956, viii), and supplied questions at the end of each case and short reading included in his book. Johnston's text supplies brief introductions to the ethical frameworks of Aristotle, Kant, Mill and John Dewey and even includes an assessment of the criticism of ethics by logical positivists such as A.J. Ayer and Charles Stevenson (Johnston 1956, 9–11). As a Catholic philosopher, Johnston advocated using the classical virtue of prudence if students wished to "bridge the gap" between conscience and reaching ethical conclusions. The textbook is dominated by its chapters on rights, justice and truth understood from a Catholic perspective, with Johnston citing Maritain (1951) and the UN Declaration as well as making widespread citations to Aquinas.

Including brief readings from Tawney's *Acquisitive Society* (1921), Peter Drucker's *Practice of Management* (1954) and congressional hearings on banking and currency, and the Labor Relations Act 1947, Johnston's textbook also included a section on Aristotle and Aquinas on economic life, criticisms of the private enterprise system and an account of the proper role of government in commerce. A section on labour relations begins with a summary of the 1949 address by Pius XII to members of UNIAPAC and further references to Pius XI's encyclical *Quadragesimo anno* (1931), explaining the role of labour unions envisaged in Catholic social thought. Justice is introduced as a virtue and treated in its usual neo-Thomist manner, including a section on social justice as it was articulated in *Quadragesimo anno*. Discrimination against "Negroes or Jews or Mexicans or Catholics" is characterised as "social injustice" (Johnston 1956, 92) and the issue of married women working (bad) and equal pay for women (good) also receive considerable attention (Johnston 1956, 246–51). So strongly Catholic and neo-Thomist in its approach, it is not surprising that Johnston's textbook did not achieve greater acclaim in a country still particularly noted at the time for its anti-Catholic sectarianism.

A more significant influence from a Catholic source was the appearance of Raymond Baumhart's survey of the ethical values of American businessmen. Published in 1961 in the *Harvard Business Review*, Baumhart's survey was further explained in the 1968 monographic exposition of his Harvard University dissertation completed as part of his doctorate in business administration (DBA). Baumhart was a Jesuit, having joined the priesthood in 1946, and went on to become the dean of business at Loyola University, where he also served as its long-standing president (until 1993). Baumhart's 1961 paper is often cited as a seminal social science study of American business ethics.

Baumhart observed that "during the past decade, much has been written about ethics in business. Most of the books and articles are based on the experiences of one man, or on a priori reasoning" (Baumhart 1961, 7). Baumhart's survey of 1,700 readers of the *Harvard Business Review* painted "a picture of executives' deep concern over business behavior". The findings included an acknowledgement that "executives are alert to the social responsibilities of business as these are expressed in general terms". Baumhart's respondents agreed that "the man most likely to act ethically is one with a well-defined personal code. If he also has a boss who is highly ethical, his behavior will be consistently upright" (Baumhart 1961, 7). *Harvard Business Review* readers contended that "top management must lead the way. The men at the top must be individuals of principle, who unmistakably reveal their ethical attitude, not only verbally, but also by forceful actions". Baumhart reported the common opinion that "most executives would welcome a written code of ethics for their industry" and that "organized religion and clergymen have been lax in providing guidance for the ethical problems of business" (Baumhart 1961, 7). Five out of six respondents agreed that "For corporation executives to act in the interest of shareholders alone, and not also in the interest of employees and consumers, is unethical", and four out of every seven executives believed that businessmen "would violate a code of ethics whenever they thought they could avoid detection" (Baumhart 1961, 19).

In a paper read at the sixteenth annual meeting of the American Catholic Theological Association, the Redemptorist priest Daniel Lowery of Holy Redeemer College, Washington, D.C., pointed out the problem with theological approaches to business ethics at the time. Citing Johnston's textbook as "excellent", Lowery (1962) quoted American businessmen dismissing theological advice:

> "When I need moral guidance," one man said, "the last place in the world I would go for it is to the Church". Another said, "If I took the advice of the clergy I would either be out of business in a month or be involved in twice as many moral perplexities as I started out with".
> (Lowery 1962, 131)

Lowery pointed to the pioneering 1949 sociological study of white-collar crime by Edwin Sutherland in light of the 1961 price-fixing scandal in the US electricity market that had been revealed in the press that April (Walton and Cleveland 1963). Lowery bemoaned the lack of agreement among theologians concerning moral problems in business and instead suggested that a "new cultivation of business ethics" should occur along the lines as had occurred in medical ethics:

> Moralists long ago recognized that the problems of medicine are intricate, that certain moralists must specialize in a reasonably complete knowledge of the facts about certain surgical and medical procedures, and then present a moral evaluation . . . business ethics needs the same thorough treatment, needs its specialists who are familiar with the real world and the "muddy waters" of American business.
> (Lowery 1962, 131)

The response of the Kennedy Administration to the electricity scandal was to establish a Business Ethics Advisory Council, organised by the Secretary of Commerce Luther Hodges. In 1962 the council published a "Statement on Business Ethics and A Call for Action". The statement included an acknowledgment that the key issue in American business ethics was its complex nature:

> The ethical standards of American businessmen, like those of the American people, are founded upon our religious heritage and our

traditions of social, political, and economic freedom . . . but new ethical problems are created constantly by the ever-increasing complexity
of society. . . . Business enterprises, large and small, have relationships
in many directions—with stockholders and other owners, employees,
customers, suppliers, government, and the public in general. The traditional emphasis on freedom, competition, and progress in our economic system often brings the varying interests of these groups into
conflict, so that many difficult and complex ethical problems can arise
in any enterprise . . . we, therefore, now propose that current efforts
be expanded and intensified and that new efforts now be undertaken
by the American business community to hasten its attainment of those
high ethical standards that derive from our heritage and tradition.

(Thau 1962, 137–8)

The statement then went on to list conflicts of interest, entertainment, gifts
and expenses, customers and suppliers, and social responsibilities as
areas where American businesses needed stronger management of ethical
standards. The council, led by William Decker, the chairman of Corning
Glass Works, New York, included nine senior corporate executives, the
presidents of Northwestern University and the University of Minnesota,
the deans of the graduate schools of business at Columbia, Harvard and
Stanford Universities, Episcopalian, Presbyterian, Catholic and Jewish
clergy, Victor Nyberg from the Association of Better Business Bureaus
and Lawrence Appley of the American Management Association.

The main response of US business was the creation of a wave of corporate business ethics codes, replacing or supplementing the over 100 docu-
ments known as business ethics creeds in the 1950s. Ethics codes were
advocated by Hodges in his resultant book, *Business Conscience* (1963):
"few companies can survive without some kind of policy regarding ethical
questions", Hodges stressed, but it was important that any such code "has
teeth" (Hodges 1963, 204–5). The American Management Association
had published a study of *Management Creeds and Philosophies* in 1958
(Thompson 1958) and was offering to help businesses design ethics codes
and training. But the most striking feature of the Business Ethics Advisory
Council was the absence from the body or the initiatives promoted in light
of its work of the involvement of any of the recognised experts in business
ethics of the day, clerical or philosophical. The council (and Hodges) relied
only on Baumhart's survey, the American Management Association study
and a survey the council undertook of American business schools.

The mid-1962 Business Ethics Advisory Council survey of what ethics content was being taught in American business schools found that
"few schools offered a separate course in business ethics. The tendency
was to weave an ethical content into all the specialized courses" (Hodges
1963, 224). One exception was the University of Wisconsin that had
offered a separate business ethics course since 1907. "More common was

the experience of another school which said it dropped an ethics course because it became too preachy and was shunned by the student body" (Hodges 1963, 224). Hodges recommended business ethics seminars be established in all American business schools, but "keep the seminars geared to practical business affairs" (Hodges 1963, 225).

The founding of the council was quickly followed by a series of academic conferences and business initiatives. In December 1961 the winter conference of the American Marketing Association focused on the social responsibilities of marketing (Stevens ed. 1962), and in 1963 a two-day conference for 100 executives at St Joseph's College, Philadelphia, was organised by the Business Ethics Advisory Council (Sporn 1963). A symposium on the same theme was held at Columbia Graduate School of Business, also sponsored by the council (DeLucca 1964), and Robert Bartels hosted a similar seminar on business ethics at Ohio State University (Bartels 1963), while the University of Washington's business ethics conference brought together academics, managers and religious leaders (Towle ed. 1964). The American Management Association had started running business ethics training sessions four times a year as the *Annals of the American Academy of Political and Social Science* dedicated a volume to an investigation of the "ethics of business enterprise" (Miller 1962). Wroe Alderson's pioneering1964 report on ethical standards and professional practice for the American Marketing Association quickly followed, and another survey published in 1965 of over 800 executives by Thomas F. Schutte revealed that marketing was by far the area of firms where most executives (including marketing executives) thought unethical practices were found. Marketing ethics also became an interest of researchers such as Bartels (1967), the author of a seminal paper on ethical decision-making in marketing who is now best known for his historical studies of marketing thought (Bartels 1962).

Clerical ethicists continued to write on business morals throughout the 1960s. The University of Scranton's Thomas M. Garrett S.J. published a well-received guide for businessmen on the *Ethics of Business* in 1963, although as Tom McMahon pointed out in 1966, standard introductions to theological ethics still generally lacked considerations of business morals at the time. But that year, another Jesuit, John W. Clark, concluded from a study of 103 managers on the US West Coast that formal education was not a strong influence on the ethical behaviour of businessmen (Clark 1966). In 1969, Baumhart pointed out that most ethics content in business schools was being taught by people without any ethical training themselves. Baumhart also described the resistance of some corporate executives to allow business ethicists to publish work they had undertaken researching ethical issues in their firms:

> At times I am tempted to try the Ralph Nader approach to solving unethical business practices. . . . For the present, however, I am sufficiently impressed by the responsible behavior of the majority of

businessmen, by the great pressures and complexity of the economic and social problems which they face and, by and large, solve in laudable ways, that I will continue to rely on research in cooperation with businessmen as the better way to improve business behavior.

(Baumhart 1969, 72)

Applied Ethics

Yet a transformation in medical ethics was also occurring at the time. Medical ethics had been understood to constitute a specialist field since at least the nineteenth century when Thomas Percival published a Code of Medical Ethics in England, updating the ancient Hippocratic Oath (Percival 1803). The Principles of Medical Ethics adopted by the American Medical Association in 1957 were the latest in a series of guidelines published since the nineteenth-century founding of the national medical body in 1846 (Baker 1999). The 1960s had proved to be a particularly contentious time in American medical ethics, however. An emphasis on the rights of patients had emerged that saw considerable change in the focus of medical ethics, or bioethics as it was increasingly called after 1970 (Jonsen 1988; Stevens 2000).

Philosophers had long considered matters such as abortion as a proper matter for ethical investigation. In 1967, for example, Philippa Foot and Elisabeth Anscombe had argued over the Thomist approach to abortion in the *Oxford Review* (Foot 1967; Anscombe 1967). But by the late 1960s, the development of an increased focus on bioethics had led to the founding of medical ethics institutes such as the Hastings Centre in New York (in 1969) and the Kennedy Institute of Ethics at Georgetown University in Washington, D.C. (in 1971). Conferences on medical and biological ethics had been held by bodies such as the World Health Organization (1960), but the foundation of dedicated research institutes as well as ethics boards at American hospitals saw a significant change in the scope and nature of the intellectual production in bioethics occur over the course of the 1960s and 1970s.

A similar development subsequently occurred in business ethics. A new tradition of conferences dedicated to business ethics began in the late 1970s, with the first annual series of conferences beginning in 1977 at Bentley College (now Bentley University) in Boston. The papers of the first conference proceedings in business ethics from the 1970s (Hoffman 1977; De George and Pichler 1978) show some confusion regarding what business ethics should comprise, with theologians, sociologists and even activists such as Nader appearing at the early meetings. What is particularly notable is the lack of any sense of continuity with earlier writings, however. The Scottish philosopher Alasdair MacIntyre (1977) claimed at the first conference at Bentley College that issues of business ethics were essentially unresolvable; a few years later, in his celebrated *After Virtue*

(1981), he went on to criticise managers as essentially amoral, as being concerned only with efficiency. Philosophers had begun analysing business ethics from outside American business schools largely without making reference to the earlier traditions that had arisen in the area.

The pioneers of the new philosophical ethics were all members of philosophy departments. W. Michael Hoffman had come to Bentley College only in 1974 as chair of the philosophy department, but he had quickly applied to the National Endowment for the Humanities for a grant to develop courses in business ethics and, in 1976, founded the Bentley Center for Business Ethics. In 1978, with the philosopher Thomas Donaldson, he co-founded what in 1979 became the Society for Business Ethics, with the group sponsoring a Workshop on Issues, Courses, and Programs in Business and Professional Ethics at the Eastern Division of the American Philosophical Association in December that year. By 1980, the Society had 185 members, and over 500 by 1983 (De George 2005). Business ethics quickly began to be formally institutionalised in American philosophy departments.

In 1978, the first publication on business ethics by the philosopher Richard De George appeared. De George had begun his career at the University of Kansas as a specialist in Soviet ethics and was much better established by the late 1970s than was Hoffman. Already a university distinguished professor after serving as chairman of the philosophy department, in 1976 De George had hosted a conference on business ethics (on "Ethics, Free Enterprise and Public Policy") at the University of Kansas in collaboration with Joseph Pichler, the dean of the university's business school. The conference was funded by a $25,000 grant from Peat, Marwick, Mitchell and Co., now part of the international accounting partnership KPMG (Donaldson et al. 2015). De George's first publications in business ethics were on the social responsibility of business and other moral issues, and his approach was clearly anti-communist rather than religious or liberal.

At the time of the conference hosted by De George and Pichler, Tom Donaldson was still a graduate student in philosophy at the University of Kansas. His first paper in business ethics was presented at the second annual conference on business ethics at Bentley (Donaldson 1979), and by the time his first book on business ethics had appeared (Donaldson 1982), he was an associate professor of philosophy at Loyola University of Chicago. As Donaldson would later recall, there was still considerable cynicism in business schools about what business ethics could contribute to their curricula. "Business schools saw 'business ethics' as tantamount to business bashing; anyone who believed that business ethics needed special study must be someone who wanted to shame business" (Donaldson 2015, 784). Donaldson points to the importance of the appearance of De George's book *Business Ethics* (1982) as establishing the field as a topic worthy of study in US business schools.

Another monographic treatment that appeared as part of the new business ethics of the day was Norman Bowie's *Business Ethics* (1982). Bowie's first publication in business ethics was a paper originally presented at the twelfth Conference on Value Inquiry that appeared in 1978. At the time he was director of the Center for the Study of Values at the University of Delaware, where Bowie had been on the staff of the Department of Philosophy since 1975. He was also serving as the project director of a National Endowment for the Humanities sponsored project to prepare curriculum materials in business ethics. His first business ethics paper, "Why Should a Corporation Be Moral?" was soon followed by essays on the social responsibilities of multinational corporations and the effectiveness of business ethics codes (Bowie 1978a and b, 1979). With his earlier studies of the philosophy of Kant and John Rawls (Bowie 1971, 1974), Bowie would become a leading American voice in promoting deontological perspectives in business ethics.

By 1982, Hoffman could report that business ethics was well-established in American academic institutions. In a survey of American colleges and universities undertaken in 1980, 317 schools of the 655 that had responded reported that a business ethics course was being offered by the institution (Hoffman and Moore 1982a). In some cases more than one course was noted with 386 units being offered in all, more than 50 percent of the colleges and universities that had responded. Hoffman and Moore (1982a) estimated that between 35,000 and 40,000 students were undertaking the subjects, with most being offered in philosophy and religion departments (186), but with a comparable number (147) being offered by business schools. Some 322 of the 386 courses had been set up after 1973, with the most common textbooks used including the collection *Ethical Theory and Business* by bioethicist Thomas Beauchamp and Norman Bowie (1979), the anthology *Ethical Issues in Business* collected by Thomas Donaldson and his fellow Loyola University philosopher Patricia Werhane (1979), and *Moral Issues in Business* by the Bakersfield College philosopher Vincent Barry (1979). Hoffman's survey appeared in the first volume of the *Journal of Business Ethics*, edited by Alex C. Michalos, professor of philosophy at the University of Guelph in Canada.

The range of topics to be covered in the courses these textbooks sought to cater for was diverse rather than standardised (or even clear). Barry's book (continued later by William Shaw) featured discussions of consequentialism and deontology, justice, capitalism and socialism, theories of property, corporate personhood and CSR. It had more of a political philosophy quality to it than the other business ethics textbooks of the time which tended to be more focused on particular issues—bribery, business responsibility, product safety and ethics codes. Rather than works which set out a standard or canonical set of topics, the early business ethics textbooks were characterised by their heterogeneity although some standard, classic readings (such as Friedman's *New York Times* attack on CSR) already appear in some of the earliest versions of the textbook anthologies.

The clearer philosophical bent of these works sets them apart from the early business and society works produced by figures such as Davis—or even the works of Taeusch. Produced by trained moral philosophers, they focused on providing explicit ethical frameworks within which to evaluate business practices. But taking a course in business ethics was still considered a novel experience, as was reflected in the 1980s adage that the description "business ethics" is an oxymoron, a dismissive quip that had first appeared in print in the *Wall Street Journal* in response to a survey of business ethics courses by Hoffman (Tannenbaum 1983). Peter Drucker complained that "to the moralist of the Western tradition 'business ethics' would make no sense. . . . There is only one ethics, one set of rules of morality, one code, that of individual behavior in which the same rules apply to everyone alike" (Drucker 1981, 18–19). But his call to dismiss business ethics as a form of casuistry was not accepted by the growing numbers of philosophers who entered the burgeoning field of business ethics at the time (Hoffman and Moore 1982b).

American business ethics had become a fully fledged form of applied philosophy. But it was a different story in Europe. There had been a long tradition of publications on commercial ethics and summaries of Catholic social teaching and its applications in business in Europe. The philosopher and priest Octave Lemarié's popular French survey *La morale des affaires* [*Business Ethics*] (1928) was subtitled "a short introduction to economic morals" and concentrated on matters such as how managers should treat employees according to Catholic social teaching. The French political economist André Arnou's *La morale des affaires* [*Business Ethics*] (1925) was similarly focused on workers and participation, declaring ownership rights in modern business to be "exaggerated". The Catholic bishop Franz Xaver Eberle's *Katholische Wirtschaftsmoral* [*Catholic Business Ethics*] (1921) was followed by Protestant contributions in the 1920s including the Calvinist lawyer Ernst Cahn's *Christentum und Wirtschaftsethik* [*Christianity and Business Ethics*] (1924) and the Lutheran theologian Georg Wünsch's *Evangelische Wirtschaftsethik* [*Lutheran Business Ethics*] (1927). Works such as the German pedagogical reformer Berthold Otto's *Moral und Wirtschaft* [*Morality and Business*] (1931) continued to be produced into the 1930s, and Otto Schilling's *Katholische Wirtschaftsethik* [*Catholic Business Ethics*] (1933) was reissued in a second edition after the Second World War. More post-war works included the German social ethicist Walter Weddigen's conceptual and historical survey *Wirtschaftsethik* [*Business Ethics*] (1951) and the Austrian economist Anton Tautscher's similarly named 1957 work (that was published in a moral theology series). A key Italian contribution was

Monsignor Giuseppe Bicchierai's *Il mondo degli affari e la morale* [*The Business World and Ethics*] (1935) while the Jesuit political economist Joaquín Azpiazu's 701-page *La moral del hombre de negocios* [*The Ethics of the Businessman*] (1944) also appeared in two post-war Spanish editions (in 1952 and 1964).

In 1958, the Australian Methodist Clarence Northcott published a study of *Christian Principles in Industry* in the United Kingdom. Northcott was a former personnel manager at Rowntree's cocoa works in York and president of the Institute of Personnel and Development. In the 1930s, he had been involved in the *Incentives and Contentment* (Hall and Locke 1938) studies at Rowntree's and emphasised, in contrast to his compatriot Elton Mayo, an approach to human relations explicitly based on moral responsibilities (Weatherburn 2019). Comparable Continental European publications at the time, however, tended to be produced by university scholars. In 1968, Johannes Messner, the professor of ethics and the social sciences at the University of Vienna, produced a short summary of *Das Unternehmerbild in der katholischen Soziallehre* [*The Image of the Entrepreneur in Catholic Social Teaching*], which was published in Cologne by the Bund Katholischer Unternehmer, the German branch of UNIAPAC; while in 1969 a collection of case studies in business ethics was assembled under the direction of Gilbert Olivier, the head of the École supérieure des sciences économiques et commerciales (ESSEC) in Paris by members of the Mouvement des cadres, ingénieurs et dirigeants chrétiens (Movement of Christian Executives, Engineers and Managers) (Gueneau et al. 1969).

The United Kingdom proved rather slower to adopt a formal tradition of business ethics. Reflections of American concerns with the ethical behaviour of businessmen first began to appear in British publications in the late 1960s but became more widespread in the 1970s, informed by earlier religious traditions. The Second Ecumenical Council of the Vatican (Vatican II), held from 1962 to 1965, had promoted dialogue between the Catholic Church and other Christian denominations, and UNIAPAC had renamed itself, accordingly, as the International Christian Union of Business Executives, allowing Protestant groups to join. The Catholic Industrialists' Conference in London was renamed the Christian Association of Business Executives (CABE) and opened up to all Christian executives, and in 1974 it produced its own American-style business ethics code (CABE 1974). The Industrial Relations Act of 1971 had included a code of practice which spurred the Confederation of British Industry and the British Institute of Management to begin work on developing codes of corporate conduct, and most of the early ethics codes of groups such as the British Computer Society, the Institute of Public Relations and the Law Society date to this period (Adams 1973; Filios 1985). CABE's code appeared after two surveys of British business ethics had been undertaken by the Anglican economist Simon Webley (1971, 1972), and Webley's surveys of directors and managers were followed by the publications *Ethical Choice and Business Responsibilities* by Major Kenneth Adams (1975), the director of studies at St George's House, Windsor (cf. Adams 1973), and the British Institute of Management's *Business Ethics and Responsibilities* (BIM 1975).

Webley had undertaken his first business ethics survey for the Foundation for Business Responsibilities, set up in 1966 as the Industrial Educational and Research Foundation by Aims of Industry (Webley 1973). In 1968, CABE (which sponsored Webley's second survey) had produced a draft report on employee participation in collaboration with UNIAPAC (CABE/UNIAPAC 1968), but Aims of Industry was principally known in the 1970s for its anti-union propaganda and promotion of industrial relations reform. Adams, on the other hand, had joined the royal charity the St George's House Trust in 1969, where he began its mid-service clergy courses on the issues of modern society and its "Attitudes to Industry" consultations (funded by Demetrius Comino's Comino Foundation) that sought to address anti-business sentiment in the United Kingdom (Adams 1971, 1979, 1986). In 1973, Webley had noted early moves to establish formal business ethics curricula by British management educators had begun, including the formation of an ethics group among the Association of Teachers of Management (cf. Hope and Dowling 1975). In 1973, the Heath government's White Paper on Company Law Reform even included a proposal for a business code of conduct (Department of Trade and Industry 1973, 19–20). After adopting its own code in 1974, the British Institute of Management continued to promote work in the area, producing a survey in 1976 on ethics codes comparable to that produced the previous year by the Business Roundtable in New York (Business Roundtable 1975; Melrose-Woodman and Kverndal 1976).

The call for business to raise its ethical standards was also felt in Continental Europe at the time. Prepared during the Third European Management Symposium by the European Management Forum, the Davos manifesto of 1973 was a one-page code of ethics (in German) particularly focused on social responsibility:

A. The purpose of professional management is to serve customers, employees, investors and society, and to balance conflicting interests.
B. 1. Management must serve its customers. It must satisfy its customers' needs in the best possible manner. Fair competition among companies is necessary to ensure that customers receive the best value for money, quality and range of products. Management's aim must be to translate new ideas and technological advances into marketable products and services.
    2. Management must serve its employees. In a free society, leadership will only be accepted if it respects the interests of employees.

Management must aim to secure jobs, increase real incomes and contribute to the humanisation of work.

3. Management must serve its investors. It must guarantee them a return on their investment, higher than the return on government bonds. This higher return is necessary to integrate a risk premium into capital costs. Management is the investors' trustee.

4. Management must serve society. It must ensure a liveable environment for future generations. It must use the knowledge and resources entrusted to it for the good of society. It must continuously expand the frontiers of knowledge in management and promote technological progress. It must ensure that the business pays tax in order to allow the community to fulfil its objectives. Management should also put its knowledge and experience at the service of society.

C. Management can only serve customers, employees, investors and society by securing the long-term future of the business. This requires sufficient corporate profit. Therefore, profit is necessary, but not the ultimate goal of business leadership.

(Steinmann 1973, 472–3)

The Davos forum had been established in 1971 by the Swiss industrialist Klaus Schwab, whose 1971 book *Moderne Unternehmensführung im Maschinenbau* [*Modern Enterprise Management in Mechanical Engineering*] encouraged managers to recognise the importance of other interests (*Interessenten*) such as employees, investors and customers to business (Schwab 2009). Schwab had studied at Harvard's John F. Kennedy School of Government in 1966–67, and the first Davos meeting had been chaired by George P. Baker, the dean of the Harvard Business School.

Far from a matter only for philosophers and theologians, business ethics was becoming more and more important in Europe. In 1977, the German business journalist Rosemarie Fiedler-Winter published a book based on interviews with sixty leading figures in European industry, politics, unions and the churches on business ethics; and Ernst H. Plesser, the general manager of Deutsche Bank, published an essay on managerial ethics that appeared that same year. A similar collection was published in the Netherlands in 1978 as the proceedings of a conference held two years earlier at Nijenrode, The Netherlands School of Business (Van Dam and Stallaert eds. 1978). Ethics codes had also been discussed by Plesser at UNIAPAC's 1975 symposium (Plesser 1975; 1977), the same year that the United Nations took the first steps towards establishing a Code of Conduct on Transnational Corporations. The need for a UN code was proposed in light of ITT's interference in the Chilean presidential elections after Salvador Allende had drawn attention to the issue during a 1972 address to the UN General Assembly (Sauvant 2015). Allende had accused ITT of trying to overthrow his Popular Unity administration:

ITT, a huge corporation whose capital is greater than the budget of several Latin American nations put together and greater than that of some industrialized countries, began, from the very moment that the people's movement was victorious in the elections of September 1970, a sinister action to keep me from taking office as President. . . . Last July the world learned with amazement of different aspects of a new plan of action that ITT had presented to the US Government in order to overthrow my Government in a period of six months. . . . They wanted to strangle us economically, carry out diplomatic sabotage, create panic among the population and cause social disorder so that when the Government lost control, the armed forces would be driven to eliminate the democratic regime and impose a dictatorship.

(Allende 1972)

ITT had its way when the Chilean military seized power on September 11, 1973, with Augusto Pinochet's murderous junta remaining in power in Chile until 1990.

The institutionalisation of business ethics was much slower in Europe, but in 1983, a research position in business ethics was created at the University of St Gall in Switzerland (Hajduk and Beschorner 2015), and in 1984 Henk van Luijk took up the first chair in business ethics at Nijenrode (now Nyenrode Business Universiteit). In 1980, Brian Griffiths, the dean of City University Business School, had given one of the London Lectures in Contemporary Christianity on the subject of business ethics (Griffiths 1982) and in 1986 CABE created the Institute of Business Ethics in London. The teaching of specialised university-level business ethics courses did not begin in the United Kingdom until Andrew Likierman began offering a graduate option in the area at the London Business School in 1988, however. Sheena Carmichael and John Drummond from the University of Strathclyde published *Good Business* in 1989, and after organising conferences on teaching business ethics in 1990, the Scottish Jesuit Jack Mahoney reported that several other schools had established similar courses or were investigating offering them (Mahoney 1990). But by this time the international adoption of the new American style of business ethics had seen the 1987 establishment of the European Business Ethics Network followed in 1989 by the founding of the International Society for Business, Economics and Ethics (Van Luick 1990).

By the 1980s business ethics had largely been secularised as earlier figures such as Baumhart retired from active involvement in the discipline and applied ethicists in philosophy departments such as Richard De George contested whether neo-Thomists had any contribution to make to business ethics at all (De George 1986). The field had rapidly institutionalised and the generation of clerics who had helped revive business ethics in the 1950s and 1960s mostly withdrew from the field, leaving the impression among many that business ethics was a later development than business and society scholarship. But just as CSR had grown out of a broader concern with the ethical behaviour of business and the negative effects of industrial capitalism, a new area of concern, first raised substantially in the early 1960s, developed more strongly in the following decade in light of broader debates concerning the social responsibilities of business and more revelations of misconduct by American corporate officials.

6 Corporate Governance

With the adoption of business ethics by a new generation of academic philosophers, American university educators finally seemed to have discovered a comprehensive manner in which to address issues of business wrongdoing and scandal. But as Frederick (2006) adumbrates, a third strand of American responses to corporate wrongdoing emerged in the 1970s and 1980s that was articulated in a separate manner than advocates of CSR and applied philosophy had developed. The critique raised in the new discourse of business ethics had been presaged by Eells and the Davos manifesto, and it also reflected a key criticism of corporate boards raised by figures such as Nader. Much of the reform called for was legal, however, and was most evident initially in the form of codes of conduct promoted in countries other than the United States.

The notion that American corporations had duties to parties affected by their activities other than employees and shareholders had been widely acknowledged by the 1930s. Yet in the 1970s, challenges to the traditional model of firm governance had been put forward by "Nader's Raiders" that influenced the development of a new formal model of business responsibility and ethics. Where the 1950s and 1960s had seen the widespread uptake of industrial democracy in Western Europe, a different "variety of capitalism" had emerged in the United States (Hall and Soskice eds. 2001). A full-blown form of "stakeholder theory" arose in America in the 1980s that attempted to describe the model of the corporation advanced by earlier figures such as Dodd and Eells in terms of secular ethics.

At the same time, however, a revival in classical economic thought saw a new approach to business ethics develop and a decline in traditions of state ownership. Encapsulated in the "agency theory" of two Harvard economists, Michael Jensen and William Meckling (1976), two very different approaches to business had emerged: a neo-classical economic view bolstered by the adoption of Hayekian economic thought, and an ethicalised social perspective that tried to serve as a catch-all for social liberal understandings of the proper role of business in society. With the international development of formal corporate governance requirements, codes of ethics regained a popularity they had not had since the 1920s, and ethics came more and more to be something articulated in semi-legal terms as a new form of social control of corporations arose.

Corporate Democracy and Stakeholders

In November 2001, the Houston-based energy trader Enron collapsed. The $62 billion champion of American energy deregulation would soon be revealed to have been the home of one of the biggest frauds in corporate history. Formed in 1985 as part of a merger between two gas companies, InterNorth and Houston Natural Gas, from 1987 Enron had begun aggressively expanding into the newly deregulated US energy markets. But Enron's businesses were unprofitable, and to hide the losses it was accruing, its managers had engaged in widespread accounting fraud. Its senior executives were convicted, its 21,000 employees lost their jobs and its shareholders were wiped out. Described by the journalists who first revealed the scandal as *The Smartest Guys in the Room* (McLean and Elkind 2003), Enron's managers had developed a comprehensive ethics policy and its corporate values were "respect, integrity, communication and excellence". Its corporate strategy had been developed by McKinsey & Co. and the firm was audited by Arthur Andersen, one of the country's "big five" accounting firms. The collapse of Enron shocked corporate America and led to a comprehensive recasting of US corporations and securities law.

Most commentators claimed that the biggest problem with Enron was with its corporate governance, a concept that had first been popularised by Nader and his supporters in the 1970s. Considerations of the proper relationship between employees, owners and directors of firms in a democratic society have a long history in Western business. Yet the traditional focus on the interests of capital and labour which informed Marxist criticism and the conservative and Catholic responses to socialism had been transformed in the early twentieth century by what Berle and Means (1932) had first described as the separation of ownership from control. The Berle/Dodd debate in the 1930s presented two different perspectives: one focused on the relationship of corporate management with shareholders, the other on a wider range of claimants on the corporation. The rights of employees and the maintenance of social order had been the main focus of European debates, but the emergence of the idea of corporate social responsibility and the consumer movement associated with Nader had broadened the focus of American theorists of business ethics.

Debates over worker representation and the effective functioning of governing boards were particularly common in Continental Europe in the 1950s and 1960s (Neuloh 1956; Clegg 1960; Blumberg 1968; Czubek 1968; Emery and Thorsrud 1969). Yet the discourse around how firms should be constituted and the proper role of corporate directors had undergone a very different path in the United States. Works councils and employee involvement in industrial decision-making had first been advocated during the First World War but had subsequently been advanced more successfully by advocates of Taylorism as a method for improving production processes. Joint labour-management arrangements were advocated most notably by Morris Cooke, Frederick Taylor's ghostwriter (i.e. the actual author of *The Principles of Scientific Management*), as the Taylor movement (particularly after Taylor's death) attempted to extend Taylor's "mental revolution" by engaging union support (Cooke and Murray 1940; Derber 1970; Wrege and Stotka 1978; McCartin 1998). But American employers had been able to resist industrial democratisation, particularly through the efforts of human relations programmes of the type recommended by Elton Mayo (Bruce and Nyland 2011; Nyland et al. 2014).

Instead, the American focus on corporate governance reform remained managerialist or corporatist in focus. In 1932, Dodd had observed that American corporations were taking on more responsibility for the welfare of employees, but that they were also permitted to engage in philanthropy, suggesting that corporate managers recognised that they had a broader responsibility to society. With the growth in claims that corporations had broader responsibilities than just to their shareholders, less focus on the rights of employees necessarily ensued. Advocates of CSR envisaged a different post-war settlement than that which had occurred in Europe—one between managers and the broader public rather than simply a partnership between capital and labour. Indeed, in 1960 Eells had expanded Dodd's 1932 list of corporate claimants and organised them into two groups: direct and indirect claimants. For Eells, direct claimants on the corporation included security holders, customers, employees and suppliers, while indirect claimants were competitors, local communities, the general public and governments. But rather than just in terms of responsibility, Eells (1960) described the way that corporations should be constituted and directed as a matter of what he dubbed "corporate governance".

Eells was particularly interested in the social role that corporations had as institutions in society—philanthropic, statesmanlike and what he called the "well-tempered corporation" (Eells 1960, 330). The stated purpose of his 1962 study *The Government of Corporations* was to establish corporate governance as a field in light of what he had earlier described as the "excessive materialism", the "cynical disregard for moral and religious standards" and the "undemocratic values" of US business in the early 1960s (Eells 1960, 52). Eells defined corporate governance as "the structure and function of the corporate polity", and his call "to develop a theory of corporate governance consistent with the ideals of a democratic society" made it clear that he saw corporate governance largely in terms of moral and institutional reform (Eells 1960, 19, 21). By 1970, Eells was using the expression mostly in terms of directors and shareholder rights, but the description "corporate governance" was clearly understood to represent an extension of business ethics when it was first adopted into mainstream business discourse (Eells 1970).

Another model of the corporation that was proposed in the 1960s was Gary March's notion that businesses were "political coalitions" (March 1962). But it would be Eells's terminology and focus that would be adopted in American legal debates in the 1970s when critics such as Nader began to emphasise the role that corporate directors had had in the ongoing scandals that seemed especially to characterise American business at the time. In a report released in 1976 as *Taming the Giant Corporation* (Nader et al. 1976), Nader and his colleagues Mark J. Green and Joel Seligman stressed particularly how senior management groups had in many instances proved contemptuous of both consumers and shareholders. Nader and his supporters argued that US corporations needed to be regulated federally to force them to be more responsible not just to their shareholders, but also to societal concerns more generally.

The first use of the expression "corporate governance" in the *Wall Street Journal* was in a review of *Taming the Giant Corporation* by UCLA Business School dean Neil H. Jacoby (1977). In their report, Nader, Green and Seligman had devoted an entire chapter to corporate governance subtitled "Who Rules the Corporation?" bemoaning the "failure of modern corporate governance" in terms of a "political state in which all powers are held by a single clique" (Nader et al. 1976, 75, 86, 186). In a reply to Jacoby's review, Nader and Green further observed that "corporate governance is often undemocratic and ineffective"—they proposed a major restructuring of boards, elevating the rights of stockholders, employees and the general public, and rescuing corporations from managerial domination (Nader and Green 1977). Yet later that year, the *Wall Street Journal* journalist William D. Hartley still thought that the expression required definition for his readers, describing shareholder activists proposing resolutions "around what is termed 'corporate governance' such as voting procedures for directors" (Hartley 1977).

With its popularisation, though, Eells's expression soon began appearing in more conservative legal discourse, in mainstream legal publications and even textbooks, and the June 1976 hearings on "corporate rights and responsibilities" held before the US Senate further established the broader usage of the term (Committee on Commerce 1976; Conard 1976, 317–415; Schwartz 1976). Soon the US Congress and the Securities and Exchange Commission were considering wide-ranging changes to federal corporations law and securities regulation—law conferences were held linking corporate governance with social responsibility, public statements for and against regulatory reform were thrashed out by lobbyists and scholars and, in 1978, the American Law Institute inaugurated a corporate governance project which had the aim of standardising and rendering explicit the many issues of common law that informed and impinged upon US "corporate directorship" (Securities and Exchange Commission 1977, 35–6; Ruder 1979; Small 1979; Fischel 1982; Scott 1983). Securities and Exchange Commission chairman Harold M. Williams had begun his four-year term in 1977 amid a hail of public criticism of corporate behaviour and weaknesses in securities regulation (Gerth 1981; Seligman 2003, 516–68). But after the flurry of reform proposals and institution of legislation like the 1977 Foreign Corrupt Practices Act, the drive for corporate governance reform soon slipped off the mainstream American political agenda.

Yet already the notion of corporate governance seemed to have undergone a bifurcation. The main issues surrounding the new concern were summarised by "corporate doctor" Victor H. Palmieri in the *Wall Street Journal* in 1978 in a manner that is clearly consistent with how the notion is often still understood today:

> The subject of "corporate governance" has become a favorite preoccupation of Congressmen, SEC commissioners, legal scholars and Naderites. "How can we improve the way corporations are run?" is the question they are asking. The answers come in three clusters: (1) Making sure that directors are "independent" (i.e. not under management domination); (2) increasing the responsibility of the audit committee of the board for monitoring sensitive disclosure issues such as questionable payments; and (3) raising the level of federal and state standards for corporate behavior in relation to investors and the public.
>
> (Palmieri 1978)

By the beginning of the 1980s, however, much of the heat had gone out of the debate over corporate governance reform. The movement begun in the early 1970s to install more non-executive directors on corporate boards and increase the number of listed firms with audit committees had largely been completed by that time, with the annual studies of executive recruiters Korn/Ferry tracking the number of organisations that had accepted the need for greater board independence particularly in light of the scandals that had emerged at the start of the decade such as the spectacular Penn Central Transportation Company bankruptcy of 1970 (Korn/Ferry 1973ff.). The Penn Central was the sixth-largest corporation in the United States, and its bankruptcy occurred after ongoing losses that had been so well hidden by its managers that even the board members were not aware of them (Sobel 1977). Williams had promoted a goal of only one executive director on corporate boards, and audit committees (first recommended by the Securities and Exchange Commission in 1940) had become a mandatory requirement under the listing rules of the New York Stock Exchange in 1978. But John S.R. Shad, the incoming head of the Securities and Exchange Commission in 1981, did not hold the same ambitions as had his Democrat-appointed predecessor as the main ambition of corporate reform in the Reagan years became deregulation. As former SEC commissioner Roberta S. Karmel put it to a *New York Times* columnist in 1982, the moral dimension of reform encapsulated in the expression "corporate governance" had fallen off the SEC's agenda at the expense of economic efficiency (Noble 1982).

The (tentative) corporate governance common law restatement published by the American Law Institute in 1982 was particularly opposed by the Business Roundtable (which had been set up in 1972 with the support of the Nixon administration as the leading US advocate of big business) (Lewin 1982; Business Roundtable 1983; Seligman 1987). Some of the 1970s progress on matters of corporate disclosure and accountability for bribery in foreign subsidiaries had remained intact, but a proposed bill on corporate democracy that would force corporate boards to be more representative of stakeholder interests did not survive the 1980 congressional elections (Green et al. 1979; Wall Street Journal 1980; Green 1980; Ruder 1981). The incoming Reagan administration showed little stomach for further corporate law reform—the focus of the new administration would instead be on economic and regulatory modernisation.

Another new feature of the period was the employment of the use of the legal term "stakeholder" to refer to Eells's "claimants" and the Davos manifesto's "interests". Yet when "stakeholder theory" had first been formally propounded by William R. Dill (1975), the dean of New York University's Graduate School of Business Administration, it was presented principally from the perspective of firm strategy—how could a business best manage its relationships with each of its key constituencies? Dill's 1975 article was written in response to "Naderites"—or "Kibbitzers", as Dill called them (employing a Yiddish word for people who did not play chess, but watched other people who did, making comments on their play). Dill had misused the term stakeholder (which properly referred to a disinterested party that held a stake as a custodian for someone else), but the expression had rapidly caught on as a replacement for Eells's "claimants". Despite calling his book *Strategic Management*, however, in the 1980s, Edward Freeman (1984) further developed the stakeholder approach by giving it a philosophical perspective. Freeman (1984) buttressed his version of stakeholder theory by employing the Harvard philosopher John Rawls's (1971) *Theory of Justice*.

Freeman's articulation of stakeholder theory was derived separately from Dill's, in Freeman's case from Russell Ackoff's *Redesigning the Future* (1974). In Ackhoff's book "stakeholder theory" is ascribed to the repudiation of Dodd's approach by the strategic management pioneer Igor Ansoff:

> "responsibilities" and "objectives" are not synonymous, [but] they have been made one in a "stakeholder theory" of objectives. This

theory maintains that the objectives of the firm should be derived balancing the conflicting claims of the various "stakeholders" in the firm: managers, workers, stockholders, suppliers, vendors.

(Ansoff 1965, 34)

The original misuse of the legal term seems to have arisen at the Stanford Research Institute in the early 1960s (Freeman et al. 2010, 30–2). But by the 1970s, the description "stakeholder" had spread from being used irregularly by Ansoff and his colleagues into general American management parlance. Freeman's key contribution was to match the notion with a philosophical understanding of justice, his 1984 work popularising the stakeholder concept more widely outside the strategic management literature.

Yet Rawls's *Theory of Justice* was more important to the development of business ethics than just making an appearance in Freeman's 1984 book. In 1958, the English philosopher Elizabeth Anscombe had published a key criticism of ethical philosophy, particularly taking aim at approaches she called "consequentialist". Anscombe excoriated secular philosophers for their obsession with consequentialism even where their approach could lead to justifications for murder. A Catholic, Anscombe not only named consequentialist ethical philosophy for the first time, she equally complained that deontological ethics seemed to lack a proper judge. Shorn of reference to God, deontological ethicists were practicing a secularised kind of Christian ethics without wanting to admit it. Pointing to moral psychology, Anscombe challenged philosophers to stop making judgements about what is morally right or wrong as if there were a universal legislator:

It would be most reasonable to drop it. It has no reasonable sense outside a law conception of ethics; they are not going to maintain such a conception; and you can do ethics without it, as is shown by the example of Aristotle.

(Anscombe 1958, 8)

Anscombe's intervention eventually led to a revival of virtue ethics separate from the neo-Thomism promoted by the Papacy. But some of Anscombe's Oxford colleagues offered a different solution, arguing that normativity could be derived from the social dimension of morality (Toulmin 1950, 223; Foot 1958, 510–11). In the United States a group of ethicists, most notably John Rawls, began to argue instead that morality was grounded in human nature (Bok 2017). Rawls worked at first from a Protestant perspective, but he later came to insist that ethical judgement merely needed a "competent judge", not a supernatural one. Developing on the work of the Swiss psychologist Jean Piaget (1932), Rawls (1963) argued that children develop a sense of morality as their understanding of their parent's love matures and hence of fairness and justice. Rawls was able to bring aspects of Christian ethics (such as an emphasis on love) into secular philosophy. The publication of his *Theory of Justice* in 1971, however, allowed Catholic social justice teaching to be reconciled with the philosophy of social contracts developed by secular figures such as Jean-Jacques Rousseau (1762).

Rawls's secularisation of social justice became a key feature of Freeman's stakeholder theory but also began to appear separately in business ethics textbooks. Despite its appearance first in a strategic management context, the stakeholder approach to the corporation rapidly took the place that calls for corporate democracy had in the Naderite movement. The use of the term "stakeholder" seemed not only to crystallise the notion that corporations had multiple claimants, Freeman's application of Rawls's understanding of justice gave the concept a philosophical sheen that its managerialist forebear had not. The idea of interests of or claimants on business had already been adopted in European practice in terms of expressions such as the Davos manifesto. But with the adoption of the irregular term "stakeholder" in works such as Freeman's 1984 book, a new way of thinking about corporate governance and corporate strategy seemed to have emerged that was reconcilable with the earlier traditions of social justice that informed social liberal politics.

Yet at the same time as stakeholder theory was emerging, a rather different approach developed in economics. With the advent of public choice theory in the 1960s, economists had grown increasingly confident that economic arguments could be used to promote clearer thinking in areas that previous generations had not thought properly part of the purview of economic theory (Buchanan and Tullock 1962). Beginning in 1970, economic theoreticians began to propose ways of modelling the behaviour of agents employed by the public—for example, public officials such as police officers (Ross 1973; Mitnick 1975). In 1976, Jensen and Meckling published a paper which argued that similar theorising could be applied to listed corporations.

Jensen and Mecking's theory of the firm was based on the assumption that stakeholder theory was wrong and the only valid economic claimants a corporation had were its owners—that is, its shareholders. Enlarged by later scholars such as Eugene F. Fama (Fama 1980; Fama and Jensen 1983), the agency approach to corporate governance served to establish a canonical body of scholarship that would come to represent the intellectual mainstream of 1980s corporate governance discourse in a development hailed by conservative critics of Nader and his supporters. The main focus of agency theory was corporate efficiency, as Jensen became a hero of conservative business commentators. His focus on what became known as "shareholder primacy" seemed to represent a major challenge to business ethics.

Industrial Democracy

By the 1980s, corporate governance had started to take a foothold also in the United Kingdom. Bob Tricker's *Corporate Governance* (1984), however, seemed quite detached from the talk of stakeholders, principals and agents that were being advanced in the United States at the time. Instead, the calls for more independent directors by Jonathan Charkham of the reform group Promotion of Non-Executive Directors (ProNED) in the United Kingdom was couched in terms of board professionalisation and improving the performance of British firms (Charkham 1983, 1984). ProNED, which had been established in 1981 under the auspices of the Bank of England, performed a similar public function to Korn/Ferry and its annual reviews of US boards. When the expression "corporate governance" was used at all in British (or European) commentary at the time, it was clearly an Americanism used to describe a particular approach to improving the productive functioning of company boards that lacked a clear ethical dimension.

In Europe, American-style corporate governance seemed to be a challenge to industrial democracy. First coined as an expression (*démocratie industrielle*) by Proudhon in the fifth edition of his *Manual of the Stock Exchange Speculator* (1857, 461), industrial democracy contrasted with corporate governance genealogically as originally representing a radical discourse inherited from the nineteenth-century worker movement (Mees 2017b). Workers' councils had played a key role in the revolutionary movements in Germany, Italy and Russia, although in most cases they had been brought under union control by the 1920s (Eley 2002, 160–4). Yet European industrial democracy also drew on Catholic social thought as expressed in *Rerum novarum* and Pius XII's 1949 address to UNIA-PAC which advocated seeing a business as a community of work. The external notion of industrial democracy, as articulated by Sidney and Beatrice Webb (1897), concerned the rights of workers to join trade unions and to be represented by these external bodies in industrial bargaining, grievance handling and other kinds of employment matters. Internally, however, industrial democracy had usually been envisaged in the form of works councils and the election of worker directors to the supervisory boards of publicly listed business undertakings (Markey et al. 2010).

By the 1970s, advocacy of industrial democracy had spread to the United Kingdom. Ever since Great Britain had entered the European Economic Community (EEC) in 1973, questions had been raised over the traditional structure of publicly quoted British companies. After the war, the continental European model of two boards—one managing and one supervisory—had been further adapted in countries such as West Germany to accommodate the often-opposing interests of management and non-executive employees. Works councils of various forms had been current in

German experience since the late nineteenth century, and these bodies had been strengthened after the war by the adoption of the first West German codetermination (*Mitbestimmung*) legislation (McGaughey 2015). First developed in 1951 at a time when employers were still in a particularly weak political position, in 1976 the German parliament had even extended the number of employee-elected positions on German supervisory boards to 50 percent in large enterprises (i.e. those with over 2,000 employees). German-style codetermination was duly presented as an alternative business structure, tried and tested in the EEC's dominant economy, and constituted a quite different model for the modern British public company (Mertens and Schanze 1979; Havlovic 1990; Fetzer 2010).

British support for industrial democracy had always been mixed. The Webbs had opposed worker involvement in management originally because of the low reputation that British employee shareholding schemes had achieved in the late nineteenth century, but by 1920 had come around to an acceptance of union involvement in the management of industry (Webb and Webb 1920; McGaughey 2014). Whitley Works Committees had also been formed in many industries between the two World Wars in a Taylorist attempt to "tap labor's brains" (Cooke and Murray 1940), but most of the UK's Joint Industrial Councils had been abolished by the 1970s (Patmore 2016). British trade unions did not actively seek to become involved in German-style codetermination arrangements until the 1960s (McGaughey 2014; Williamson 2016).

The UK's industrial democracy proposals of the late 1970s, however, also reflected a uniquely British concern in which industrial relations was largely unregulated, an environment that had led to an ungoverned industrial system where wildcat strikes and disputes even within unions were very much the order of the day (Fox 1985). In 1975, the Labour government of Harold Wilson had consequently appointed a commission of inquiry to respond to the matters raised in the European Commission's Draft Fifth Company Law Directive, the first version of which (published in 1972) proposed the institution of a modified West German system of firm governance right across the EEC. The Draft Fifth Directive was intended as an EEC-wide company-law harmonisation measure that would protect West German businesses from "social dumping"— i.e. it would stop multinationals from employing their staff in member countries that had the worst employment protections (Commission of the European Communities 1972; Dalton 1974; Conlon 1975; Bullock 1977; Davies and Wedderburn of Charlton 1977). The Conservative Party had duly proposed amending British company law to include a statutory duty for directors to take into account the interests of both shareholders and employees (Department of Trade and Industry 1973). But when the Labour government responded with a White Paper on industrial democracy in 1978, British business groups were appalled. The committee of inquiry led by the historian (and Labour peer) Allan

Bullock concentrated on how electing union representatives to company boards might lead to less industrial conflict in light of the undeniable economic success of West German firms under codetermination. Nonetheless as the government of James Callaghan (Wilson's Labour Party successor) moved into crisis during the strike-riddled "Winter of Discontent" of 1978–79, the UK's industrial democracy model for the public company soon disappeared from the mainstream policy agenda (Lopez 2014; Williamson 2016).

The majority report of the Bullock committee had proposed the adoption of a single board in British public companies of over 2,000 employees with worker-elected directors making up as many members of the board as shareholder-elected directors, with the remainder being independent of both unions and shareholders (the 2x + y model). As the committee noted:

> it seems to us (as it did to most witnesses) that to regard the company as solely the property of shareholders is to be out of touch with the reality of the present day company as a complex social and economic entity, subject to a variety of internal and external pressures, in which the powers of control have passed from the legal owners to professional management.
>
> (Bullock 1977, 41)

The minority report, prepared by the industrialists on the committee (who were constrained by the committee's terms of reference to advise on *how*, not *whether* codetermination should be implemented), instead recommended a dual-board model more along the lines that applied in West Germany.

Yet the Bullock report proved an immediate failure. Upon its publication in January 1977, its industrial democracy proposals were loudly criticised by the Confederation of British Industry. The confederation opposed the matter of union-appointed directors outright. The Callaghan government in turn quickly retreated, its White Paper published in May 1978 refusing to "impose a standard pattern of participation on industry by law" (Department of Employment 1978, 2), calling instead for the extension of participation through industrial agreements (Wedderburn of Charleton 1984; Carter 1989; Williamson 2016). Yet with the 1979 replacement of Callaghan as British Prime Minster by the Conservative Party's Margaret Thatcher, experiments with worker directors in nationalised industries were ended and the EEC proposals for codetermination were comprehensively rebuffed. Rather than adopting German-style codetermination, the response under Thatcher was to regulate union activity and industrial relations more generally (Marsh 1991; Shackleton 1998). The idea of industrial democracy quickly disappeared from the British public agenda.

The Globalisation of Corporate Governance

The development of a new discourse of corporate reform in the United States in the 1970s rapidly led to the dominance of a renewed shareholder-primacy approach to corporate management. As Milton Friedman had argued since the 1960s (Friedman 1962), corporations existed to make money, and the main claimants on that profit had been intended to be shareholders historically, not management elites or workers. The new American economic approach to corporate governance that first arose in the 1970s quickly became principally focused on maximising returns to shareholders, not issues of democratisation (Mees 2015). Much of the discussion of industrial democracy in the Anglo-Saxon countries has subsequently seen the scope of the democratising narrative retreat to an etiolated, management-controlled model of "participation" or "voice" (Bixler 1985; Mitchell 1998; Budd 2004). Industrial democracy in this understanding is restricted to the right of workers' voices to be heard through their unions—bodies external to the firm—or are reduced to a purely consultative (and often only token) role. Under codetermination, it is the firm itself which is democratised, as shareholder rights to be represented on the board of governance are balanced with those of the right of employees to be heard. The American discourse of corporate governance, however, did not consider democratisation at all, with emphasis on the rights of shareholders (over management) often serving as a proxy for democratisation more generally.

By the 1980s, Nader had despaired of achieving real reform from the perspective of corporate governance (Nader 1984). Yet his focus on consumers lived on. Further reform of American corporate law occurred with the introduction of conservation laws, prohibitions on discrimination in hiring and the further strengthening of legal rights of shareholders, employees and consumers. In 1986 the US Supreme Court confirmed the right of female employees to sue for sexual harassment, and in 1992 federal proxy rules for shareholders were amended in a manner that allowed investors to increase their ability to communicate with each other (Anderson 1987; Schwab and Thomas 1998). But Nader had criticised industrial-democracy initiatives as unworkable in the United States, and codetermination has remained only a peculiarly European aspect of corporate regulation (Nader et al. 1976).

Yet the 1990s saw a great growth in corporate governance reform particularly in terms of what the German scholar Klaus J. Hopt later styled the "code of conduct movement", a development whose genesis is usually linked to the appearance of the UK's Cadbury Report in 1992 (Hopt 2007). The Cadbury Report, produced by a committee chaired by former confectionary-industry executive Sir Adrian Cadbury, was not the first such body of its kind, as a similar document had been released by the US Business Roundtable in 1990 and a comparable attempt to provide a national code of conduct (or "compact") for directors had appeared in the *Harvard Business Review* in 1991 (Business Roundtable 1990; Working Group on Corporate Governance 1991). The corporate code movement can also be seen to be adumbrated by both the American Law Institute project and the various standards and surveys of directorship promoted by long-standing organisations such as the American Bar Association, the National Industrial Conference Board and the British Institute of Directors (Read 1953; Watson 1953; Ethe and Pegram 1959; Tangley 1961; Bacon 1967; Conference Board 1972; Bacon and Brown 1977; American Bar Association 1978; Mills 1981). Yet the Cadbury committee had to create its corporate governance code largely from scratch and featured a particular emphasis on "standards of conduct". This included the recommendation "We regard it as good practice for boards of directors to draw up codes of ethics or statements of business practice and to publish them both internally and externally" (Cadbury 1992, 4.29). Above all, however, the Cadbury committee served to popularise the notion of corporate governance internationally in a way that comparable American developments did not.

The 1990s saw an explosion of interest in corporate governance internationally. The Cadbury committee had been established after several lesser-known company collapses had occurred in Great Britain whose likelihood had not been signalled in their audited reports. The committee was supported by the UK's Financial Reporting Council, the London Stock Exchange, the Institute of Business Ethics and the accounting profession, and it was clear that the Cadbury committee was primarily focused on an ethics initiative (Cadbury 2002, 10–12; Jones and Pollitt 2002; Spira and Slinn 2013). The number of securities quoted on the London Stock Exchange had greatly expanded over the course of the 1980s as the Thatcher government had privatised a range of previously state-owned enterprises. But it was the much more public business scandals that were revealed only after the establishment of the Cadbury committee which most informed the reception of its final report. The collapse of the Bank of Credit and Commerce International (in light of Central Intelligence Agency accusations that the London-listed Pakistani bank had become involved in money laundering and gun running) and the revelation that the Czech-born British newspaper tycoon Robert Maxwell had raided his employees' pension fund during the implosion of his Mirror Group gave the Cadbury Report much of its moral authority (Truell and Gurwin 1992; Greenslade 1992). Nonetheless the British code did not ask as fundamental questions of corporate governance reform as had Nader or other early American critics of corporate behaviour. Corporate governance was to remain a fundamentally conservative project aimed at improving the productive functioning of company boards.

One of the main economic developments which informed the Cadbury Report was the rapid internationalisation of financial markets over the course of the 1980s, one of the key emerging economic features later to be associated with globalisation (Giddens 1999). The company scandals of the late 1980s and early 1990s in Britain threatened to undermine the reputation of London as a financial centre. The drive to maintain the City of London as Europe's leading financial hub seemed to be at stake. But the development of the corporate governance code established by the Cadbury committee set in train a number of similar bodies and the promotion of international "Cadburyfication" (as the code of conduct movement was called at the time) first in South Africa (with the King Report), then in Canada, France, Japan, the Netherlands, India and Germany (King 1994; Dey 1994; Vienot 1995; Keidanren 1997; Peters 1997; Confederation of Indian Industry 1998; Cromme 2002). The Organisation for Economic Cooperation and Development report which outlined the first international set of corporate governance principles (albeit developed by an advisory group led by the American lawyer Ira M. Millstein) also predates the major American corporate governance reforms which occurred only after the collapse of Enron (Millstein 1998; OECD 1999).

Significant corporate governance reform, then, occurred later in the United States than it did in many other advanced economies. It was not until 1997 that the US Business Roundtable prepared a statement that seemed to support corporate governance reform after the American Law Institute had finalised its second corporate governance report in 1994 (ten years after it had begun working on the project). By this time, institutional investors (particularly the American state and city pension funds and their Council of Institutional Investors, founded in 1985) had begun to join other shareholder activists in the United States in their efforts to reform corporate boards. Yet the first institutional pressure on corporate governance in America had become noticeable only in the late 1980s. Before that time shareholder activism had usually been confined to small groups of irate stockholders, union-controlled pension funds and responsible investment groups such as the Investor Responsibility Research Center, founded in 1972 by a consortium of Ivy League universities, and the Interfaith Center on Corporate Responsibility, established in 1974 to protest against corporations involved in Apartheid South Africa (Drucker 1976; Gray 1983; Harrington 1992, 8–30; Robinson 2002). The main reason for the emergence of the corporate governance code movement internationally had been the growing financialisation of international business (and the consequent desire to win the trust of "impatient capital") that has become such an evident characteristic of globalisation. Having a Cadbury-style set of national corporate governance principles became a necessity if a local securities industry was to attract and retain international finance capital (Ireland 2009).

This aspect of international financialisation explains why the major corporate governance reforms in the United States arose only in the aftermath of the 2001 collapse of Enron and the contemporary scandals at

Worldcom, Tyco, Adelphia Communications, Imclone and Global Crossing. But perhaps the most characteristic feature of the American discourse on corporate governance after the collapse of Enron and the promulgation of 2002's Sarbanes-Oxley Act is how little public comment concerning corporate governance had appeared in the American financial press in the years leading up to the scandals. A constant stream of corporate criticism had characterised American reporting during the 1970s hey-day of figures such as Nader, but little mention of such matters appeared in papers like the *Wall Street Journal* in the years leading up to 2002. Confidence in the self-regulating nature of financial markets had been unreasonably bolstered by the claims of economists such as Jensen and his supporters. But when the change of 2002 did come in the United States, it came hard and spectacularly fast—previous propensities for *laissez-faire* laxness and accommodation of accounting irregularities would no longer be considered acceptable in the wake of the collapse of Enron.

Many of the issues which informed later debates on corporate governance first became apparent in the United States, but with the emergence of agency theory, much academic discourse since that time had tended to be of a form acceptable to or even supported by managerialist conservatives in the business world. Reaching its most preposterous extreme in the 2001 claim by Henry Hansmann and Reinier Kraakman of an "end of history" in corporate law reform, the narrowing and winnowing of the discursive formation arraigned about the notion of corporate governance that occurred during the 1980s clearly represented a form of moral erosion of concepts originally developed in business ethics. Corporate governance as it stands today is best seen as a movement to improve the performance and standards of the directorial and executive teams at the top of listed companies, and to improve the confidence of international investors in local securities markets. But it was originally a moral discourse, first promoted by Richard Eells, a key figure in the business and society movement that had developed in American business ethics in the 1960s before the entry of secular philosophers into the field.

7   Ethical Leadership

As Raymond Baumhart's 1961 survey of *Harvard Business Review* readers had revealed, ethical behaviour in American corporations was generally thought to be primarily a matter for "top management", for "individuals of principle, who unmistakably reveal their ethical attitude" (Baumhart 1961, 7). The key to corporate governance scandals such as those at the Penn Central and at Enron had not just been a failure of moral leadership, however, but also a lack of financial prudence. Prudence is often seen today in terms of aversion to risk, but it is often forgotten that it was originally a key ethical concept in Western philosophy. In Aristotelean ethics, prudence was considered the main ethical virtue required of politicians, princes and generals—those in positions of authority who found themselves in charge of social institutions. Indeed, one of the aspirations of ancient Greek and Roman philosophers was that they could inculcate moral behaviour into political figures; Alexander the Great, for example, was tutored by Aristotle. But no mention of "leadership" is to be found in classical sources. Nor is one preserved in nineteenth-century philosophy, religious teachings or social science. The abstract concept of leadership is an American creation of the early twentieth century and soon became a key feature of business studies, particularly in the form of grants offered to university researchers by large American corporations.

The need for moral leadership had been a recurrent trope in American business since the 1930s when the telecommunications executive Chester Barnard had devoted an entire chapter to the concept in his *Functions of the Executive* (1938). But by the 1970s the idea seemed to have disappeared from business ethics discourse, only to reappear in a charismatised form in the 1980s. By the 1930s, what had previously been called prudence was increasingly being called leadership, but typically in a manner shorn of much of its ethical valence. As Josef Pieper (1966) had explained, prudence had come to be associated with "mere utility . . . in colloquial use, prudence always carries the connotation of timourous, small-minded self-preservation" (Pieper 1966, 4). A prudent person, Pieper maintained, "is thought to be one who avoids the embarrassing situation of having to be brave" (Pieper 1966, 4). With the revival of discourses of business leadership in the 1980s, however, ethics again came to be seen as a key feature of leadership, but in organisational psychology rather than philosophical ethics.

Rather than philosophers, it was industrial psychologists who rediscovered the early twentieth-century notion of moral leadership. An idea most strongly associated with American presidents such as Franklin D. Roosevelt and John F. Kennedy, ethical leadership became a key concept in "transformational leadership" and, from the 1990s, would also become strongly associated with organisational culture. By the 1990s a field of psychological business ethics had emerged, as long-standing philosophical understandings of ethical decision-making were rediscovered and promoted by moral psychologists. The role and effectiveness of ethics codes, ethics training and the nature of ethical reasoning also became key issues in the new psychologised form of business ethics and ensured the continued flourishing of the field.

Leadership and Prudence

The term "leadership" was first applied to religious and political leaders in the nineteenth century, but in a much more restricted manner than it is today. The expression "leadership" was most commonly used in the Victorian period as a collective noun applied to the people who led religious organisations (e.g. the "leadership" of the Methodist church) or in politics (the "leadership" of a political party). An 1894 article in Funk & Wagnalls' *Literary Digest* recorded a "revolt against bad leadership" (i.e. against the Democratic Party) by "business men who have found their business shrinking in volume; manufacturers who have had to close their mills because no one would buy a dollar's worth of goods beyond such demand as was immediately in sight" (The Literary Digest 1894). Leadership was not something that businesses had—the wider conceptual notion of leadership was a twentieth-century development.

In 1909, the "origins of leadership" was the subject of Eben Mumford's doctoral dissertation in sociology at the University of Chicago. Mumford declared that leadership was "a universal function of association" but was unable to explain why social scientists had not written about the concept before. Mumford described leadership as having evolved as hunter-gatherer societies emerged, citing a range of anthropological literature. The rise of the notion of leadership in business, however, was more closely associated with the notion of moral leadership. In 1932, just before he was inaugurated as president, Franklin Roosevelt opined to the *New York Times* that the presidency was "pre-eminently a place of moral leadership" (McCormick 1932). The notion was borrowed into business discourse by Barnard (1938), and as Baumhart (1961) had found, by the 1960s the idea that "top management" had an especially important ethical role was widespread in American business. But the notion that being a political leader or even a business manager meant having a significant moral duty was not a particularly new one at the time—moral leadership seemed merely to be a new way of describing the nineteenth-century notion of stewardship.

Yet in the Aristotelian tradition, the key contributor to moral leadership was prudence (*phronēsis*), or "practical wisdom". Aristotle differed from other prominent ethical thinkers of classical times in giving such prominence to the concept, separating it from "philosophic wisdom" (*sophia*), the form of wisdom especially stressed by the Stoic thinkers who dominated classical philosophy in Roman times. Philosophic and practical wisdom were both considered virtues of the intellect and of morality by Aristotle, but prudence was the key moral virtue in the Aristotelian tradition. Aristotle made it clear that "prudence is bound up with action" and that it was fundamental to all moral practice (Aristotle 2011, vi, 7). Accordingly, it was Aristotle's notion of prudence that featured in Aquinas's ethics and was reflected in the advocations of prudence in nineteenth-century business.

As Robert Hariman (2003) describes it, however, prudence suffered an "erosion" during the Enlightenment. It was largely dismissed by Kant, but in Adam Smith's *Theory of Moral Sentiments*, prudence was separated into two different forms. Smith's "inferior prudence" was mainly concerned with personal propriety and the frugality and restraint required of successful business managers. Notions such as thrift and caution were closely connected to prudence—extravagance and speculation were imprudent behaviours. Inferior prudence was the kind of practical wisdom most associated with accounting and running a small business. But by the nineteenth century, the concept of prudence had lost most of its appeal to philosophers of all varieties (Pieper 1966).

Smith's superior form of prudence was the practical wisdom of princes and kings—prudence used in government. The *Mirrors of Kings* (*Specula Principum*) that were written to educate princes in the Middle Ages were manuals of royal leadership, but most of them do not feature a focus on prudence (Anton 1968). "Prudence takes measure of the results to come from all things", Boethius advises in his *Consolations of Philosophy*, one of the first works to have come down to us translated into (Old) English. But Aristotle's discussion of practical wisdom was mostly unknown in medieval Europe until Robert Grosseteste's complete translation of Aristotle's text appeared in about 1248.

Yet Aristotelian prudence takes a key role in the system of ethics set out in Thomas Aquinas's *Summa Theologica* (written in 1265–74). In his explanation of prudence, Aquinas quoted Isidore of Seville: "A prudent man is one who sees as it were from afar, for his sight is keen, and he foresees the event of uncertainties" (Aquinas 1952, I, 47). He also added that Aristotle advised "a prudent man is one who is capable of taking good counsel" and that "prudence is right reason applied to action" (Aquinas 1952, I, 47). Prudence was also concerned with practical matters, not theological or abstract concerns: "it is clear that prudence is wisdom about human affairs: but not wisdom absolutely, because it is not about the absolutely highest cause, for it is about human good". Prudence is also not merely a virtue, but "prudence is in every virtue" (Aquinas 1952, I, 47).

As the most important of the four cardinal virtues in Aristotelian ethics, prudence was personified in medieval European art as carrying a mirror in one hand (to indicate reflection) and holding a serpent in the other (to indicate perspicacity). Its legal use preserved in the contemporary "prudent person" standard of the law of trust and fiduciaries, and the similar "prudence principle" of accounting reflect a sense of conservatism which represents a semantic narrowing of the original philosophical concept. Prudence had become the opposite of risk and reflected a sense of undue caution. Yet prudence underwent a further reduction in early management thought that is even less well understood.

The French engineer Henri Fayol's *General and Industrial Management* (1916) sets out five key functions of management: *prévoyance, organisation, commandement, coordination* and *controle*. These were translated in the 1949 English edition by Constance Storrs as "planning, organising, commanding, coordinating and controlling" (which are typically rebadged as "planning, leading, organising, coordinating and controlling" in undergraduate management textbooks today). But Storrs translates Fayol's *prévoyance* as both "planning" and "foresight" in the English edition of his key work, as *prévoyance* is the usual word for "foresight" or "forethought" in French, not "planning" (French *planification*). As M. Bernard Brodie (1962) pointed out, Storrs's "planning" is one of several poor glosses that appear in her translation of Fayol's main contribution to modern management.

Fayol began his chapter on *prévoyance* by citing the French saying *gouverner, c'ést prévoir* which Storrs translated as "managing means looking ahead". But the expression was a well-known French political adage, usually attributed to the nineteenth-century French politician Émile de Girardin, and is best understood in a political context (Naszályi 2017). The expression is perhaps put in its clearest light by its use by Jacques François Dupont de Bussac in the first issue of the *Revue républicaine* in 1838:

> *Gouverner, c'est prévoir, c'est vouloir, c'est ordonner l'exécution des choses conçues, c'est en surveiller l'exécution, c'est l'assurer par le choix et la nomination des principaux agens, c'est se faire rendre compte de l'exécution.*

> To govern is to foresee, it is to will, it is to order the execution of things conceived, it is to supervise their execution, it is to assure this by the choice and the appointment of the principal agents, it is to be accountable for execution.

> (Dupont 1838, 41)

For Fayol, *prévoyance* was merely a practical form of foresight, prudence as an intellectual virtue, without the overt moral sense stressed in Aristotle and Aquinas. It was a largely amoral form of prudence. The Aristotelian "common good" had become the good of the firm—Fayol's *prévoyance* was a form of practical wisdom applied in the furtherance of industry and was quite different in this way from the prudence advocated in traditional philosophy. But the amoral term "planning" was the word used for thinking ahead in British and American business at the time of Storrs's 1949 translation, so it is little surprise that she wavers so frequently between "foresight" and "planning" in her translation of Fayol's unvarying term *prévoyance*.

Yet by the 1960s, business planning had become strategy, a military term originally (cf. Greek *strategos* "(military) general", *strategia* "(military) generalship"). Before the appearance of Alfred Chandler's *Strategy and Structure* (1962), it was more common to speak of business policy or planning; it was not until Chandler's landmark 1962 analysis of decision-making at the highest levels of corporate America appeared that textbooks like William Newman's *Administrative Action* (1951) began to include the description strategy. Economic thought in the 1940s and 1950s stressed planning in a sense similar to wartime planning, but after Chandler the military notion of strategy (learnt, for example, by the Ford "whiz kids" while they served in the US Air Force) replaced the earlier notion (Byrne 1993).

This change in business *prévoyance*, from foresight to strategy, reflected a key change in the way the principal function of business leadership was conceptualised. Where the role of senior management had typically been thought of previously in American discourse as one of stewardship, the adoption of the military metaphor strategy represented an adoption of the economic language of competition. Rather than holding to the traditional virtue of prudence or a Protestant notion of stewardship, from the 1960s the key attribute of business leaders came to be seen as martial or fighting. This development is one of several themes that entered business thinking at the same time as Friedman's 1962 advocacy of a return to economic liberalism was first published, but has since become a key aspect of management thought and education.

By the 1970s strategy seemed to have become all encompassing, to the point even where the notion of a business having responsibilities to a different range of stakeholders had come to be understood in terms of strategy. Ansoff had dismissed the "stakeholder" concept, but Dill's 1975 articulation of "stakeholder theory" included "Naderites" as one of the groups for which businesses needed to show some concern. Freeman's key 1984 work on stakeholder theory was also simply called *Strategic Management: A Stakeholder Approach*. But there is no sense of prudence or leadership in Freeman's 1984 book, only justice. Barnard, the first management writer to talk about moral leadership, is mentioned only as a (possible) precursor of systems theory in Freeman's key 1984 work (Freeman 1984, 50). Barnard's focus on moral leadership had largely been forgotten. It would be up to organisational psychologists to ensure that an ethical facet to leadership would return to the literature of business management.

Leadership and Moral Psychology

After the Second World War, the work of Elton Mayo and Fritz Roethlisberger inspired the advent of the human relations movement, a development that made psychology central to the new science of management. First applied to American industry by Hugo Münsterberg (1912), psychology was a German invention that Edwin Boring in his *History of Experimental Psychology* (1929) connected especially with the key nineteenth-century German pioneer Wilhelm Wundt. Over the course of the 1950s, management studies developed a much stronger social science foundation than it had had in Taylor's day, albeit mostly only in psychology. Psychology graduates such as Douglas McGregor and Frederick Herzberg, famous now for their leadership and motivation studies (McGregor 1960; Herzberg 1966), found positions in business schools and were supported in their research by corporate benefactors (Wren and Bedeian 2009).

The success of the human relations movement saw industrial psychology (or organisational psychology as it is now usually called) transform management research. Taylor, Barnard and Drucker had written the most influential books in management studies by the 1950s. But hypothesis testing and the use of quantitative methods soon began to dominate intellectual production in post-war management research. Early psychological studies of workplaces tended to focus on matters such as increasing "human efficiency" and developing psychometric tests to gauge employee aptitude for certain kinds of occupations (Münsterberg 1912; Scott 1912; Sokal 1984). These approaches were modelled on the work of Taylor and his supporters and fell out of fashion after the results of the Hawthorne studies became widely known. Most of the quantitative studies produced by psychologists before the Second World War proved of little use to later generations of management scholars. In contrast, the psychological studies of members of the human relations movement soon threatened to overwhelm the emerging discipline.

Leadership studies were promoted especially by psychologists from the 1930s onwards, particularly in terms of the social psychology of the Massachusetts Institute of Technology's Kurt Lewin. With Mayo, Lewin was a key figure in the development of the human relations movement, but particularly from the perspective of leadership. Lewin was most interested in leadership for political reasons; a Jewish refugee from Nazi Germany, Lewin's leadership studies (of schoolchildren) were clearly aimed at promoting (American) democracy over (Hitlerian) autocracy (Lewin et al. 1939). His work on leadership was expanded after the war by Ralph M. Stogdill and other industrial psychologists at Ohio State University, where in their studies of navy personnel, democracy and autocracy were refined into subordinate "consideration" versus "initiation of structure" orientations (Stogdill and Shartle 1948; Stogdill et al. 1953). Advocates of employee-focused rather than production-oriented management used the findings of psychologists to justify the superiority of their relational management style over the directive, task-structuring approach associated with Taylor and scientific management (Wren and Bedeian 2009).

By the 1960s, leadership studies had developed further into what Fred Fiedler (1967) styled a situational or contingency approach—different management styles (employee or production focused) appeared to work better in different environments. Much psychological research into leadership favoured a developed form of the human relations approach as researchers adopted the humanising rhetoric of Abraham Maslow and his "Eupsychian" or psychologically "healthy" approach to business management (Maslow 1965). Chris Argyris had argued in his *Personality and Organisation* (1957) that Taylorist-style industrial production retarded the psychological development of employees, making them defensive and inward looking; and McGregor had taken Argyris's approach further in his *Human Side of Enterprise* (1960), where he argued that lack of creativity among employees reflected negative attitudes held by management. By the 1960s, the University of Michigan's Rensis Likert (1967) thought he could prove that more humanistic management made employees more productive and firms more profitable—hundreds of quantitative studies that Likert had led seemed to show that greater consideration of the needs of employees tended to correlate with higher profitability and performance. Proponents of leadership studies of the human relations type showed a keen interest in producing morally better, more humane organisations and argued that their approach led to more profitable businesses as well.

In the 1970s, however, a significant change in emphasis in business leadership studies arose under the influence of the presidential biographer James McGregor Burns. Burns (1978) promoted an understanding of political leadership focused on Weber's sociological notion of charisma (Weber 1922). Burns had developed the idea from his political biographies, particularly those he had written of Franklin D. Roosevelt and John F. Kennedy (Burns 1956, 1960, 1970). A member of the Massachusetts delegation to the Democratic National Conventions from 1952 to 1964 and a professor of political science at Williams College in Massachusetts, Burns promoted in his works a social liberal ideal of moral leadership.

The model of charisma employed by Weber had been developed from the religious history of Rudolf Sohm (1888). According to Sohm, charisma was the "gift of grace" that was recognised in leaders of the early

Christian church who led their faith communities without election, hierarchy or coercion. Weber's understanding of charisma was derived in part and is typical of the romantic stream of German history of religions epitomised in Weber's later years in the form of the theorising of holiness by Rudolf Otto (1917). But by the 1950s, charisma was increasingly being promoted in American political science as an explanation not only for the rise of figures such as Hitler, but also of Democratic presidents.

Burns's 1960 biography of Kennedy, written before the presidential election, has an entire chapter on leadership. Where Roosevelt had spoken about "moral leadership", Burns proclaimed that Kennedy would need to show "creative leadership" in order "positively to change the shape of public opinion" (Burns 1960, 276–81). He would also require "charismatic leadership" which Burns described as "the capacity to inspire, to lift the hearts, to exalt, to make people lose themselves in a cause" (Burns 1960, 276–81). Burns cited some of the early psychological writings on leadership in the endnotes of his 1960 work, but the notion of charismatic leadership he accepted mostly reflected 1950s American developments on Weber's formulation.

Burns's second biographical work on Roosevelt, *Roosevelt, the Soldier of Freedom*, won him the 1971 Pulitzer Prize, but it was his 1978 book *Leadership* and his model of what he dubbed "transforming leadership" that would revolutionise business leadership studies in the 1980s. Charisma, now for Burns, had become "so overburdened as to collapse under analysis" (Burns 1978, 241)—Burns had come instead to accept that leadership came in two types: transforming and transactional. Transforming behaviours were those which fostered commitment in followers, giving them something to believe in, making them willing to sacrifice above and beyond the usual in politics. Transactional leaders, on the other hand, only encouraged normal behaviour—getting the job of a politician done effectively, but without necessarily being able to win followers to support their policy agenda. Yet by 1978 Burns had clearly come to be influenced by a psychologised understanding of leadership. "The transforming leader", he wrote in *Leadership*, "seeks to satisfy higher needs . . . the result of transforming leadership is a relationship of mutual stimulation and elevation that converts followers into leaders and may convert leaders into moral agents" (Burns 1978, 4). But apart from learning to invoke Maslow's theory of a hierarchy of needs (Maslow 1943, 1954), Burns seemed to have little interest in psychology or its application to business management.

The key figure in introducing Burns's transforming leadership into business studies was Bernard M. Bass (1985), a professor of management at the State University of New York at Binghamton. Bass had originally noted Burns's work in his continuation of Stogdill's *Handbook of Leadership* (Stogdill and Bass 1981) and in 1982 and 1983 the University of Southern California's Walter Bennis had promoted the need for "transformative leadership" in articles in *Industry Week* and the *Harvard University Newsletter* (Bennis 1982, 1983). Bass admitted quite openly how much he was influenced by Burns and his portraits from "psychohistory", dedicating his 1985 book to the political scientist. Bass seemed quite unaware of how poor a reputation psychohistory had among historians, but like Burns, he was inspired by the example of Kennedy as he became the key proponent of the notion he called transformational leadership in organisational psychology.

The *Annales* school historian Fernand Braudel had downplayed the ability of individual political actors to influence broader historical developments, dismissing the apparently great leaders of the past as "surface disturbances, crests of foam" (Braudel 1949, 21). In management studies, Jeremy Pfeffer (1981) had similarly written of the "symbolic" manager whose individual endeavours made little difference to the performance of a firm. But as the American economy began to show signs of revival after the extended period of low growth since the 1970s, Burns's approach offered the prospect that a new style of management could arise that would throw off the gloom of the "stagflation" years as the new US president Ronald Reagan promised to "make America great again".

According to Bass, "charismatic leadership is central to the transformational process" (Bass 1985, xiv). "Charismatic leaders have insight into the needs, values, and hopes of followers. They have the ability to build on the needs, values, and hopes through dramatic and persuasive words and actions" (Bass 1985, 47–8). But "a subfactor within charismatic leadership behaviour" was inspiration which "employs or adds nonintellectual, emotional qualities to the influence process" (Bass 1985, 63). This led to "intellectual stimulation" through the leader's "problem awareness and problem solving, of thought and imagination, and of beliefs and values" and "followers' conceptualization, comprehension, and discernment of the nature of the problems they face, and their solutions" (Bass 1985, 99). Leaders should also employ "individualized attention and a developmental or mentoring orientation", according to Bass, in order to have a transformational effect on their subordinates (Bass 1985, 83).

Whatever the truth behind these claims, the development of transformational leadership in management studies certainly proved inspirational for Bass's followers. As James G. Hunt (1999) observed in his historical overview of the development of transformational leadership studies:

> a crucial contribution of transformational/charismatic leadership has been in terms of its rejuvenation of the leadership field. . . . This rejuvenation came about because of what most would consider a paradigm shift that has attracted numerous new scholars and moved the field as a whole out of its doldrums.
>
> (Hunt 1999, 129)

Indeed, by the 1980s, something evangelical had seemed to come to grip the part of management studies which concentrated on leadership. Over the course of the decade, an obsession with heroes and charisma appeared to become characteristic of the field. As the American economy surged during the years of the Reagan administration, scholars who were not doing transformational leadership study or were not devouring the associated literature increasingly seemed not to be keeping up with the cutting edge. The key aspect of transformational business leaders was argued to be their moral stimulation of employees, revealed in quantitative survey after survey. Transformational leadership seemed to make firms more profitable, gave staff a reason to turn up to work; it energised those who experienced it to do their best for their employers. Transformational leadership entailed a focus on values, vision, belief and trust—it was adopted with an almost religious fervour by many of its advocates at the time.

Yet the 1980s was not just a particularly inspirational period in leadership studies. A similar development occurred in organisational psychology in the 1980s with the development of theories of organisational culture. The idea first became prominent in 1982 in a popular work on *Corporate Cultures* by Terrence Deal and Allan Kennedy which, like Bass's 1985 book, focused on hopes and values. Deal was an education professor at the time at Vanderbilt University and Kennedy a corporate consultant in Boston, and their book set forth a view of organisations through an anthropological lens, talking about the rituals and heroes of modern business. Organisational culture was developed further in 1985, however, by the Massachusetts Institute of Technology Sloan School of Management professor Edgar Schein. Schein put the notion of organisational culture on a surer social science (and less charismatic) basis, defining it as the "basic assumptions and beliefs that are shared by a member of an organization" (Schein 1985, 6).

In Schein's model, organisational cultures were rooted in the philosophy of a firm's founders. The founders encouraged adoption of the firm-specific culture by selecting employees with similar sets of values and by top management socialising staff into the organisation's culture. Organisational culture was so important to Schein he maintained that "culture and leadership, when one examines them closely, are two sides of the same coin, and neither can really be understood by itself" (Schein 1985, 2). Leadership and organisational history became the key determinants of organisational culture in Schein's model, which he developed in line with Deal and Kennedy's anthropological flourishes but also with older ideas (such as employee socialisation) that had already been present in organisational studies in the 1970s.

In 1989, Charles R. Stoner of Bradley University, Illinois, first applied Schein's model specifically to business ethics. Ethics codes for Stoner were "merely starting points" and could be effective only if they were accompanied by an organisational culture that promoted ethical behaviour. If values could be set by management and inculcated into staff, as Schein advocated in his work, then so could ethical behaviours. Indeed if the values adopted by management were clearly ethical, an ethical organisational culture could be developed by executives both espousing and enacting ethical organisational values.

Nonetheless, by this time the development of a quantitative form of ethics had emerged in social psychology. A form of moral psychology had developed in a manner at first quite removed from business studies. The key figure in the emergence of moral psychology in the United States was Lawrence Kohlberg, who had first developed his theory of cognitive moral development in his 1958 University of Chicago doctoral dissertation. At a time when most American psychologists had adopted behaviourialism, Kohlberg's work was characterised by its concentration on cognitive phenomena.

Kohlberg developed his theory over the course of the 1960s, with it receiving its most developed form in a paper he published in 1976. Like Rawls, Kohlberg's approach was based on the observation of Piaget (1932) that children's moral development could be seen to emerge in stages. In Kohlberg's fuller model, children developed from a natural state of psychological egotism to more mature understandings of morality based on interpersonal expectations and relational conformity, and then ultimately, as they developed into adults, social contract, utility, rights-based and finally Kantian stages of cognitive moral development.

With Kohlberg demonstrating that quantitative techniques could be used to give ethics a psychological basis, a new form of business ethics soon emerged. The most influential figure in this new psychological wave of business ethics has been Linda K. Treviño of the Smeal College of Business at the Pennsylvania State University. In 1990, Treviño published a paper on ethical decision-making in organisations in collaboration with Texas Christian University's Stuart Youngblood that sought to measure whether Kohlberg's theory of cognitive moral development influenced ethical decision-making. This first study assessed decision-making by MBA students, in line with an approach Treviño had first adopted in a paper published in 1986 before she had completed her doctoral studies in management at Texas A&M University. The 1990 paper was an attempt to measure whether the key problems in business ethics stem from "bad apples" or from "bad barrels". With bad apples, unethical behaviour in an organisation could be attributed to a few unsavoury individuals, but with bad barrels, unethical behaviour was more likely to stem from "competition, management's results orientation, the lack of reinforcement of ethical behavior . . . requests from authority figures to behave unethically . . . and peer behavior" (Treviño and Youngblood 1990, 378).

Kohlberg's approach to ethics had been further developed by the University of Minnesota psychologist James Rest, however, in a manner indebted to Kohlberg (Rest 1994). As Rest and his colleagues would later reflect: "Kohlberg's fusion of Piaget and Rawls excited many researchers because of its interdisciplinary approach (taking seriously the questions and contributions of developmental psychology and of normative ethics), and because it addressed issues of the day (e.g. what is social justice?)" (Rest et al. 2000, 381). The experiments undertaken by Rest's Minnesota group suggested that the capacity for moral decision-making in individuals not only developed much as Kohlberg had argued, but that moral decision-making was actuated in terms of four stages: (1) moral sensitivity, or an individual's ability to recognise that a situation contains a moral issue; (2) moral judgement, or formulating and evaluating which possible solutions to the moral issue have moral justification; (3) moral motivation, or the intention to choose the moral decision over another solution representing a different value; and (4) moral courage, or the ability to follow through with the moral decision.

In 1991, Rest's model was adapted by Thomas M. Jones of the Foster School of Business at the University of Washington to become moral awareness, judgement, intent and behaviour (Jones 1991). But Jones developed Rest's moral decision-making model further to include what he called moral intensity. Moral intensity was determined by six issues according to Jones: (1) the magnitude of consequences, (2) temporal immediacy, (3) social consensus, (4) proximity, (5) probability of effect and (6) concentration of effect. Adopting the quantitative methodologies used by Kohlberg, Rest and other moral psychologists, a new, fully psychologised form of business ethics had developed, where specialists in moral psychology could attempt to measure and test all matters of moral decision-making in organisations.

In 1999, in collaboration with Gary R. Weaver of the University of Delaware, Treviño published the results of an attempt to measure the effectiveness of business ethics codes. Two main approaches had developed in American organisations to implementing ethics codes. In 1991, organisational sentencing guidelines had been adopted federally in the United States that allowed for reduced penalties for corporate offenders if an ethics code was in place in the organization. Ethics codes had become so common by the 1990s that very few large corporations were without one, and they were hailed for the formal accountability they sought to provide (Ferrell et al. 1998). In research supported by the Ethics and Responsible Business Practices group at Arthur Andersen, Weaver and Treviño found in their 1999 paper that American businesses seemed to fall into two camps. There were organisations with compliance-based approaches to ethics that saw business ethics mainly as an issue of avoiding legal sanctions. According to this type of approach, employees could be made to behave ethically by management's threat of punishment.

The other approach, Weaver and Treviño (1999) found, was evident in firms that took an employee-focused line based on modelling and rewarding good behaviour. Such a positive approach could even involve employees establishing the set of values that the firm wished to follow. Staff would then be encouraged to "give voice" to the firm's values, presuming those values aligned with those held by staff in the first place (Stevens 2008). Weaver and Treviño advocated for more focus on quantitative assessments of business ethics, pointing to Baumhart's 1961 *Harvard Business Review* survey as a pioneering example of this approach (Treviño and Weaver 2003).

Yet by the late 1980s, organisational culture was increasingly being seen as coercive, as another neo-Durkheimian attempt to wean employees off union representation and to coerce them into following dictates set by management (O'Reilly et al. 1991; Starkey 1998). Corporate ethics initiatives were argued to represent a form of social control that often did not see employees as a means in themselves, but instead as a means to an end (Laufer and Robertson 1997; Reynolds and Bowie 2004). "Shared meanings provide alternatives to control through external procedures and rules", the British organisational theorist Gareth Morgan (1997, 143) admitted.

The focus on employees expressing their values eventually gave rise to a "Giving Voice to Values" method of management education (Gentile 2010). Yet the talk of "values", which had been typical of American management since at least the 1940s, had largely been confused with moral virtues. In the explanation for how business managers gain a reputation for ethical leadership put forward by Treviño, Laura Hartman and Michael Brown in 2000, the characteristics of a moral person (integrity, honesty, trustworthiness) are all virtues (but are not designated as such) or reflect their expression (hold to values, be objective/fair, have concern for society, follow ethical decision rules). Organisational psychologists seemed to have done away with philosophical ethics altogether.

Yet an approach more in keeping with traditional philosophical understandings was being developed at time by the University of Virginia's Jonathan Haidt. Haidt was influenced by Carol Gilligan, a student of Kohlberg who in 1982 had published a key critique of his cognitive moral development framework. Gilligan set forth how sexist moral psychology had generally been since Sigmund Freud (1925) had first postulated that women "show less sense of justice than men" and were otherwise (apparently) prone to allowing emotions to cloud their moral judgement (Freud 1925, 258). Gilligan focused her analyses on the ethical concerns of young women and declared that Kohlberg was wrong: their "failure to develop within the constraints of Kohlberg's system", was a problem with the system itself. Modelling their moral understandings on their mothers and seeing their role primarily in terms of caring for children, women's moral development, according to Gilligan (1982), was best seen principally in terms of an "ethics of care". For Gilligan's women:

> the moral problem arises from conflicting responsibilities rather than from competing rights and requires for its resolution a mode of thinking that is contextual and narrative rather than formal and abstract. This conception of morality as concerned with the activity of care centers moral development around the understanding of responsibility and relationships, just as the conception of morality as fairness ties moral development to the understanding of rights and rules.
>
> (Gilligan 1982, 19)

Haidt (2001) developed Gilligan's insights further, arguing that most moral reasoning is intuitional, not consciously rational, and that the schemes of Enlightenment figures such as Bentham and Kant were not a good guide to understanding moral behaviour.

Basing his work on cross-cultural research, Haidt along with Craig Joseph of the University of Chicago developed a model of moral psychology based on a set of basic moral intuitions (Haidt and Joseph 2004). The first of these was Gilligan's category of care, to which they added fairness (or justice), loyalty (to in-groups), authority (or respect) and sanctity (or purity). Most moral decision-making, according to their moral foundations theory, occurred at the intuitive level and was influenced by what moral philosophers had traditionally considered virtues. Anscombe's 1958 criticism of consequentialism and deontology had led to a resurgence of interest in virtue ethics, and Haidt and his colleagues seemed to have found a justification for focusing on virtues in moral psychology.

Cross-cultural work by the Dutch scholar Fons Trompenaars (1993) had similarly brought focus on the influence of cultural factors in ethical decision-making. Commitment to principles such as honesty seemed to vary across countries where "in-groups" were concerned. Trompenaars had shown that some national cultures seemed to support ethical decision-making that promoted the interests of "in-groups" over "out-groups" in a manner that conflicted with Kohlberg's assumptions that moral development was chiefly a product of intellectual maturity. Cultural influences mattered, and Haidt and Joseph explained such cross-cultural variables in terms of the relative development of their five intuitive moral foundations.

Moral foundations theory was later tested and apparently validated in a large quantitative survey led by the University of Utah's Jesse Graham (Graham et al. 2011). Nonetheless the late-twentieth-century revival in virtue ethics in philosophy had only ever been partial. Most secular virtue ethicists have been neo-Aristotelians, although some concern with Confucian ethics has also been important, particularly with the rise of

East Asian economies. The "Confucian ethics" stressed in most accounts of East Asian business bears little in common with traditional Confucian discourse, however, as "Confucian" has been increasingly conflated with a sense of cultural "Chineseness" (Chan 2008). Yet within business studies the most noted adoption of the Aristotelian tradition has occurred since 2003 among proponents of "Positive Organisational Scholarship", a revival of the human relations concern with establishing humane organisations that has principally been couched in terms of virtue (Cameron et al. 2003). Advocates of the notion have attempted to develop measures of "organizational virtuousness", adopting a notion of collective virtue comparable to that employed in ancient times by Plato in his *Republic* (Bright et al. 2014).

Yet the leading contemporary figure in the study of virtue ethics in business is the American philosopher Joanne Ciulla, formerly of the Jepson School of Leadership Studies at the University of Richmond, but now at Rutgers Business School. A former colleague of Burns, Ciulla has returned the discussion of leadership in her works to a broader philosophical approach of a type that methodologically predates Mumford's first social science study of leadership. Ciulla's work has ranged widely over the philosophical past and has brought out especially the importance (as she sees it) of distinguishing why it is so difficult to be an ethical leader from studying "ethical leadership" as an ideal. Ciulla stresses that leadership is "morality magnified" (Ciulla 2004, 302) and that it is often judged in terms of "moral luck" (Ciulla 2004, 308–9). She advocates more excavation of past discourses on moral leadership, looking back into the long-standing traditions found in all cultures that have described what it is to be a morally good leader.

As Ciulla put it in her 2017 Verizon lecture at the W. Michael Hoffman Center for Business Ethics at Bentley University: "Unlike ordinary people we hold leaders responsible for things that they do not do" (Ciulla 2018, 372). Leaders have greater responsibilities than their followers, but "some leaders are fortunate because of the social-historical context that they are in and the fact that their initiatives turn out well for them. Others are unlucky because a hurricane, accident, or other unforeseeable event ruins their best-laid plans" (Ciulla 2018, 372). Ciulla takes a long historical view on leadership, concluding that "throughout history and across cultures, we find that people want the same moral qualities in their leaders". From ancient Egyptian times up to today, people want leaders who inspire trust and who are not obviously governed by self-interest. Ciulla cites Plato advocating in his *Republic* that "anyone who is really a true ruler doesn't by nature seek his own advantage but that of his subjects" (Plato 1992, 23). Self-mastery, compassion and care are also perennials of traditional leadership lore—what makes a good leader is the perception of virtue among others (Ciulla 2018). In Ciulla's work, philosophical ethics takes a full turn; hers is a historian's ethics that mines traditional sources of wisdom.

Although Barnard had argued that moral leadership was one of the key requirements for successful business management, much of the early development of leadership studies was not overtly concerned with ethical issues other than a broader commitment to promoting more humane forms of leadership. When a sense of moral leadership did make its way decisively into organisational psychology, however, it seemed to be more excitable and manipulative than it was clearly a theory of business ethics. The employment of organisational psychology explicitly in business ethics was more focused on instrumental matters originally, such as how to ensure that as many employees as possible engaged with the ethical systems designed by senior management. Much of this literature encouraged forms of coercion, as if employees lacked moral autonomy, and presumed that the role of managers was to inculcate ethical behaviours into employees with the key aim being to minimise the possibility of a business scandal emerging.

What was still lacking from psychological approaches to ethics was any engagement with the wider issues that had occasioned many of the debates that had arisen since the 1950s regarding the social responsibilities of corporations. Ethics codes still seemed not to work, even if corporate governance reforms appeared to have done a better job at protecting shareholders from losing their capital in financial scandals. Key issues concerning pricing and marketing, discrimination and harassment had been subject to regulatory reform, but widespread public concerns still remained over a new ethical challenge. Beginning in concerns over industrial pollution, the issue of the environmental sustainability of business activity became the key ethical issue for business during the 1990s, a concern that only seemed to heighten with the dawn of the new millennium.

8   Sustainability

With the emergence of moral psychology and a revival of interest in the ancient notion of virtue, business ethics had developed significantly since it had first become of such interest to applied philosophers in the 1970s. But another development reaching back to the time of Nader and his supporters emerged more fully in the 1990s. At first it seemed to return business ethics to the more political form it had often assumed in Western Europe, but it eventually became a cause adopted even by all manner of multinational corporations. The new political concern was environmentalism, and it was articulated initially especially in terms of a distinctively "green" form of left-wing politics.

Yet the contemporary environmental movement has its origins in the United States, and its best-known early expression is Rachel Carson's 1962 book *Silent Spring*. Carson blamed American chemical companies for destroying the natural environment, but it was not until the late 1960s that the conservation cause developed into a left-wing political movement. Environmental scandals led to the development of environmental protection legislation as the emergence of issues such as acid rain saw the founding of Green political parties. But a more elaborate critical response to environmental issues has been the notion of sustainability. This time, however, the main institutional proponent of the notion has been the United Nations.

Sustainability became particularly associated with the United Nations from the 1980s and the three pillars development policy adopted by the UN at the time was bolstered by growing international awareness of climate change. Sustainability soon became a catch-all umbrella under which all sorts of ethical, economic, developmental and even investment issues could be grouped and moralised from a global perspective. With the development of the discourse of sustainability, business ethics had become a truly global notion as ideas such as ethical consumption and corporate environmentalism developed. The environmental challenge has not yet abated, however, as a growing sense of ecological crisis has meant the development of even more pressure on businesses to behave ethically and assume social responsibilities internationally.

The Rise of the Environmental Movement

The environmental movement has its origins in romanticism and the nineteenth-century adoration of nature. As Western cities grew and urban poverty increased, an anti-urban sentiment arose among the middle and upper classes of industrial Europe and North America. Back-to-nature groups developed that championed forests, mountains, rivers and lakes, as hiking, boating and mountain-climbing became favoured pastimes of Westerners of all persuasions. From the German Youth Movement to the British Boy Scouts, the young of the industrial cities were encouraged to return to nature. National parks were created by governments as mountain and beach resorts became popular. Celebrated in the arts and literature, Europeans and Americans were encouraged to reclaim their natural souls through direct encounters with Mother Nature.

Environmentalism was practiced by both sides of politics at first, but mostly initially by conservatives. Socialists were too busy fretting about the fate of the poor in the industrial neighbourhoods of Paris, London and New York. Edgar Heermance, for example, was a leading conservationist in Connecticut where he was recently honoured as the founder of the Connecticut blue-blazed system of hiking trails (Lambert 2018). A section of the Quinnipiac Trail is named after him, near where he once owned a summer house. Heermance was the Connecticut Forest and Park Association secretary from 1936 to 1948, and in 1935 he wrote *The Connecticut Guide*, an early sightseeing book.

By the 1960s, however, conservation had become associated with left-wing politics throughout much of the West. In 1962, the marine biologist Rachel Carson published her most famous book, *Silent Spring*, and helped found a new movement. The image of a springtime in the future where birds no longer sang, wiped out by chemical pollution created by American pesticide manufacturers, caught the public imagination. As Carson wrote:

> Since the mid-1940s over 200 basic chemicals have been created for use in killing insects, weeds, rodents, and other organisms described in the modern vernacular as "pests"; and they are sold under several thousand different brand names. These sprays, dusts, and aerosols are now applied almost universally to farms, gardens, forests, and homes—nonselective chemicals that have the power to kill every insect, the "good" and the "bad", to still the song of birds and the leaping of fish in the streams, to coat the leaves with a deadly film, and to linger on in soil—all this though the intended target may be only a few weeds or insects. Can anyone believe it is possible to lay down such a barrage of poisons on the surface of the earth without making it unfit for all life?

> (Carson 1962, 8)

Carson had already developed a career producing publications for the Fish and Wildlife Service of the US government, publishing the bestselling *The Sea Around Us* in 1951. By the late 1950s, however, she had become increasingly alarmed by the deleterious effect that pesticides were having on the natural environment, and Carson's 1962 book especially focused on the pesticide dichlorodiphenyltrichloroethane (DDT). Since the 1940s, DDT had been widely used to kill lice and other disease-carrying insects as part of attempts to combat typhus and malaria. After a long scientific and policy debate, in 1972 DDT was finally banned in the United States, ten years after the publication of *Silent Spring* (Dunlap 1981; Conis 2010).

Another negative effect of industrialisation that became the subject of public debate was the issue of air pollution. The first movement towards establishing health initiatives to combat smoke caused by the burning of coal had begun in the late nineteenth century, but continued concern had led to the development of smoke abatement movements in St Louis and Pittsburgh in the 1930s and 1940s (Stradling 1999). Smoke had changed from being a sign of progress to representing an urban blight, a symptom of a broader problem with industrialisation. But air pollution would continue to worsen in Western cities after the end of the Second World War. In 1952, London had been enveloped in a great smog that killed 12,000 people and the English Parliament responded by passing the Clean Air Act 1956 (Dawson 2017). In 1955, the US government similarly passed the Air Pollution Control Act to enable the Surgeon General to undertake research into the effect that industrial pollution was having on the public. Most of the air pollution in Western cities in the 1950s was caused by the domestic burning of coal for heating and an increase in automobile emissions.

A new Clean Air Act was passed in the United States in 1963, which, after further amendment, was significantly enhanced in 1970. A new form of urban air pollution, photochemical smog, had been discovered in the 1950s, as chemical reactions produced unnaturally high levels of ozone over American cities. Yet in the late 1960s, the conservation movement of the time of Heermance had developed into an environmental movement characterised by left-wing radicalism. Adam Rome (2003) demonstrates that this process began in the late 1950s when the environment had become connected with the Democratic Party as figures such as the economist J.K. Galbraith had bemoaned the ills associated with the success of consumer society. As Galbraith wrote in 1958 in his *The Affluent Society*:

> The family which takes its mauve and cerise, air-conditioned, power-steered, power-braked automobile out for a tour passes through cities that are badly paved, made hideous by litter, blighted buildings, billboards, and posts for wires that should long since have been put

underground. They pass into a countryside that has been rendered largely invisible by commercial art. . . . They picnic on exquisitely packaged food from a portable icebox by a polluted stream and go on to spend the night at a park which is a menace to public health and morals. Just before dozing off on an air mattress, beneath a nylon tent, amid the stench of decaying refuse, they may reflect vaguely on the curious unevenness of their blessings. Is this, indeed, the American genius?

(Galbraith 1958, 196–97)

The problem of pollution soon entered the rhetoric of Democratic politicians. As John F. Kennedy wrote in *Life* magazine in 1960 during the US presidential campaign:

But the good life falls short as an indicator of national purpose unless it goes hand in hand with the good society. Even in material terms, prosperity is not enough when there is no equal opportunity to share in it; when economic progress means overcrowded cities, abandoned farms, technological unemployment, polluted air and water, and littered parks and countrysides; when those too young to earn are denied their chance to learn; when those no longer earning live out their lives in lonely degradation.

(Kennedy 1960, 75)

With the appearance of Carson's book, the earlier movement for conservation became increasingly associated with American social liberalism. Concern for the environment was a pronounced theme of the speeches of Lyndon B. Johnson, Kennedy's successor as president, on what he called the "Great Society":

A second place where we begin to build the Great Society is in our countryside. We have always prided ourselves on being not only America the strong and America the free, but America the beautiful. Today that beauty is in danger. The water we drink, the food we eat, the very air that we breathe, are threatened with pollution. Our parks are overcrowded, shores overburdened. Green fields and dense forests are disappearing.

(Johnson 1965, I.704–5)

The World Wildlife Fund had been founded in Europe in 1961, and the US Wilderness Act was passed in 1964 as a result of advocacy by the Wilderness Society (founded in 1935 on the initiative of the forester Robert Marshall). Rome (2003) also stresses the importance of women's activist groups such as Citizens for Clean Air and the League of Women Voters. Yet by 1967, the first hippy communes had been established, and in 1969 the outrage over an oil leak at Santa Barbara, California, signalled to many New Left thinkers that the environment was a cause around which they could rally (Rome 2003). In April 1970, the first Earth Day saw an estimated 20 million Americans demonstrate concern for the environment, with over 1,000 colleges hosting Earth Day "teach-ins". In response, in late 1970 the Nixon administration established the federal Environmental Protection Agency as concern for the environment quickly became a key feature of left-wing politics internationally (Rome 2013).

Environmental concerns of another type also influenced public sentiment at the time. In 1949, the United Nations had hosted a Scientific Conference on the Conservation and Utilization of Resources. But it was not until 1972 when the Club of Rome published their *Limits to Growth* (Meadows et al. 1972) that a broader concern became widely apparent about the future of international development. Founded in 1968 at the Accademia dei Lincei in Rome, the Club of Rome was initially led by the former Fiat executive Aurelio Peccei and the British chemist Alexander King. Peccei's group was founded to investigate internationally significant problems such as malnutrition, poverty and pollution, and the *Limits to Growth* report relied on computer modelling by a team led by Dana Meadows at the Massachusetts Institute of Technology funded by the Volkswagen Foundation. *Limits to Growth* made a series of wildly inaccurate predictions regarding overpopulation, oil production and ecological crisis. The report concluded:

> If the present growth trends in world population, industrialization, pollution, food production, and resource depletion continue unchanged, the limits to growth on this planet will be reached sometime within the next one hundred years. The most probable result will be a rather sudden and uncontrollable decline in both population and industrial capacity.
>
> (Meadows et al. 1972, 129)

Dubbed "Models of Doom" by one group of critics (Cole et al. 1973), *Limits to Growth* became the most famous of a series of ecological catastrophe works produced since the 1950s. But its predictions seemed more dire than M. King Hubbert's theory of peak oil production (Hubbert 1956) or Paul Ehrlich's warnings about overpopulation in his bestselling *Population Bomb* (1968).

Despite the many technical failures of the Club of Rome's models of doom, over the 1970s the environmental movement grew, adding nuclear energy to a growing list of concerns. In 1974, Nader had formed a "Citizen's Movement to Stop Nuclear Power" two years after a Bundesverband Bürgerinitiativen Umweltschutz (Federal League of Citizen Initiatives on Environmental Protection) had formed in West Germany. In the early 1970s, scientists had first noticed that European forests were beginning to be affected by acid rain—rain ionised by air pollution was beginning to affect treasured wilderness areas such as the Black Forest in Bavaria (Likens et al. 1972). By 1977, the first Green list politicians had started campaigning in state elections in West Germany, and in 1980 a federal Greens Party had been formed. Similar Greens parties quickly sprang up in other Western countries as the adjective "green" changed its political connotation from "young" or "immature" to "environmental" (Dominick 1988; Frankland and Schoonmaker 1992).

The United Nations had been holding environmental conferences since the 1960s, but the UN Conference on the Human Environment, held in Stockholm in 1972, seemed to crystallise the growing sentiment that the world was facing an ecological crisis. The conference ended with the declaration:

> A point has been reached in history when we must shape our actions throughout the world with a more prudent care for their environmental consequences. Through ignorance or indifference we can do massive and irreversible harm to the earthly environment on which our life and well being depend. Conversely, through fuller knowledge and wiser action, we can achieve for ourselves and our posterity a better life in an environment more in keeping with human needs and hopes. . . . To defend and improve the human environment for present and future generations has become an imperative goal for mankind.
>
> (United Nations 1972, 6)

In the late 1970s, the environmental challenge faced internationally first came to be described in terms of sustainability (Du Pisani 2006). In 1974, George P. Mitchell, the president of Mitchell Energy & Development Corp., decided with his wife Cynthia to offer a prize "to those individuals demonstrating the highest degree of creativity in designing workable strategies to achieve sustainable societies" (Coomer 1979, ix). From 1975 to 1979, three conferences were held at Mitchell's The Woodlands commuter town development near Houston, Texas, with the resultant publications of proceedings stressing "sustainable futures", "sustainable growth" and "the quest for a sustainable society" (Meadows ed. 1977; Coomer ed. 1979; Cleveland ed. 1981). In 1980, in a World Conservation Strategy jointly issued by the International Union for the Conservation of Nature, the United Nations Environment Programme and the World Wildlife Fund, sustainability was articulated in terms of "sustainable development" or "development that is likely to achieve lasting satisfaction of human needs and improvement of the quality of human life" (Allen 1980, 23). In 1983, the UN General Assembly duly voted to establish a World Commission on Environment and Development to further initiatives in the area. Headed by the former Norwegian prime minister Gro Harlem Brundtland, the commission's report *Our Common Future*

(1987) would establish the notion of sustainability internationally. Originating in reactions to the Club of Rome's *Limits to Growth*, the Brundtland commission defined sustainability as "development that meets the needs of the present without compromising the ability of future generations to meet their own needs" (Brundtland 1987, 13). The Brundtland commission would also articulate the United Nations' three pillars development model of economically, socially and environmentally sustainable growth.

In 1992, the Earth Summit, the UN Conference on Environment and Development in Rio de Janeiro, saw the formation of the Business Council for Sustainable Development at the suggestion of Maurice F. Strong, the Canadian secretary general of the Earth Summit. Occurring twenty years after the UN's 1972 Stockholm conference, the Earth Summit was held with the aim of helping national governments rethink economic development and find ways to halt pollution and the destruction of the natural resources of the planet. The council was aimed specifically at helping corporations to take a long-term global view of the role of business in environmental management and development. As the Swiss entrepreneur Stephen Schmidheiny, Strong's chief adviser for business and industry and founder of the Business Council for Sustainable Development, reflected: "Business will play a vital role in the future health of this planet. As business leaders we are committed to sustainable development. This concept recognizes that economic growth and environmental protection are inextricably linked" (Schmidheiny 1992, xi). Not only had businessmen such as Peccei and Mitchell taken the lead in promoting awareness of the global challenges associated with environmental degradation, the Business Council for Sustainable Development thought that corporations should take a leading role in promoting solutions to the growing problem.

Corporate Environmentalism

Yet the adoption of environmental principles by Western businesses was not only a reflection of an ethical change that occurred over the course of the 1980s and 1990s. Reflecting back in 1998, Michael A. Berry and Dennis A. Rondinelli, two colleagues at the University of North Carolina, remarked on the widespread change in business practice that had occurred over the course of the decade. In the 1960s and 1970s, the response of corporations to environmental matters was characterised by Berry and Rondinelli as "coping" and of "attempting to control the resulting damage". By the 1980s, corporations had instead begun to act in a manner that Berry and Rondinelli typified as "reactive" as they struggled with "rapidly changing government environmental regulations" and minimised the "costs of compliance". In the 1990s, though managers were becoming "proactive":

corporations began to anticipate the environmental impacts of their operations, take measures to reduce waste and pollution in advance of regulation, and find positive ways of taking advantage of business opportunities through total quality environmental management.

(Berry and Rondinelli 1998, 39)

Berry and Rondinelli made it sound as if this move to adopt a "proactive" form of corporate environmentalism was voluntary. But in many cases, it rather obviously was not.

A more empirically considered historical analysis was undertaken by Andrew Hoffman in 2001. In his history of corporate environmentalism in the American chemical and petroleum industries, Hoffman broke down the historical development of corporate reactions to environmental challenges in the United States into four stages. The premise of his book was "How did industry move from a posture of vehement resistance to environmentalism to one of proactive environmental management?" (Hoffman 2001, 4) and Hoffman employed institutional theory (DiMaggio and Powell 1983) to help answer his question. Hoffman characterised the 1960s as a period in which the American chemical and petroleum industries were able to resist pressures to improve their environmental management practices, whereas the 1970s was an era of "regulatory environmentalism" in which the Environmental Protection Agency acted as a mediator between environmental critics and industry. A 1974 Conference Board survey found that the majority of American corporations surveyed at the time still saw environmental issues as a "threat" rather than a social responsibility (Lund 1974, cited in Hoffman 2001, 3).

During the 1980s, American corporations gradually began to cooperate more with government in a period Hoffman characterised in terms of a "dynamic isomorphism" of social responsibility as new managerial solutions to environmental problems were developed that spread across industry in the mimicking manner described by DiMaggio and Powell (1983) in their neo-Weberian model of collective institutional rationality. Industry associations and non-profit actors took the position previously held by government in the decade punctuated by the disastrous 1984 gas leak at a Union Carbide plant in Bhopal, India, the 1985 discovery of a hole in the ozone layer (caused by chlorofluorocarbon emissions) and the 1986 nuclear accident at Chernobyl, Ukraine (Farman et al. 1985; Park 1989; Shrivastava 1992). After the gigantic Exxon *Valdez* oil spill in Prince William Sound, Alaska, in 1989, however, a form of "strategic environmentalism" eventually emerged as the chemical and petroleum industries developed proactive responses to environmental protection requirements. Yet with the publication of a key paper by strategic management specialist Michael Porter and his Swiss colleague Claas van der Linde (1995), corporate environmentalism had developed into a new stage Hoffman dubbed "environmental management as an opportunity". In 1991 Porter had asserted:

> Properly constructed regulatory standards, which aim at outcomes and not methods, will encourage companies to re-engineer their technology. The result in many cases is a process that not only pollutes less but lowers costs or improves quality. Processes will be modified to decrease use of scarce or toxic resources and to recycle wasted by-products.
>
> (Porter 1991, 168)

Over the course of the 1990s, many leading American businesses had adopted such an eco-efficiency approach which recognised that corporations that developed a leading market position in pollution reduction, clean energy and recycling could compete more successfully than less responsive rivals.

A key issue lost in this scheme of economically rational responses, however, is the emergence of a broader movement, particularly in the United Kingdom, towards green entrepreneurship and ethical consumption. Harvard business historian Geoffrey Jones (2017) traces the history of green entrepreneurship back to individuals such as the Austrian philosopher and education reformer Rudolph Steiner. In the years before the First World War, Steiner had founded an esoteric spiritual movement called anthroposophy, whose practices influenced childhood education (in the form of Steiner schools) as well as the organic and biodynamic farming movements (particularly in Germany), and green building design. In 1964, the British charity Oxfam established Oxfam Trading as the first formal expression of the burgeoning Fair Trade movement, and the rise of the environmental movement in the 1970s also inspired entrepreneurs such as Anita Ruddock to found for-profit businesses based on ethical consumption—in the case of Ruddock's the Body Shop, founded in 1975, by producing and selling cosmetics not first tested on animals.

In 1988, the first Friends of the Earth UK green consumer week was held in mid-September. John Elkington and Julia Hails took the opportunity to launch their *Green Consumer Guide* (1988), a practical handbook on how consumers could change their lifestyles so that they were more environmentally sustainable. The book was an immediate success, eventually selling almost a million copies in the United Kingdom, with Canadian, Australian and American versions all eventually appearing (McCormick 1991, 107–11). But the success of the *Green Consumer Guide* would soon be outstripped by Elkington's 1997 book *Cannibals with Forks*. In it Elkington proposed a novel business framework that would transform corporate reporting:

> Future market success will often depend on an individual company's (or entire value chain's) ability to simultaneously satisfy not just the

traditional bottom line of profitability but also the two emergent bottom lines: one focusing on environmental quality, the other on social justice. As a result, companies and their boards will need to think in terms of the *triple bottom line*.

(Elkington 1997, xiii, emphasis in original)

Elkington's influence was particularly important to the 1998 establishment of the Shell reports. In April 1995, Greenpeace activists had occupied a 40-storey-tall oil storage platform owned by Royal Dutch/Shell. The Brent Spar platform was due to be sunk in the waters of the North Atlantic, creating what the activists called a "toxic timebomb". In October that year protestors at Shell's annual general meeting had demanded that the Anglo-Dutch giant's executives be held accountable for the despoliation of the homeland of the Ogoni people in southern Nigeria and for the death sentence given tribal leader Ken Saro-Wiwa by the Nigerian government (Mirvis 2000). Shell's response was to publish a 1998 report, *Profit and Principles—Does There Have to be a Choice?* (Royal Dutch/Shell 1998). Issued with "Tell Shell" reply cards, the report included sections on Shell's ethics principles and on "contributing to society" written by Elkington (Royal Dutch/Shell 1998, 5–30, 46–7). The report also provided a candid assessment of Shell's human rights and environmental record and was widely hailed as marking a profound change in the ethical direction taken by Shell management.

The first Shell report was not merely a public relations exercise, but was part of the outcome of a three-year process that began in 1994 when Shell had employed the services of Noel Tichy, a professor of management at the University of Michigan, as a consultant. Tichy assembled a group of "change agent" consultants whose role was to investigate ways to make Shell more profitable. The team discovered a culture at Shell of arrogance and insularity when dealing with customers, shareholders, environmental groups and the general public. What the consultant and member of Tichy's team Phillip Mirvis calls a "remaking" of Shell began in the aftermath of the Brent Spar protest and led to Shell committing itself to a programme of "corporate citizenship" (Mirvis 2000). Shell quickly became a leader in sustainability reporting, adopting Elkington's approach to the "triple bottom line".

The Exxon *Valdez* oil spill in 1989 also led to another voluntary development—the creation of the Valdez Principles, later renamed the CERES Principles for Corporate Environmental Responsibility (Smith 1993). Formally the Coalition for Environmentally Responsible Economies, CERES was founded by a group of investors, environmentalists, religious organisations and public interest groups, led by Joan Bavaria, the founder of the employee-owned investment manager Trillium Asset Management. CERES's 1989 press release announcing the launch of principles quoted Harrison J. Goldin, the Comptroller of New York, saying that the principles represented "a starting point from which corporations can help us develop a workable approach to environmentally responsible corporate policy making" (Smith 1993, 309). The original ten CERES principles were grouped under the following headings:

1. Protection of the Biosphere
2. Sustainable Use of Natural Resources
3. Reduction and Disposal of Wastes
4. Wise Use of Energy
5. Risk Reduction
6. Marketing of Safe Products and Services
7. Damage Compensation
8. Disclosure
9. Environmental Directors and Managers
10. Assessment and Annual Audit

(CERES 1989)

In 1997, CERES went further and convened a Global Reporting Initiative that in 1999 released a draft of its proposal for Sustainability Reporting Guidelines "to assist those enterprises and other organisations that choose to publish reports about their performance and progress toward the environmental, social, and economic aspects of sustainable development" (GRI 1999, 3). With the support of the United Nations Environment Programme, the Sustainability Reporting Guidelines of the Global Reporting Initiative were officially launched in 2000 as the first globally recognised standards for sustainability reporting (Willis 2003).

There remained a considerable amount of popular scepticism regarding the adoption of environmentalism by large corporations, however. In 1985, the American petroleum corporation Chevron had started running its "People Do" advertising campaign in print and on television. The "People Do" advertisements showed pictures of bears, sea turtles and endangered birds while the voiceover or accompanying text read, "Do people sometimes work through the winter so nature can have spring all to herself?" The answer, beneath a Chevron logo, was an affirmative "People do". By the late 1980s, corporations flaunting superficial commitments to the environment were being criticised as engaging in "greenwashing". American environmentalists began counter-campaigns to expose cases of misleading corporate co-option of environmentalism (Greer and Bruno 1996; Bowen, F., 2014). Claims that corporations had "hijacked" environmentalism persisted as green activists called for more profound change. The University of Huddersfield economist Richard Welford despaired that "business practices and current business education are failing us", pointing to a range of what he characterised as "very tangible environmental crises" (Welford 1997, 3–4). "Change will have to be quite radical . . . there really is no alternative" (Welford 1997, 16).

Global Warming

Another environmental factor that was first raised in the 1970s was the issue of the greenhouse effect—the heating of the planet caused by atmospheric gases such as carbon dioxide (Sawyer 1972). The effect had been broadly understood by scientists since the nineteenth century, but in a time of warnings of ecological catastrophe, the greenhouse effect began to be raised by concerned scientists. By the 1980s the United Nations had begun warning about the effect of the continued expansion of carbon dioxide emissions as more and more coal-fired power plants were built and demonstrations by environmental groups had limited the adoption of nuclear energy plants.

A key development from the Earth Summit in 1992 was the United Nations Framework Convention on Climate Change. By 1997 negotiations had led to the signing of the Kyoto Protocol that committed its signatories in the developed world to stabilising and then reducing national levels of carbon emissions. In 2005, the year that the Kyoto Protocol came into force, the European Union adopted an Emissions Trading System run by the European Commission, and other signatory states began to take action to reduce the greenhouse gas emissions in their respective countries.

In 2006 the British government released the Stern Review on the Economics of Climate Change, headed by the economist Nicholas Stern of the Grantham Research Institute on Climate Change and the Environment at the London School of Economics. The review warned that "The scientific evidence is now overwhelming: climate change is a serious global threat, and it demands an urgent global response", and that "the benefits of strong and early action far outweigh the economic costs of not acting" (Stern 2006, vi). Stern further warned:

> Using the results from formal economic models, the Review estimates that if we don't act, the overall costs and risks of climate change will be equivalent to losing at least 5% of global GDP each year, now and forever. In contrast, the costs of action—reducing greenhouse gas emissions to avoid the worst impacts of climate change—can be limited to around 1% of global GDP each year.
>
> (Stern 2006, vi)

The following year the Intergovernmental Panel on Climate Change (IPCC), established in 1988 by the World Meteorological Organization, released its fourth assessment report that advised "warming of the climate system is unequivocal" and that "most of the observed increase in global average temperatures since the mid-20th century is *very likely* due to the observed increase in anthropogenic greenhouse gas concentrations" (IPCC 2007, 2 and 5, italics in original). Moreover, the fourth IPCC report included predictions of increase in frequency of "hot extremes, heat waves and heavy precipitation", "sea level rise, storm surges and river flooding", "progressive acidification of oceans" and "increased risk of extinction" for some species (IPCC 2007, 8, 9, 13 and 52). Together with the Kyoto Protocol and the Stern review, the fourth IPCC report made climate change an increasingly mainstream and alarming concern.

Government policies were quickly adopted to encourage the use of "clean" energy, and as Jones (2017) argues, the solar industry soon became one of the few areas of green entrepreneurship where entrants to the industry were attracted by the prospect of financial returns rather than predominately ethical or political considerations. Public policies adopted by Western governments in response to the Kyoto Protocol such as the solar roof programmes and feed-in-tariffs adopted in Germany, the United States and Japan were instrumental in encouraging production. But as Jones explains, there were downsides to industry dependence on tax breaks and subsidies. When coupled with unpredictable government policy, boom and bust cycles occurred in the solar industries in Europe and America.

As Denis G. Arnold and Keith Bustos noted in 2005, however, despite the growing evidence that the climate was changing under the influence of greenhouse gases, very little focus on the matter had arisen among business ethicists. Yet even those business ethicists who had written on the ethics of sustainability had mostly done so without reference to the decades-old tradition of environmental ethics. Environmental ethics had emerged in the 1970s as papers such as the American historian Lynn White's 1967 ascription of Western "anthrocentricism" to Christianity began to be discussed more formally. By the 1970s the English scientist James Lovelock (1972) had started promoting his "Gaia hypothesis"— that living organisms interact with their inorganic environments in a complex, self-regulating system. And in 1973, the Norwegian philosopher Arne Næss had begun talking about a "deep ecology" focused on respecting nature and the inherent worth of other beings as opposed to a "shallow" ecology which promoted causes such as recycling without looking more deeply into the consumption-oriented values that underpin industrial economies.

When sustainability was raised by business ethicists such as Norman Bowie (1990), it was not discussed in terms of environmental ethics, but rather in anthropocentric terms such as harm to members of society. Arnold and Bustos (2005) similarly conceptualise the ethics of climate change predominately in terms of anthropocentric "citizens", "consumers" and "others" (in the sense of "every person on the Earth"). Environmental ethics has long been used as a conceptual basis by those arguing for animal rights (e.g. Katz 1990). But most business ethicists have typically approached the issues of sustainability and climate change from within pre-established traditions of business ethics, such as considerations of consumer rights, or in reference to the Brundtland Commission or other UN initiatives. It has only been quite recently that scholars such as the Hungarian business ethicist Laszlo Zsolnai (2011) have tried to ground their analyses of sustainability in terms of environmental ethics.

By 2006, growing awareness and state actions concerning climate change had begun to see scholars engaging with the issue of "green-collar jobs" and the ethics of the transition to a "green economy" (Pinderhughes 2006). The closing down of coal-fired power stations and the growing number of positions in sustainability management and clean energy industries developed into labour union calls for "just transitions" for workers losing their jobs as the result of efforts to reduce the dependence of Western economies on carbon-based energy production (Rosemberg 2010).

The focus on just transitions, however, was one of many emerging issues regarding "social sustainability", a description that covers problems such as poverty, income inequality, disease, access to health care, sanitation and education. As Bobby Banerjee stressed in 2011,

> Despite more than 50 years of research on stakeholders and corporate social responsibility, we know very little about the outcomes of CSR for society because the primary focus in the literature is on the financial impact on the company of CSR initiatives.
>
> (Banerjee 2011, 720)

The assumption, Banerjee asserted, is "if environmental and social initiatives do not provide growth opportunities or go beyond the 'limits of private enterprise,' business firms should not pursue it" (Banerjee 2011, 721). Banerjee (2011) cited the example of the Tata Group having developed a comprehensive eco-efficiency programme on the one hand, but having a reputation in India for bullying local communities and denying that the firm has any responsibility for the social upheavals its development policies were causing on the other.

Yet since at least 2013, a new term had joined sustainability in the vocabulary employed by businesses seeking to demonstrate their social responsibilities: the "social licence to operate" (SLO). The term was first used in the late 1990s, but since 2013 it had enjoyed a marked rise in employment, particularly in the resource-rich countries of Canada and Australia. The expression was used especially in the context of mining, oil and gas development and other resource-related projects. As Neil Gunningham and colleagues described the notion in 2004: "The social license [to operate] is based not on legal requirements but, rather, on the degree to which a corporation and its activities meet the expectations of local communities, the wider society, and various constituent groups" (Gunningham et al. 2004, 313). The concept of a social licence to operate originated in the mining industry, where it had been employed since the late 1990s to describe the informal acceptance or approval of a local community of a mining operation or development.

The idea of social licence to operate was first developed in light of the 1996 Placer Dome mining disaster (Gehman et al. 2017). Placer Dome had been widely criticised after a tailings dam burst at one of the mines it had operated since 1969 on Marinduque Island in the Philippines, releasing toxic waste into a local river and burying a village in one of the worst environmental disasters in Philippine history (Boutilier 2014). Mining disasters were being reported widely in the press at the time, and in 1997, James Cooney, the vice-president for External Relations at the Canadian gold mining company, was invited to give an address at a conference hosted by the World Bank in Quito, Ecuador. Cooney characterised the mining industry's problems as a matter of retaining their "social licence to operate" (McMahon 1998; Gehman et al. 2017).

In 2013, Leeora Black, the managing director and founder of the Australian Centre for Corporate Social Responsibility, published a book on the social licence to operate "for managers in any company facing rising social scrutiny due to unwanted social or environmental impacts" (Black 2013, 16). The expression social licence to operate has also begun to appear in UN publications and in Europe as a way of describing the social expectations that any business is expected to meet (United Nations Global Compact 2008, 17; Buhmann 2016). Originally proposed in the light of environmental failings in the mining industry, the term had come to be used to articulate a wider form of corporate social responsibility.

In the twenty-five years since the Brundtland commission had set out the UN claim that sustainable development had three pillars, many changes had occurred in the way businesses operated. A 2013 German study by Sarah Windolph and colleagues, however, showed that environmental matters still often remained the main preserve of business corporate affairs departments, suggesting that being environmentally responsible was still understood to be mainly an issue of public legitimacy for many firms. Yet another 2013 survey of sustainability managers in Australian corporations headed by the University of Sydney's Chris Wright suggested that these "hippies on the third floor" saw themselves as internal corporate environmental activists. Carl Rhodes's (2016) analysis of the 2015 Volkswagen emissions scandal, however, suggested that management at the giant German carmaker had seen sustainability only as an input to their decision-making processes—an instrumental issue rather than an ethical concern—as they developed emissions-testing "defeater" mechanisms to make their cars appear much "greener" than they truly were. Sustainability had been adopted into the language and thinking of large business concerns, but it had not always been understood in an ethical sense, despite the issues of environmental degradation and climate change widely being held as essentially ethical challenges.

9 Responsible Management

The issue of sustainability had seen the United Nations begin to take a key role in business ethics. One of the more recent projects of the United Nations, however, has been its Principles for Responsible Management Education (PRME). The establishment of the PRME reflects a long-held understanding that universities should have a moral duty and not just be content to inculcate technical skills. The Global Financial Crisis has seen widespread criticism of economic and regulatory policies, derided by their opponents as "neo-liberalism", and responsible management education represents an attempt to entrench a moral component into business education. The PRME also appeared at the time of the emergence of a new form of business ethics that developed under the influence of the liberal arts. The field of Critical Management Studies was established by academics with liberal arts backgrounds who found positions in European business schools. Approaches such as those of critical theory have now been brought into business ethics as a more radical form of politicised business scholarship has emerged. Expressions of Marxisant academic critique have now found a position in business ethics in a manner that takes the field even further away from its roots in Christian moral thought and business philanthropy.

The United Nations Global Compact

On the evening of November 9, 1989, the Socialist Unity Party chief in Berlin announced an easing of travel restrictions to the west. East German border police opened the gates at crossing points in the Berlin Wall, allowing large numbers of citizens of the German Democratic Republic to cross through. The opening of the Berlin Wall started a night of unbridled celebrations as people crossed freely back and forth through the gates of the wall, climbed on it, and danced and partied on it. The opening of the Berlin Wall triggered a series of events that led to the unification of Germany on October 3, 1990, with the annexation of East Germany to the Federal Republic. It also presaged the collapse of the Soviet bloc of nations and the end of the Cold War.

In the weeks after the opening of the Berlin Wall, a peaceful transition to democratic government transpired in Czechoslovakia, and more bloody political changes occurred in Romania and Bulgaria, as it became clear the Soviet Union was no longer prepared to prop up communist governments in Eastern Europe. Poland had already held democratic elections by this time, as a growing sense of euphoria gripped European capitals. The period of *die Wende* ("the Change") was followed by the collapse of communism in Russia, as after an abortive military coup, on December 8, 1991, the presidents of the Russian Federation, Ukraine and Belarus announced the dissolution of the Soviet Union.

In Rome, the Vatican had been preparing a new encyclical for the hundredth anniversary of *Rerum novarum*. Pope John Paul II's *Centesimus annus* was filled with hope that the end of communism was near and a new period of social peace would prevail. The Polish Pope's document reaffirmed the Catholic Church's social teaching regarding the "dignity of the worker", the "right to private property" and workers' right to join trade unions, to a living wage, and to "discharge freely one's religious duties" and particularly "Sunday rest" (John Paul II 1991, 6–9). The "new things" (*rerum novarum*) of 1991, however, were the "harshness" and "evil" of state socialism where "the concept of the person as the autonomous subject of moral decision disappears". The "first cause" of this degradation, according to *Centesimus annus*, is atheism which "consequently leads to a reorganization of the social order without reference to the person's dignity and responsibility" (John Paul II 1991, 13).

Centesimus annus set out a series of standards, including

> a continuous effort to improve workers' training and capability so that their work will be more skilled and productive, as well as careful controls and adequate legislative measures to block shameful forms of exploitation, especially to the disadvantage of the most vulnerable workers, of immigrants and of those on the margins of society.
>
> (John Paul II 1991, 15)

Workers' rights to "adequate free-time" were stressed as was "the right to express one's own personality at the work-place without suffering any affront to one's conscience or personal dignity" (John Paul II 1991). Unions "serve the development of an authentic culture of work and help workers to share in a fully human way in the life of their place of employment", but governments must also endeavour to create "favourable conditions for the free exercise of economic activity, which will lead to abundant opportunities for employment and sources of wealth" (John Paul II 1991, 15). *Centesimus annus* also called for development in poorer parts of the world to help "needy people to acquire expertise, to enter the circle of exchange, and to develop their skills in order to make the best use of their capacities and resources" (John Paul II 1991, 34). The encyclical also recognised the right of business to make a profit:

> The Church acknowledges the legitimate *role of profit* as an indication that a business is functioning well . . . [but] it is possible for the financial accounts to be in order, and yet for the people—who make up the firm's most valuable asset—to be humiliated and their dignity offended. . . . Profit is a regulator of the life of a business, but it is not the only one; other human and moral factors must also be considered which, in the long term, are at least equally important for the life of a business.
>
> (John Paul II 1991, 35, emphasis in original)

John Paul II's encyclical, with its acclamation of the defeat of Marxism, looked back at what the Church saw as the errors of Soviet Communism, but looked forward at the same time to "prepare for the moment" of the new millennium, walking with Christ "towards eternal destiny" (John Paul II 1991, 62).

Yet rather than let UNIAPAC remain the focus of the Church's outreach to employers, the Vatican established a new body, the Foundation "Centesimus Annus—Pro Pontifice". Established by Cardinal Castillo Lara and Archbishop Giovanni Lajolo, the foundation's key role was to explain *Centesimus annus*, first to Italian business, and then more generally to European and American Catholics. The foundation's first conference, "Confronting Globalization: Global Governance and the Politics of Development", was held in 2004 and included Catholic thinkers such as Michael Novak, the American author of the best-selling *The Spirit of Democratic Capitalism* (1982).

Instead of by a better-known body such as UNIAPAC, however, in 1994 the first international business standards were produced by the Caux Round Table. The Caux Round Table for Moral Capitalism had been established in 1986 by Frederik Philips, the chairman of the Dutch electronics company Philips, and Olivier Giscard d'Estaing, the founding dean of INSEAD, the Institut européen d'administration des affaires (Young and Straub 2006). Phillips and Giscard d'Estaing chose Mountain House in Caux, Switzerland, as the site for their gatherings because it had been the place where Moral Re-Armament had organised meetings between French and German industrialists after the Second World War. Moral Re-Armament was an organisation established by the American Lutheran Frank Buchman at Oxford University in 1938 that sought to enrol business leaders in an effort to re-introduce Christian principles into political and economic decision-making (Sacks 2009). The original Caux meetings had helped lead to the creation of the European Coal and Steel Community, a body whose supranational principles served as the model for the 1957 foundation of the European Economic Community (Luttwak 1994).

Phillips and Giscard d'Estaing had established the Caux Round Table at a time when accusations had arisen that Japanese firms had been engaged in "dumping" goods on the European market at uncompetitive prices. Their invitation of Japanese industrialists to Caux in turn led Ryuzaburu Kaku, then chairman of Canon, to propose that the Caux Round Table adopt a philosophy of *kyosei* in their efforts to promote a "moral capitalism". The key premise of *kyosei* was that "business and society exist in a mutually supportive, living and organic relationship". In 1992 Kaku had presented Canon's philosophy of *kyosei* to a meeting of business leaders in Minneapolis, where he met Robert MacGregor, who was preparing a set of business principles based on the stakeholder approach of American business ethics and Protestant traditions of community stewardship. Later in 1992, MacGregor travelled to Mountain House with a group of other Minnesotans, and they proposed that the Caux Round Table should draft a set of principles for international business incorporating *kyosei* and key aspects of the Minnesota guidelines. The European participants argued that any proposed set of principles should also draw on the social teachings of the Catholic Church, particularly in light of the appearance of *Centesimus annus*. Two years later, in 1994, the Caux Round Table published its Principles for Business, the first considered attempt at developing a set of international standards of business ethics.

Previous attempts to develop national standards, such as the Davos manifesto, had not had any input from Asia, and unlike the earlier business creed adopted by UNIAPAC in 1968, the Caux Round Table principles were not a statement primarily focused on defending the moral bases for business activity. The Caux Round Table principles were also much wider in scope than previous attempts to provide international standards for business conduct. The Caux principles were arranged in five areas: principles for responsible business (including stakeholder management guidelines), principles for government, principles for good citizenship, principles for the ownership of wealth and principles for non-government organisations. The Caux principles contain elements such as "respect stakeholders beyond shareholders" and "living wages" that obviously reflected American and Catholic concerns, whereas the "living and working together" of *kyosei* was most strongly evidenced in advocations in the principles such as "True justice is the expression of honest citizenship living in community".

The Caux Round Table's principles were presented to UN Secretary General Kofi Annan. The Ghanaian did not respond, however, until 1999 when he issued a call to establish a global compact between the agencies of the United Nations and business leaders at the annual meeting of the World Economic Forum at Davos (as the European Management Forum had been retitled in 1987). A set of nine principles had been drawn up and the Global Compact was launched on July 26, 2000, at UN headquarters in New York. Attempts to formulate a UN code of conduct on transnational corporations in light of Salvador Allende's 1972 speech to the General Assembly had collapsed in 1992. Annan's initiative proved more successful, with its positive reception by advocates such as John Browne, the chairman of the privatised British petroleum company BP.

The first UN Secretary-General with a business management degree, Annan introduced the Global Compact as part of his attempts to modernise the United Nations in light of the end of the Cold War. Annan had spent much of his first term as Secretary-General setting out the need for the United Nations to become involved with facilitating international business and had already built up relationships with international business groups such as the International Chamber of Commerce and the International Organization of Employers (Kell 2005). Accordingly, the UN Global Compact's nine principles were especially focused on globalisation. "Unless globalization works for all", Annan said at Davos in 1999, "it will work for nobody". He emphasised that

> a global compact of shared values and principles [would] give a human face to the global market. The spread of markets outpaces the ability of societies and their political systems to adjust to them, let alone to guide the course they take. History teaches us that such an imbalance between the economic, social and political realms can never be sustained for very long.
>
> (Annan 1999)

Annan argued that the United Nations had a role to play in globalisation because of international agreements such as the Universal Declaration on Human Rights, the International Labour Organization's 1999 Declaration on fundamental principles and rights at work, and the Rio Declaration of the United Nations Conference on Environment and Development from 1992. The Global Compact's nine principles were derived by the United Nations from these three sources and were separated into three areas: human rights, labour and the environment (Kell and Ruggie 1999). A tenth was added in 2004 after the United Nations Convention Against Corruption was agreed by the General Assembly in 2003, bringing the principles to their present form:

Human Rights

Principle 1: Businesses should support and respect the protection of internationally proclaimed human rights; and

Principle 2: make sure that they are not complicit in human rights abuses.

Labour

Principle 3: Businesses should uphold the freedom of association and the effective recognition of the right to collective bargaining;

Principle 4: the elimination of all forms of forced and compulsory labour;

Principle 5: the effective abolition of child labour; and

Principle 6: the elimination of discrimination in respect of employment and occupation.

Environment

Principle 7: Businesses should support a precautionary approach to environmental challenges;

Principle 8: undertake initiatives to promote greater environmental responsibility; and

Principle 9: encourage the development and diffusion of environmentally friendly technologies.

Anti-Corruption

Principle 10: Businesses should work against corruption in all its forms, including extortion and bribery.

(Fussler et al. 2004, 9)

By 2001, however, it was clear that the UN Global Compact would become much more than a set of principles. The original nine principles proposed by the Secretary-General were reviewed and influenced by organisations such as Amnesty International and the World Business Council for Sustainable Development. But given its fractious history a body like the General Assembly did not seem an appropriate one to develop an international corporate code to Annan's team (Ruggie 2002; Kell and Levin 2003). Business participants would not accept a binding code, and at the meetings held after Annan's speech at Davos, it was agreed instead that an approach based around "learning, dialogue and partnerships" would be adopted where business and other concerned groups would come together and discuss how the Global Compact would work (Ruggie 2002; Kell 2005). The German Georg Kell would head the Global Compact's office (under the supervision of a Global Compact Advisory Council) and build links not just with individual businesses (43 had signed up by July 2001), but also bodies such as the World Business Council for Sustainable Development and Business for Social Responsibility (Kell and Levin 2003).

The involvement of the United Nations in a corporate initiative was opposed by many activist groups. In 1999, anti-globalisation protests at the World Trade Organisation Ministerial Conference in Seattle had descended into riots, and works like Canadian journalist Naomi Klein's *No Logo* (1999) brought wider attention to the sweatshop conditions that existed in developing countries where many of the goods produced by big brands were being made. A group of environmental, development and human rights groups protested to Annan (including the Institute for Policy Studies, CorpWatch and Greenpeace) that the United Nations was allowing companies such as Nike, Shell and Rio Tinto "to gain all the benefits of association with the U.N. without any responsibilities" (Bruno and Karliner 2002, 154).

Several years later, in January 2004, Annan wrote to over 50 chief executives of major financial institutions, inviting them to participate in a joint financial sector initiative, "Who Cares Wins" under the auspices of the UN Global Compact, with the support of the International Finance Corporation and the Swiss Government. Subsequently a report was prepared by the Swiss investment banker Ivo Knoepfel (2004). The Knoepfel report argued that improving corporate environmental, social and governance standards (ESG) made good business sense and led to more sustainable investment markets and better outcomes for societies. Shortly after the release of the Knoepfel report, the United Nations Environment Programme's Financial Initiative released a second report prepared by the London-based international law firm Freshfields Bruckhaus Deringer (2005) which argued that active monitoring of ESG issues by pension fund trustees could be allowed under national investment laws, as such issues could be seen as important for the financial valuation of listed business stocks. As the co-chairs of the Asset Management Working Group of the United Nations Environment Programme's Financial Initiative wrote in the foreword to the Freshfields report:

> In our business, the investment business, ethical conduct extends beyond not breaking the law to properly interpreting what is in the best interests of the savers who are the ultimate beneficiaries of the institutional pools of money we are engaged to oversee or manage. This is where the interesting questions concerning fiduciary responsibility come to the fore: are the best interests of savers only to be defined as their financial interest? If so, in respect to which horizon? Are not the social and environmental interests of savers also to be taken into account?
>
> (Freshfields Bruckhaus Deringer 2005, 3)

The answer to these rhetorical questions was argued to be "yes", validating the ESG approach proposed in the Knoepfel report to pensions-fund management. The Knoepfel and Freshfield reports were the justification for the UN Global Compact's 2006 launch of the Principles for Responsible Investment (PRI) at the New York Stock Exchange.

Demands by asset managers for firms to report on and manage ESG risk first became common in Europe and Australia, but they are now a generally accepted part of the investment landscape internationally. In opposition to the American practice of socially responsible investing (SRI), as pioneered in the 1970s by American university schemes and labour union pension funds, ESG investing involves active engagement of investment industry professionals with the boards of listed businesses. SRI is principally a form of screening, of eliminating holdings of stocks by investors worried about the ethics of the business model pursued by a listed firm—for example, a tobacco business or one involved in the arms trade. Under the ESG framework, pension fund trustees engage with the boards of firms whose stock their fund holds and attempt to manage ESG risks, whether they are linked with climate change, human rights issues or traditional corporate governance concerns such as excessive executive remuneration (Louche and Lydenberg 2010).

In 2006, a third initiative of the UN Global Compact was announced at the triannual Global Forum at the Center for Business as an Agent of World Benefit at Case Western Reserve University: the Principles for Responsible Management Education (PRME) (Alcaraz and Thiruvattal 2010). Jose Alcaraz had been working with the UN Global Compact in New York since 2005, and as Alcaraz recalled in 2010: "PRME started in the staircase of Case Western Reserve University in Cleveland, in the Weatherhead School of Management, in a conversation with David Cooperider . . . the director of the Center for Business as an Agent of World Benefit at Case Western" (Alcaraz and Thiruvattal 2010, 544). The European Foundation for Management Development had joined the UN Global Compact in 2003 "to focus on the question of how to develop a next generation of globally responsible leaders" (United Nations Global Compact 2007, 54), and Alcaraz had already begun working in New York on the "synergy between responsible business and responsible business education . . . [and] defining the policy of engagement for business schools". Cooperider's "answer was so enthusiastic that we prepared the first announcement of the launch of PRME in that forum" (Alcaraz and Thiruvattal 2010, 544).

An international taskforce of sixty deans, university presidents and other representatives of leading business schools and universities internationally worked on the project, led by Ángel Cabrera, the president of the Thunderbird School of Management at Arizona State University. In 2007, the PRME task force developed a set of six principles which were published at the 2007 UN Global Compact Leaders Summit in Geneva in the presence of a new UN Secretary-General, the South Korean diplomat Ban Ki-moon. The six Global Compact principles focus on purpose, values, method, research partnership and dialogue:

> Purpose: We will develop the capabilities of students to be future generators of sustainable value for business and society at large and to work for an inclusive and sustainable global economy.

Values: We will incorporate into our academic activities, curricula, and organisational practices the values of global social responsibility as portrayed in international initiatives such as the United Nations Global Compact.

Method: We will create educational frameworks, materials, processes and environments that enable effective learning experiences for responsible leadership.

Research: We will engage in conceptual and empirical research that advances our understanding about the role, dynamics, and impact of corporations in the creation of sustainable social, environmental and economic value.

Partnership: We will interact with managers of business corporations to extend our knowledge of their challenges in meeting social and environmental responsibilities and to explore jointly effective approaches to meeting these challenges.

Dialogue: We will facilitate and support dialog and debate among educators, students, business, government, consumers, media, civil society organisations and other interested groups and stakeholders on critical issues related to global social responsibility and sustainability.
(United Nations Global Compact 2008)

Cardinal Newman (1873, ix) had argued that the purpose of university training was "intellectual, not moral", but Weber had disagreed with him, stressing the "moral authority" of universities (Weber 1908, 55–7). With the launch of the PRME, business ethics educators now had the authority of the United Nations to appeal to and a local PRME chapter to join.

Critical Management Studies

After the 2006 launch of PRME, however, a new sense of urgency seemed to emerge in business ethics and management education. In March 2008, the American investment bank Bear Stearns collapsed after it had incurred substantial losses in its mortgage bonds business. Six months later, Lehman Brothers, a second and larger American financial house, similarly filed for bankruptcy after having suffered a comparable crisis in its mortgage securities trading. Within a few weeks, the US government's mortgage providers Fannie Mae and Freddie Mac were also in distress, and by October the American International Group (AIG) was reported to be on the brink of collapse. AIG was one of the main underwriters of the international banking system—a full-blown financial meltdown had begun that led to the most significant global recession since the 1930s, the Global Financial Crisis.

The Global Financial Crisis had its origin in the development of complex financial instruments by American investment banks and the widespread practice of commission-based selling of financial assets and real estate. Since the 1970s, an ever-increasing number of tradable derivatives had been created in the United States—from call and put options and forward contracts, to swaps, contracts for difference and various kinds of "synthetic" stocks and bonds (Bryan and Rafferty 2006). Initially proposed as ways to "hedge" against risk, much of the trading in financial instruments had become so complex that it had become a significant risk in itself. The size of the market for derivatives had come to overwhelm the underlying value of the assets that they were notionally dependent on. With derivatives mostly unregulated by the American government, the crisis of 2008 led to sweeping criticism of all parts of the international financial system (Stiglitz 2010; Clark 2016). It also led to another round of calls to improve the ethical behaviour of corporate executives.

The Great Recession that followed internationally in the aftermath of the 2008 crisis was a key indication that a significant economic change had been occurring since the 1980s. This change was not globalisation, the buzzword of the late 1990s, but instead what sociologists called financialisation. In financialised economies, a newly dominant way of making money had developed—a "pattern of accumulation in which profit making occurs increasingly through financial channels rather than through trade and commodity production" (Krippner 2005, 14). Apart from the growth of derivatives trading, the most significant driver of financialisation had been a significant increase in the capitalisation of stock markets, particularly due to privatisations, de-mutualisations and the creation since the 1980s of large pools of retirement savings controlled by pension funds.

The debt-fuelled derivatives binge which led to the emergence of the 2008 crisis caused considerable harm to participants in the broader or "real" economy, not just in the United States but across Europe as well. The "irrational exuberance" of financial markets proved unsustainable in the United States, but in the European Union—particularly in the "PIGS" countries (Portugal, Ireland, Greece and Spain)—sharp and deep economic recessions followed. Governments responded with "austerity" budgets, and youth unemployment soared. The main victims of the financial crisis were school leavers, particularly in the less economically developed parts of the European Union.

The main derivatives of concern in the financial crisis were synthetic mortgage bonds—based on home mortgages parcelled up into securities—which had been on-sold by American investment banks to US pension funds, savings banks and even local governments. This new form of "alternative investment" which emerged in the early 2000s was often called a collateralised debt obligation (CDO) and was predominately derived from mortgages sold to families who could not really afford them. Many

American banks had become stuck with hundreds of millions of dollars worth of these mysterious CDOs—or "toxic assets" as they came to be known at the time. With the near collapse of AIG, banks stopped lending to each other, and international financial markets froze.

The collapse of international financial markets led to widespread government intervention as banks in Iceland, Britain, the Netherlands, Portugal and Ireland were nationalised. The crisis did not lead to the rise of a new approach to business ethics, however; instead it saw the continuation of several divergent approaches to business and morality. Rather than looking outwards, several of these focused on what was being taught to students in business schools. A particular criticism arose of the traditional focus of economists on business strategy and efficiency, and increasingly even traditional philosophical forms of business ethics.

In 2006, Michael Porter and Mark Kramer had sought to link CSR with business strategy in a model of what they called "Corporate Shared Value". CSR, they claimed, was usually understood in American business in light of considerations of "moral obligation, sustainability, license to operate, and reputation". Porter and Kramer noted that "the principle of sustainability appeals to enlightened self-interest" and that "a firm that views CSR as a way to placate pressure groups often finds that its approach devolves into . . . a never-ending palliative with minimal value to society" (Porter and Kramer 2006, 81). They instead promoted "strategic CSR" that moves "beyond good corporate citizenship" by unlocking "shared value by investing in social aspects of context that strengthen company competitiveness" (Porter and Kramer 2006, 89). Corporations should do good in order to bolster their bottom lines.

Similarly, Michael Jensen, the key advocate of agency theory, discovered integrity in 2009, but in a manner quite unlikely to impress a moral philosopher. As with Porter and Kramer's self-interested approach to CSR, Jensen did not understand integrity in terms of ethics. "I . . . distinguish integrity from morality and ethics. Integrity is a purely positive proposition. It has nothing to do with good vs. bad" (Jensen 2009, 16). Most commentators on the financial crisis, however, did not resort to such sophistry. Michael A. Santoro and Ronald J. Strauss stressed in their 2013 study *Wall Street Values* that the Global Financial Crisis developed from what was "fundamentally a crisis of business ethics rooted in almost three decades of moral, financial, and institutional transformation on Wall Street" (Santoro and Strauss 2013, vii). According to Rowan University's Edward Schoen, the Global Financial Crisis had been occasioned by an "erosion" of ethics that brought about "devastating effects" on the American economy "including unparalleled unemployment, massive declines in gross domestic product (GDP), and the prolonged mortgage foreclosure crisis" (Schoen 2017, 805–6). Schoen excoriated the "shoddy behavior of mortgage brokers", "the disgraceful work of bond rating firms, the abysmal risk management systems employed by financial institutions" and their "egregious conduct" (Schoen 2017, 806). Business school graduates studying the writings of leading Harvard Business School figures such as Porter and Jensen had been taught that self-interest was king in business and moral responsibility was not something that financial industry participants needed to worry about.

Very few scholars felt able to explain the crisis as reflecting anything other than unconstrained greed. The English professor of leadership Clive Boddy (2011) pointed to the abnormally high number of clinical psychopaths attracted to the finance industry. Marxism seemed to enjoy a brief revival in popularity, and the British historian E.P. Thompson's (1971) notion of a "moral economy" was also resurrected (Bolton et al. 2012). Other British business school professors cast their nets further, Martin Parker advocating in *Shut Down the Business School* (2018) that university business education produced "unreflective managers, primarily interested in their own personal rewards" (Parker 2018) and that business schools needed to be radically transformed. Parker is an advocate of "Critical Management Studies" and a co-author of the 2005 work *For Business Ethics* (Jones et al. 2005) that sought to provide an alternative approach to business ethics.

Critical Management Studies was first promoted by the Swedish business scholar Mats Alvesson and the English management lecturer Hugh Willmott in terms of an application of the critical theory of the Frankfurt School to contemporary management thought (Alvesson and Willmott 1992). Critical Management Studies scholars typically make considerable reference to key Foucauldian themes such as ideology and power, and in the first issue of *Organization: The Critical Journal of Organization, Theory and Society*, its editors proclaimed that the task of the new academic periodical was "to construct new analytical narratives and ethical discourses that speak to the radically changed structural, theoretical and ideological realities that we now face" (Burrell et al. 1994, 6). In his *Against Management*, Parker (2002) noted that the political sympathies of Critical Management Studies are "broad left, pro-feminist, anti-imperialist, environmentally concerned" and that its adherents generally expressed "a certain distrust for conventional positivist formulations of knowledge within the social sciences" (Parker 2002, 117). The 2005 reader of Critical Management Studies published by Oxford University Press makes clear the field's debt to the 1960s New Left by including a chapter from C. Wright Mills's *Power Elite*, but includes nothing by a member of the Frankfurt School (Mills 1956; Grey and Willmott eds. 2005).

The split between philosophical business ethics and critical studies-influenced work is reflected by Routledge publishing both a *Routledge Companion to Business Ethics* (Health et al. eds. 2018) and a *Routledge Companion to Ethics, Politics and Organizations* (Pullen and Rhodes eds. 2015). But according to Thomas Klikauer (2015), Critical Management

Studies is a shallow rather than intellectually deep project. Only marginally engaged with the project of the Frankfurt School, Critical Management Studies critiques "traditional" management approaches only in terms of a "vague sense of doing good" according to Klikauer (2015, 208). Business ethics may be "an apolog[y] for a neo-liberal moralization of the market and a supporter of the moral legitimacy of organizational self-determination" (Rhodes and Wray-Bliss 2013, 41), but *For Business Ethics* especially sets out to challenge business ethicists: "if we look at the philosophy that is done in business ethics, it seems clear that twentieth century philosophy is almost completely excluded" (Jones et al. 2005, 3). According to *For Business Ethics*, the discipline of business ethics has traditionally proceeded "as if twentieth century philosophy has nothing interesting to say about ethics" (Jones et al. 2005, 3). Traditional business ethics also (apparently) not only "forecloses" philosophy, it focuses too strongly on the individual, it narrows the concept of "ethical" and forecloses "politics" (Jones et al. 2005, 3–7).

Like the Frankfurt School and the New Left, Critical Management Studies is Marxisant, not a doctrinally orthodox Marxian project. Its advocates focus on political themes and bring approaches to bear to business ethics that earlier neo-Thomist and secular philosophical contributions do not. With university academics much more politically left-wing on average than Western societies are generally, the Critical Management Studies take on business ethics reflects a wider penetration of concerns more typical of liberal arts scholars than traditional business school approaches to the field. Indeed, given this broader liberal arts influence, it is not surprising to witness the appearance of the South African philosopher Minka Woermann's *On the (Im)Possibility of Business Ethics* (2012) that presents an even more radical approach than *For Business Ethics*. Woermann focuses particularly on the literary theory of Jacques Derrida and his call to analyse literature in terms of "deconstruction". The complexity of business ethics is the main theme of Woermann's book, as postmodernist literary critique is used as another perspective from which to understand business morals.

More recent advocations of feminist theory and even a form of "critical CSR" reflect this Marxisant stream that has become particularly notable in business ethics since the financial crisis (Andromachi and Selsky 2016; Grosser and Moon 2019). But it is unclear whether these approaches have had any effect on the manner in which ethics is understood in the contemporary business world or whether they only represent a retreat to the ivory tower of the Biblical Song of Songs. In 2006, Parker declared that "most of us know that neither business nor ethics are matters that can be tidied up by the application of some humanist common sense, moral philosophy or old time religion" (Clegg and Rhodes eds. 2006, x). But Parker's position might be contrasted with the warning of the British historian Sir Geoffrey R. Elton that postmodernism is "the intellectual equivalent of crack" (Elton 1991, 41). Between the Scylla of American business school "positivism" and the Charybdis of Critical Management Studies, there is a wide field of academic opinion, from unreflective economic liberalism to culturally pessimistic Marxisant critique. The latest project to introduce politicised moralising into business ethics may represent its most recent transformation, but it may equally not truly represent the future of the field.

Business ethics has been transformed by the establishment of the UN Global Compact and the adoption of international standards for multinational corporations. The Pontifical Council for Justice and Peace launched the book *Vocation of the Business Leader* at the 24th UNIAPAC World Congress in 2012, three years before Pope Francis issued the environmental encyclical *Laudatio si'* "On Care for our Common Home" (Pontifical Council for Justice and Peace 2012; Francis 2015). But the Global Compact has assumed a role similar to that which the Catholic Church has had in much of Europe since the proclamation of *Rerum novarum* in 1891. Yet unlike Leo XIII's key encyclical, the United Nations initiatives launched by Annan are founded in international treaties and hence have a universal authority that previous expressions of business ethics have not. Like the Japanese contribution to the Caux Round Table principles, they clearly reflect a global response to the ethics of international business practice and have helped further the rise of business ethics as a reflection of globalisation. The move to develop international standards of responsible management education also seemed particularly timely in the light of the Global Financial Crisis and the widespread recession that followed it in most of the Western world.

Rather than reflecting the unity represented by the Global Compact and the PRME, however, business ethics has become more fragmented since the collapse of Lehman Brothers. A politically Marxisant project unlikely to win much support in the wider business world has developed, especially in the United Kingdom, that marries a somewhat bastardised understanding of critical theory to the secular philosophical tradition of the 1970s. Mixed in with genuflections to postmodernism, environmentalism and feminism, the critical form of business ethics that has arisen in academic circles in recent years seems a long way away from the deliberations of earlier bodies such as the Business Ethics Advisory Council of the Kennedy administration. Whether it will have any more influence outside its left-wing audience than did the writings of Mills and Marcuse is difficult to predict, and whether it represents responsible management education or not might appear to reflect a matter of political taste. Much more engaged with received traditions of social critique, however, it surely represents a particularly interesting development in business ethics from the perspective of the history of ideas.

10 Conclusion

In a booklet launched to celebrate its thirtieth anniversary, Philippa Foster Back, the director of the Institute of Business Ethics in London, noted that "the challenges facing the Institute of Business Ethics are perhaps greater than ever. The financial crisis, corporate scandals and levels of public distrust have lowered the standing of business" (Montagnon 2016, 4). The Institute of Business Ethics' thirty-year report card does not look to have been much better than that of other business ethics institutions and centres, from the W. Michael Hoffman Centre for Business Ethics at Bentley University to UNIAPAC. Simon Webley noted in 1973 that the typical reaction of the person on the street to a mention of business ethics was "Are there any?" (Webley 1973, 3). It is not clear that anything had changed in that regard over forty years later.

Starting with an understanding that businesses could be run ethically or otherwise, a discourse that encouraged moral conduct in commercial matters appeared towards the end of the nineteenth century. In the United States it was largely understood in terms of what Abend calls the "Christian merchant", with a focus on stewardship, honesty and good service being its most prominent features. In Catholic countries a similar development occurred, although it was more explicitly focused on employer paternalism and maintaining the social order, and in this way it presaged a later Protestant reaction to the "social crisis" brought about by industrialisation. The two kinds of social thought—Catholic and Protestant—often seemed to take the side of the worker more often than they did the manager or owner. But together with other received notions of proper business conduct, they formed the foundation from which the modern discourse of business ethics originally arose, not just in North America but in Europe as well.

From the 1950s, peculiarly American expressions of business ethics came to develop—of corporate social responsibility, applied philosophy and stakeholder theory. As Frederick (2006) argues, these traditions largely emerged separately from one another, with university scholars who embraced one tradition rarely contributing to another. By the 1980s, however, these three more established kinds of business ethics were joined by a focus on moral psychology at the same time as the notion of sustainability was adopted by the United Nations. The UN role in business ethics was formalised in 2000 by the creation of the Global Compact and the Principles for Responsible Management Education that followed in 2006. A more critical tradition of business ethics has also developed in recent years in light of the rise of Critical Management Studies.

The key intellectual transformation to occur in the history of business ethics was its secularisation. The Vatican has not stopped its promotion of business ethics, and Protestant organisations have not abandoned the cause either. But with the adoption of business ethics first by applied philosophers and now by members of the Marxisant tradition, business ethics has clearly become less religious institutionally than it was over a century ago. This movement was predicted and encouraged by clerics in the United States, however, as a necessary corollary to the growing complexity of business, although it is the religious origins of the field that have long made it seem so politically centrist and social liberal, rather than conservative or radical.

Business ethics, however, remains an eclectic field, borrowing from philosophy, psychology and politics. It has also grown broadly in more recent years to outstrip its origins in the Western world as it is being infused with practices from other world traditions, from Confucian benevolence to Islamic finance. But business ethics now represents a recognisable discipline, with its own conferences, theories, jargon, pioneers, journals and reference works. Widely taught right around the world, it is a growing, widening and blooming endeavour, despite the ongoing propensity for the business community internationally to find itself a continuing cause for regulatory reform and to find itself the site of ever more ethical scandals.

References

Abend, Gabriel. 2013. "The Origins of Business Ethics in American Universities, 1902–1936." *Business Ethics Quarterly* 23 (2): 171–205.

Abend, Gabriel. 2014. *The Moral Background: An Inquiry Into the History of Business Ethics*. Princeton: Princeton University Press.

Abrams, Frank W. 1951. "Management's Responsibilities in a Complex World." *Harvard Business Review* 29 (3): 54–64.

Ackoff, Russell A. 1974. *Redesigning the Future: A Systems Approach to Societal Problems*. New York: Wiley.

Acquier, Aurélien, Jean-Paschal Gond, and Jean Pasquero. 2011. "Rediscovering Howard R. Bowen's Legacy: The Unachieved Agenda and Continuing Relevance of *Social Responsibilities of the Businessman.*" *Business & Society* 50 (4): 607–46.

Adams, Kenneth. 1971. *Exploring the Business Ethic*. St George's House: Windsor Castle.

Adams, Kenneth. 1973. "The Impact of Business on Changing Social Values." *Journal of Business Policy* 3 (4): 50–5.

Adams, Kenneth. 1975. *Ethical Choice and Business Responsibilities*. London: Church Information Office of the General Synod of the Church of England.

Adams, Kenneth. 1979. *Attitudes to Industry in Britain*. St George's House: Windsor Castle.

Adams, Kenneth. 1986. "The 'Encouragement of Manufactures and Commerce' in Britain Today in the Context of Industry Year, 1986." *Journal of the Royal Society of Arts* 134 (5355): 164–81.

Alcaraz, Jose M. and Eappen Thiruvattal. 2010. "*An Interview With Manuel Escudero*: The United Nations' Principles for Responsible Management Education: A Global Call for Sustainability." *Academy of Management Learning & Education* 9 (3): 542–50.

Alderson, Wroe. 1964. "Ethics, Ideologies and Sanctions." In *Report of the Committee on Ethical Standards and Professional Practices*, 1–20. Chicago: American Marketing Association.

Allen, Fred T. 1975. "Corporate Morality: Is the Price Too High?" *The Wall Street Journal*, October 17, pp. 16 & 21.

Allen, Robert P. 1980. *How to Save the World: Strategy for World Conservation*. London: Kogan Page.

Allende, Salvador. 1972. *Chile: Speech Delivered by Dr. Salvador Allende, President of the Republic of Chile Before the General Assembly of the United Nations, December 4, 1972*. Washington, DC: Embassy of Chile.

Alvesson, Mats, and Willmott Hugh. 1992. "On the Idea of Emancipation in Management and Organizational Studies." *Academy of Management Review* 17 (3): 432–64.

American Bar Association. 1978. *Corporate Director's Guidebook*. Chicago: American Bar Association.

American Law Institute. 1982. *Principles of Corporate Governance and Structure: Restatement and Recommendations; Tentative Draft No. 1*. Philadelphia: American Law Institute.

American Law Institute. 1994. *Principles of Corporate Governance: Analysis and Recommendations*. St Paul, MN: American Law Institute.

Anderson, Katherine S. 1987. "Employer Liability Under Title VII for Sexual Harassment After Meritor Savings Bank v. Vinson." *Columbia Law Review* 87 (6): 1258–79.

Andromachi, Athanasopoulou, and John W. Selsky. 2016. "The Social Context in CSR Research: A Contextualist Approach with Critical Applications." In *Research Handbook on Corporate Social Responsibility in Context*, edited by Anders Örtenblad, 46–65. Cheltenham: Elgar.

Aṅguttara, Nikāya. 1932–36. translated by Frank L. Woodward and Edward M. Hare as *The Book of the Gradual Sayings (Aṅguttara Nikāya) or More Numbered Suttas*. 5 vols. London: Oxford University Press.

Annan, Kofi. 1999. "Secretary-General Proposes Global Compact on Human Rights, Labour, Environment, in Address to World Economic Forum in Davos." United Nations Press Release SG/SM/6881.

Annas, Julia. 1993. *The Morality of Happiness*. New York: Oxford University Press.

Anscombe, G. Elisabeth M. 1958. "Modern Moral Philosophy." *Philosophy* 33 (124): 1–19.

Anscombe, G. Elizabeth M. 1967. "Who Is Wronged? Philippa Foot on Double Effect: One Point." *Oxford Review* 5: 16–17.

Ansoff, Igor. 1965. *Corporate Strategy: An Analytic Approach to Business Policy for Growth and Expansion*. New York: McGraw-Hill.

Anton, Hans H. 1968. *Fürstenspiegel und Herrscherethos in der Karolingerzeit* (Bonner Historische Forschungen 32). Bonn: Röhrscheid.

Aquinas, Thomas. 1952. *The Summa Theologica*, edited by Daniel J. O'Sullivan. Chicago: Encyclopedia Britannica.

Argyris, Chris. 1957. *Personality and Organization: The Conflict Between System and the Individual*. New York: Harper.

Aristotle. 2011. *Nicomacheam Ethics*, translated by Robert C. Bartlett and Susan D. Collins. Chicago: Chicago University Press.

Arnold, Denis G., and Keith Bustos. 2005. "Business, Ethics, and Global Climate Change." *Business & Professional Ethics Journal* 24 (1/2): 103–30.

Arnou, André. 1925. *La morale des affaires: contre le bénéfice exagéré*. Paris: Editions Spes.

Aßländer, Michael S. 2011. *Handbuch Wirtschaftsethik*. Stuttgart: Metzler.

Azpiazu, Joaquín. 1944. *La moral del hombre de negocios*. Madrid: Razón y Fe.

Bacon, Jeremy. 1967. *Corporate Directorship Practices: A Research Report* (Studies in Business Policy 125). New York: National Industrial Conference Board.

Bacon, Jeremy, and James K. Brown. 1977. *The Board of Directors: Perspectives and Practices in Nine Countries* (Conference Board Report 728). New York: Conference Board.

Bacon, Leonard. 1832. *The Christian Doctrine of Stewardship in Respect to Property*. New Haven: Nathan Whiting.

Bakan, Joel. 2003. *The Corporation: The Pathological Pursuit of Profit and Power*. New York: Free Press.

Baker, Robert B. 1999. "The American Medical Ethics Revolution." In *The American Medical Ethics Revolution*, edited by Robert B. Baker, Arthur L. Caplan, Linda L. Emanuel, and Stephen R. Latham, 17–51. Baltimore, MD: Johns Hopkins University Press.

Banerjee, Bobby S. 2011. "Embedding Sustainability Across the Organization: A Critical Perspective." *Academy of Management Learning & Education* 10 (4): 719–31.

Barnard, Chester I. 1938. *The Functions of the Executive*. Cambridge, MA: Harvard University Press.

Barry, Vincent. 1979. *Moral Issues in Business*. Belmont, CA: Wadsworth.

Bartels, Robert. 1962. *The Development of Marketing Thought*. Homewood, IL: Irwin.

Bartels, Robert, ed. 1963. *Ethics in Business*. Columbus: Bureau of Business Research, College of Commerce and Administration, Ohio State University.

Bartels, Robert. 1967. "A Model for Ethics in Marketing." *Journal of Marketing* 31 (1): 20–6.

Bass, Bernard M. 1985. *Leadership and Performance Beyond Expectations*. New York: Free Press.

Bauer, Raymond A., and Dan H. Fenn, Jr. 1972. *The Corporate Social Audit*. New York: The Russell Sage Foundation.

Baumhart, Raymond. 1961. "How Ethical Are Businessmen." *Harvard Business Review* 39 (4): 6–8, 10, 12, 16, 19, 156, 158, 160, 163–4, 166, 168, 170–2, 174–6.

Baumhart, Raymond. 1968. *An Honest Profit: What Businessmen Say About Ethics in Business*. New York: Holt, Rinehart and Winston (Also published in paperback under the title *Ethics in Business*).

Baumhart, Raymond. 1969. "Teaching and Researching Business Ethics." *Review of Social Economy* 27 (1): 65–73.

Baxter, Richard. 1682. *How to Do Good to Many: Or, the Publick Good Is the Christian's Life*. London: Robert Gibs.

Beauchamp, Thomas L., and Norman E. Bowie, eds. 1979. *Ethical Theory and Business*. Englewood Cliffs, NJ: Prentice Hall.

Beesley, Michael E. 1974. "The Context of Social Responsibility in Business." In *Productivity and Amenity: Achieving a Social Balance*, edited by Michael E. Beesley. London: Croom Hehn.

Beesley, Michael, and Tom Evans. 1978. *Corporate Social Responsibility: A Reassessment*. London: Croome Helm.

Behr, Thomas C. 2019. *Social Justice and Subsidiarity: Luigi Taparelli and the Origins of Modern Catholic Social Thought*. Washington, DC: The Catholic University of America Press.

Bell, Daniel. 1960. *The End of Ideology: On the Exhaustion of Political Ideas in the Fifties*. Glencoe, IL: The Free Press.

Bell, Daniel. 1973. *The Coming of Post-Industrial Society: A Venture in Social Forecasting*. New York: Basic Books.

Bennis, Walter. 1982. "Leadership Transforms Vision Into Action." *Industry Week*, May 31, pp. 54–6.

Bennis, Walter. 1983. "Transformative Leadership." *Harvard University Newsletter*, April 7.

Bentham, Jeremy. 1776. *A Fragment on Government*. London: T. Payne.

Bentham, Jeremy. 1789. *Introduction to the Principles of Morals and Legislation*. London: T. Payne.

Bentham, Jeremy. 1834. *Deontology; or, The Science of Morality*, edited by John Bowring. London: Longman, Rees, Orme, Browne, Green, and Longman.

Berger, Peter L., ed. 1999. *The Desecularization of the World: Resurgent Religion and World Politics*. Washington, DC: Ethics and Public Policy Center.

Berle, Adolf A., Jr. 1931. "Corporate Powers as Powers in Trust." *Harvard Law Review* 44: 1049–74.

Berle, Adolf A., Jr. 1932. "For Whom Are Corporate Managers Trustees: A Note." *Harvard Law Review* 45: 1365–72.

Berle, Adolf A., Jr. 1954. *The 20th Century Capitalist Revolution*. New York: Harcourt, Brace.

Berle, Adolf A., Jr., and Gardiner C. Means. 1932. *The Modern Corporation and Private Property*. New York: Palgrave MacMillan.

Berry, Michael A., and Dennis A. Rondinelli. 1998. "Proactive Corporate Environmental Management: A New Industrial Revolution." *Academy of Management Executive* 12 (2): 38–50.

Bicchierai, Giuseppe. 1935. *Il mondo degli affari e la morale*. Brescia: Morcelliana.

Bixler, Albert G. 1985. "Industrial Democracy and the Managerial Employee Exception to the National Labor Relations Act." *University of Pennsylvania Law Review* 133: 441–68.

Black, Leeora. 2013. *The Social Licence to Operate: Your Management Framework for Complex Times*. Oxford: Do Sustainability.

Blumberg, Paul. 1968. *Industrial Democracy: The Sociology of Participation*. London: Constenoble.

Boddy, Clive R. 2011. "The Corporate Psychopaths Theory of the Global Financial Crisis." *Journal of Business Ethics* 102: 255–9.

Böhm, Hans. 1977. "Unternehmensführung und gesellschaftliche Verantwortung." In *Personalmanagement, Band 1: Mitarbeiterführung und Führungsorganisation*, edited by Klaus Macharzina and Walter A. Oechsler, 261–89. Wiesbaden: Gabler.

Böhm, Hans. 1979. *Gesellschaftlich verantwortliche Unternehmensführung*. Weilheim/Teck: Bräuer.

Bok, MacKenzie P. 2017. "To the Mountaintop Again: The Early Rawls and Post-Protestant Ethics in Postwar America." *Modern Intellectual History* 14 (1): 153–85.

Bolton, Sharon C., Maeve Houlihan, and Knut Laaser. 2012. "Contingent Work and Its Contradictions: Towards a Moral Economy Framework." *Journal of Business Ethics* 111 (1): 121–32.

Boring, Edwin G. 1929. *History of Experimental Psychology*. New York: Century.

Bossard, James H., and J. Frederick Dewhurst. 1931. *University Education for Business*. Philadelphia: University of Pennsylvania Press.

Boutilier, Robert G. 2014. "Frequently Asked Questions About the Social Licence to Operate." *Impact Assessment and Project Appraisal* 32: 263–72.

Bowen, Frances. 2014. *After Greenwashing*. Cambridge: Cambridge University Press.

Bowen, Howard R. 1948. *Toward Social Economy*. New York: Rinehart & Co.

Bowen, Howard R. 1953. *Social Responsibilities of the Businessman*. New York: Harper & Bros.

Bowen, Howard R. 1978. "Social Responsibility of the Businessman—Twenty Years Later." In *Rationality, Legitimacy, Responsibility: Search for New Directions in Business and Society*, edited by Edwin Epstein and Dow Votaw, 116–30. Santa Monica, CA: Goodyear.

Bowie, Norman E. 1971. "Aspects of Kant's Philosophy of Law." *The Philosophical Forum* 2: 469–78.

Bowie, Norman E. 1974. "Some Comments on Rawls' Theory of Justice." *Social Theory and Practice* 3 (1): 65–74.

Bowie, Norman E. 1978a. "A Taxonomy for Discussing the Conflicting Responsibilities of a Multinational Corporation." In *Responsibilities of Multinational Corporations to Society*, 21–43. Washington, DC: Council for Better Business Bureaus.

Bowie, Norman E. 1978b. "Why Should a Corporation Be Moral?" *Human Values and Economic Activity: Proceedings of 12th Conference on Value Inquiry*, edited by James B. Wilbur, pp. 329–45. Geneseo, NY: SUNY College.

Bowie, Norman E. 1979. "Business Codes of Ethics: Window Dressing or Legitimate Alternative to Government Regulation?" In *Ethical Theory and Business*, edited by Thomas L. Beauchamp and Norman E. Bowie, 234–9. Englewood Cliffs, NJ: Prentice Hall.

Bowie, Norman E. 1982. *Business Ethics*. Englewood Cliffs, NJ: Prentice-Hall.

Bowie, Norman E. 1990. "Money, Morality and Motor Cars." In *Business, Ethics, and the Global Environment: The Public Policy Debate*, edited by W. Michael Hoffman, Robert Frederick, and Edward S. Perry, 89–97. New York: Quorum.

Bowie, Norman E. 1999. *Business Ethics: A Kantian Perspective*. Malden, MA: Blackwell.

Bradley, Ian C. 2007. *Enlightened Entrepreneurs: Business Ethics in Victorian Britain*. Oxford: Lion.

Braudel, Fernand. 1949. *The Mediterranean and the Mediterranean World in the Age of Philip II, Volume 1*, translated by Siân Reynolds. Berkeley: University of California Press.

Bright, David S., Bradley A. Winn, and Jason Kanov. 2014. "Reconsidering Virtue: Differences of Perspective in Virtue Ethics and the Positive Social Sciences." *Journal of Business Ethics* 119 (4): 445–60.

British Institute of Management. 1975. *Business Ethics and Responsibilities*. London: British Institute of Management.

Brodie, Bernard M. 1962. "Henri Fayol: Administration Industrielle et Générale— a re-interpretation." *Public Administration* 40 (3): 311–17.

Brown, Karin. 2008. "Buddhist Ethics." In *Encyclopedia of Business Ethics and Society*, edited by Robert W. Kolb, 202–6. Los Angeles: Sage.

Bruce, Kyle, and Chris Nyland. 2011. "Elton Mayo and the Deification of Human Relations." *Organization Studies* 32 (3): 383–405.

Brundtland, Gro Harlem. 1987. *Our Common Future*. Oxford: Oxford University Press.

Bruno, Kenny, and Joshua Karliner. 2002. *earthsummit.biz: The Corporate Takeover of Sustainable Development*. Oakland, CA: Food First Books.

Bryan, Dick, and Michael Rafferty. 2006. *Capitalism With Derivatives: A Political Economy of Financial Derivatives, Capital and Class*. New York: Palgrave MacMillan.

Buchanan, James M., and Gordon Tullock. 1962. *The Calculus of Consent: Logical Foundations of Constitutional Democracy*. Ann Arbor: University of Michigan Press.

Budd, John W. 2004. *Employment With a Human Face: Balancing Efficiency, Equity and Voice*. Ithaca: Cornell University Press.

Buhmann, Karin. 2016. "Public Regulators and CSR: The 'Social Licence to Operate' in Recent United Nations Instruments on Business and Human Rights and the Juridification of CSR." *Journal of Business Ethics* 136 (4): 699–714.

Bullock, Alan. 1977. *Report of the Committee of Inquiry on Industrial Democracy*. London: HMSO.

Burke, T. Patrick. 2011. *The Concept of Justice: Is Social Justice Just?* London: Continuum.

Burns, James MacGregor. 1956. *Roosevelt: The Lion and the Fox*. New York: Harcourt Brace.

Burns, James MacGregor. 1960. *John Kennedy: A Political Biography*. New York: Avon.

Burns, James MacGregor. 1970. *Roosevelt, the Soldier of Freedom*. New York: Harcourt Brace Jovanovich.

Burns, James MacGregor. 1978. *Leadership*. New York: Harper and Row.

Burrell, Gibson, Mike Reed, Marta Calás, Linda Smircich, and Mats Alvesson. 1994. "Why Organization? Why Now?" *Organization* 1 (1): 5–17.

Business Roundtable. 1975. *A Survey of Business Roundtable Members on Business Conduct Guidelines*. New York: Business Roundtable.

Business Roundtable. 1983. *Statement of the Business Roundtable on the American Law Institute's Proposed "Principles of Corporate Governance and Structure: Restatement and Recommendations"*. New York: Business Roundtable.

Business Roundtable. 1990. *Corporate Governance and American Competitiveness*. New York: Business Roundtable.

Business Roundtable. 1997. *Statement on Corporate Governance*. Washington, DC: Business Roundtable.

Butler, Josephine E., ed. 1869. *Women's Work and Women's Culture: A Series of Essays*. London: Palgrave MacMillan.

Byrne, John A. 1993. *The Whiz Kids: The Founding Fathers of American Business—and the Legacy they Left Us*. New York: Currency Doubleday.

CABE/UNIAPAC. 1971 [1968]. "Participation in the Enterprise." *International Studies of Management & Organization* 1 (2): 164–80.

Cadbury, Adrian. 1992. *Report of the Committee on the Financial Aspects of Corporate Governance*. 2 vols. London: Gee.

Cadbury, Adrian. 2002. *Corporate Governance and Chairmanship: A Personal View*. Oxford: Oxford University Press.

Cahn, Ernst. 1924. *Christentum und Wirtschaftethik*. Gotha: Perthes.

Cameron, Kim S., Jane E. Dutton, and Robert E. Quinn, eds. 2003. *Positive Organizational Scholarship*. San Francisco: Berrett-Koehler.

Campbell, Thomas C., Jr. 1957. "Capitalism and Christianity." *Harvard Business Review* 35 (4): 39–48.

Carmichael, Sheena, and John Drummond. 1989. *Good Business: A Guide to Corporate Responsibility and Business Ethics*. London: Business Books.

Carnegie, Andrew. 1886. *Triumphant Democracy; or, Fifty Years' March of the Republic*. New York: Scribner.

Carnegie, Andrew. 1901 [1889]. "The Gospel of Wealth." In *The Gospel of Wealth and Other Timely Essays*. New York: Century.

Carroll, Archie B. 1979. "A Three-Dimensional Conceptual Model of Corporate Social Performance." *Academy of Management Review* 4 (4): 497–505.

Carroll, Archie B., Kenneth J. Lipartio, James E. Post, and Patricia H. Werhane. 2012. *Corporate Responsibility: The American Experience*. Cambridge: Cambridge University Press.

Carson, Rachel. 1951. *The Sea Around Us*. New York: Oxford University Press.

Carson, Rachel. 1962. *Silent Spring*. New York: Houghton Mifflin.

Carter, April. 1989. "Industrial Democracy and the Capitalist State." In *Democracy and the Capitalist State*, edited by Graeme Duncan, 277–94. Cambridge: Cambridge University Press.

CERES. 1989. *Valdez Principles*. Boston: CERES.

Chan, Gary K.Y. 2008. "The Relevance and Value of Confucianism in Contemporary Business Ethics." *Journal of Business Ethics* 77 (3): 347–60.

Chandler, Alfred. 1962. *Strategy and Structure: Chapters in the History of the Industrial Enterprise*. Cambridge, MA: MIT Press.

Charkham, Jonathan P. 1983. "A New Way to Build Better Boards." *Financial Times*, September 30, p. 10.

Charkham, Jonathan P. 1984. "Non-Executive Directors." *Financial Times*, August 9, p. 15.

Chernow, Ron. 1998. *Titan: The Life of John D. Rockefeller, Sr*. New York: Random House.

Child, John. 1964. "Quaker Employers and Industrial Relations." *Sociological Review* 12 (2): 293–315.

Christian Association of Business Executives (CABE). 1974. *A Code of Business Ethics*. London: Christian Association of Business Executives.

Ciulla, Joanne B. 2004. "Ethics and Leadership Effectiveness." In *The Nature of Leadership*, edited by John Antonakis, Anna T. Cianciolo, and Robert J. Sternberg, 302–27. Thousand Oaks: Sage.

Ciulla, Joanne B. 2018. "Why Is It So Difficult to Be an Ethical Leader?" *Business and Society Review* 123 (2): 369–83.

Clark, David. 2016. *The Global Financial Crisis and Austerity*. Bristol: Policy Press.

Clark, John B. 1879. "Business Ethics, Past and Present." *The New Englander* 38 (March): 157–68.

Clark, John M. 1926. *Social Control of Business*. Chicago, IL: University of Chicago Press.

Clark, John W. 1966. *Religion and the Moral Standards of American Businessmen*. Cincinnati: South-Western.

Clegg, Hugh A. 1960. *A New Approach to Industrial Democracy*. Oxford: Blackwell.

Clegg, Stuart, and Carl Rhodes, eds. 2006. *Management Ethics: Contemporary Contexts*. London: Routledge.

Cleveland, Harlan, ed. 1981. *The Management of Sustainable Growth*. New York: Pergamon Press.

Clinard, Marshall B., and Peter C. Yeager. 1980. *Corporate Crime*. New York: Free Press.

Coats, Alfred William, ed. 1971. *The Classical Economists and Economic Policy*. London: Methuen.

Coffey, Joan L. 2003. *Léon Harmel: Entrepreneur as Catholic Social Reformer*. Notre Dame, IN: University of Notre Dame Press.

Cohn, Gustav. 1900. "Ethik und Reaktion in der Volkswirtschaft." *Jahrbuch für Gesetzgebung, Verwaltung und Volkswirtschaft im Deutschen Reich* 24: 839–86.

Cole, George D.H. 1925. *Life of Robert Owen*. London: Benn.

Cole, Hugh S.D., et al. 1973. *Models of Doom: A Critique of the Limits to Growth*. New York: Universe Books.

Collingwood, Robin G. 1946. *The Idea of History*. Oxford: Clarendon.

Commission of the European Communities. 1972. "Proposal for a Fifth Directive on the Structure of Sociétés Anonymes." In *Bulletin of the European Communities*, Supplement 10/72. Luxembourg: Office for the Official Publications of the European Communities.

Committee for Economic Development. 1971. *Social Responsibilities of Business Corporations*. New York: CED.

Committee for Economic Development. 1979. *Redefining Government's Role in the Market System*. New York: CED.

Committee on Commerce (US). 1976. *Corporate Rights and Responsibilities: Hearings Before the Committee on Commerce, United States Senate, Ninety-fourth Congress, Second Session*. Washington, DC: US Govt. Printing Office.

Conard, Alfred F. 1976. *Corporations in Perspective*. Mineola, NY: Foundation Press.

Condorcet, Nicholas de. 1795. *Outlines of an Historical View of the Progress of the Human Mind*. London: Johnson.

Confederation of British Industry (CBI). 1973. *The Responsibilities of the British Public Company: Final Report of the of the Company Affairs Committee*. London: CBI.

Confederation of Indian Industry. 1998. *Desirable Corporate Governance: A Code*. New Delhi: Confederation of Indian Industry.

Conference Board. 1972. *The Board of Directors: New Challenges, New Directions* (Conference Board reports 547). New York: Conference Board.

Conis, Elena. 2010. "Debating the Health Effects of DDT: Thomas Jukes, Charles Wurster, and the Fate of an Environmental Pollutant." *Public Health Reports* 125 (2): 337–42.

Conlon, Thomas. 1975. "Industrial Democracy and EEC Company Law: A Review of the Draft Fifth Directive." *International and Comparative Law Quarterly* 24 (2): 348–59.

Cooke, Morris L., and Philip Murray. 1940. *Organized Labour and Production: Next Steps in Industrial Democracy*. New York: Harper & Bros.

Coomer, James M., ed. 1979. *Quest for a Sustainable Society*. New York: Pergamon.

Corfield, Kenneth. 1972. *Business Responsibilities*. London: Foundation for Business Responsibilities.

Corson, John J., and George A. Steiner. 1975. *Measuring Business's Social Performance: The Corporate Social Audit*. New York: Committee for Economic Development.

Cox, Edward F., Robert C. Fellmeth, and John E. Schulz. 1970. *The Nader Report on the Federal Trade Commission*. New York: Grove Press.

Cressey, Donald R., and Charles A. Moore. 1983. "Managerial Values and Corporate Codes of Ethics." *California Management Review* 25 (4): 53–77.

Cromme, Gerhard. 2002. *Deutscher Corporate Governance Kodex*. Berlin: Regierungskommission Deutscher Corporate Governance Kodex.

Cunningham, Hugh. 2016. "The Multi-layered History of Western Philanthropy." In *The Routledge Companion to Philanthropy*, edited by Tobias Jung, Susan D. Phillips, and Jenny Harrow, 42–71. London: Routledge.

Czubek, Gisela. 1968. *Die Unternehmensverfassung: Wirtschaftliche Grundlagen, juristische Reformbestrebungen und rechtsdogmatische Widerstände.* Dissertation, University of Freiburg.

Dalton, Clare. 1974. "Proposals for the Unification of Corporation Law Within the European Economic Community: Effect on the British Company." *New York University Journal of International Law and Politics* 7: 59–102.

Dauman, Jan. 1981. *Corporate Social Responsibility: The Integration of a Crucial New Business Variable into the Mainstream of Corporate Activity.* Dissertation, Brunel University.

David, Donald K. 1949. "Business Responsibilities in an Uncertain World." *Harvard Business Review* 27 (3): 1–8.

Davies, Paul, and Lord Wedderburn of Charlton. 1977. "The Land of Industrial Democracy." *Industrial Law Journal* 6: 197–211.

Davis, Keith. 1957. *Human Relations in Business.* New York: McGraw-Hill.

Davis, Keith. 1960. "Can Business Afford to Ignore Social Responsibilities?" *California Management Review* 2 (3): 70–6.

Davis, Keith. 1973. "The Case for and Against Business Assumptions of Social Responsibility." *Academy of Management Journal* 16 (6): 312–22.

Davis, Keith. 1975. "Five Propositions for Business Responsibility." *Business Horizons* 18 (3): 19–24.

Davis, Keith, and Robert L. Blomstrom. 1966. *Business and Its Environment.* New York: McGraw-Hill.

Davis, Ralph C. 1958. "A Philosophy of Management." *The Journal of Insurance* 25 (3): 1–7.

Dawson, Kate Winkler. 2017. *Death in the Air: The True Story of a Serial Killer, the Great London Smog and the Strangling of a City.* New York: Hachette.

Deal, Terrence E., and Allan A. Kennedy. 1982. *Corporate Cultures.* New York: Addison-Wesley.

De George, Richard T. 1978. "Responding to the Mandate for Social Responsibility." In *Guidelines for Business When Societal Demands Conflict*, 60–80. Washington, DC: Council for Better Business Bureaus.

De George, Richard T. 1982. *Business Ethics.* New York: Palgrave Macmillan.

De George, Richard T. 1986. "Theological Ethics and Business Ethics." *Journal of Business Ethics* 5 (6): 421–32.

De George, Richard T. 2005. "A History of the Society for Business Ethics on Its Twenty-fifth Anniversary." *The Society for Business Ethics Newsletter* 16 (2): 5–10.

De George, Richard T., and Joseph A. Pichler, eds. 1978. *Ethics, Free Enterprise, and Public Policy: Original Essays on Moral Issues in Business.* New York: Oxford University Press.

DeLucca, Daniel N., ed. 1964. *The Concept of Business Ethics: Proceedings of a Workshop, Held Nov. 8–9, 1963, at St Joseph's College, Organized by the Council on Business Ethics.* Philadelphia: Council on Business Ethics, St. Joseph's College.

Dempsey, Bernard W. 1949. "The Roots of Business Responsibility." *Harvard Business Review* 27 (4): 393–404.

Department of Employment (UK). 1978. *Industrial Democracy*. London: HMSO.
Department of the Environment (UK). 1980. *Anglo-American Conference on Community Involvement, Sunningdale Park, UK, April 9–10: Papers and Proceedings*. London: Department of the Environment.
Department of Trade and Industry (UK). 1973. *Company Law Reform*. London: HMSO.
Derber, Milton. 1970. *The American Idea of Industrial Democracy, 1865–1965*. Urbana, IL: University of Illinois Press.
de Tocqueville, Alexis. 2004 [1840]. *Democracy in America*, translated by Arthur Goldhammer. New York: Library of America.
Dey, Peter J. 1994. *Where Were the Directors? Guidelines for Improved Corporate Governance in Canada*. Toronto: Toronto Stock Exchange Committee on Corporate Governance in Canada.
Dill, William R. 1975. "Public Participation in Corporate Planning—Strategic Management in a Kibitzer's World." *Long Range Planning* 8: 57–63.
DiMaggio, Paul J., and Walter W. Powell. 1983. "The Iron Cage Revisited: Institutional Isomorphism and Collective Rationality in Organizational Fields." *American Sociological Review* 48: 147–60.
Dingley, James C. 1997. "Durkheim, Mayo, Morality and Management." *Journal of Business Ethics* 16:1117–29.
Dodd, Merrick E., Jr. 1932. "For Whom Are Corporate Managers Trustees?" *Harvard Law Review* 45: 1145–63.
Dodd, Merrick E., Jr. 1935. "Is Effective Enforcement of the Fiduciary Duties of Corporate Managers Practicable?" *University of Chicago Law Review* 2: 194–207.
Dominick, Raymond. 1988. "The Roots of the Green Movement in the United States and West Germany." *Environmental Review* 12 (3): 1–30.
Donaldson, Thomas. 1979. "Moral Change and the Corporation." In *Power and Responsibility in the American Business System: Proceedings of the Second Annual Conference on Business Ethics*, edited by W. Michael Hoffman, 83–91. Waltham, MA: Bentley College.
Donaldson, Thomas. 1982. *Corporations and Morality*. Englewood Cliffs, NJ: Prentice-Hall.
Donaldson, Thomas. 2015. "Where the Facts End: Richard De George and the Rise of Business Ethics." *Journal of Business Ethics* 127: 783–87.
Donaldson, Thomas, Norman E. Bowie and Deborah G. Johnson. 2015. "Introduction." *Journal of Business Ethics* 127: 695–97.
Donaldson, Thomas, and Patricia Werhane, eds. 1979. *Ethical Issues in Business: A Philosophical Approach*. Englewood Cliffs, NJ: Prentice-Hall.
Drucker, Peter F. 1954. *The Practice of Management*. New York: Harper.
Drucker, Peter F. 1976. *The Unseen Revolution: How Pension Fund Socialism Came to America*. New York: Harper & Row.
Drucker, Peter F. 1981. "Can There Be 'Business Ethics'?" *The Public Interest* 63 (2): 18–36.
Duff, Edward. 1956. *The Social Thought of the World Council of Churches*. New York: Association Press.
Dunlap, Thomas R. 1981. *DDT: Scientists, Citizens, and Public Policy*. Princeton: Princeton University Press.
Du Pisani, Jacobus A. 2006. "Sustainable Development—Historical Roots of the Concept." *Environmental Sciences* 3 (2): 83–96.

Dupont (de Bussac), Jacques François. 1838. "Introduction." *Revue républicaine* 1: 1–53.

Durkheim, Emile. 1984 [1893]. *The Division of Labour in Society*, translated by W.D. Halls. Basingstoke: Macmillan.

Eberle, Franz Xaver. 1921. *Katholische Wirtschaftsmoral*. Freiburg i.Br.: Herder.

Editors 1960. "Declaration of Independence." *Business & Society* 1: 3–4.

Eells, Richard F.S. 1956. *Corporation Giving in a Free Society*. New York: Harper.

Eells, Richard F.S. 1960. *The Meaning of Modern Business: An Introduction to the Philosophy of Large Corporate Enterprise*. New York: Columbia University Press.

Eells, Richard F.S. 1970. "Corporate Social Responsibility in the USA." In *The Company: Law, Structure, and Reform in Eleven Countries*, edited by Charles De Hoghton, 124–37. London: Allen & Unwin.

Eells, Richard F.S., and Clarence Walton. 1961. *Conceptual Foundations of Business: An Outline of the Major Ideas Sustaining Business Enterprise in the Western World*. Homewood, IL: Richard D. Irwin.

Ehrlich, Paul R. 1968. *The Population Bomb*. New York: Ballantyne.

Eley, Geoff. 2002. *Forging Democracy: The History of the Left in Europe, 1850–2000*. Oxford: Oxford University Press.

Elkington, John. 1997. *Cannibals With Forks: The Triple Bottom Line of 21st Century Business*. Oxford: Capstone.

Elkington, John, and Julia Hailes. 1988. *The Green Consumer Guide: From Shampoo to Champagne. High-Street Shopping for a Better Environment*. London: Gollancz.

Elton, Geoffrey R. 1991. *Return to Essentials: Some Reflections on the Present State of Historical Study*. Cambridge: Cambridge University Press.

Emery, Frederick E., and Einar Thorsrud. 1969. *Form and Content in Industrial Democracy: Some Experiences From Norway and Other European Countries*. London: Tavistock.

Ethe, Solomon, and Roger M. Pegram. 1959. *Corporate Directorship Practices* (Studies in Business Policy 90). New York: National Industrial Conference Board.

Evans, Christopher H. 2017. *The Social Gospel in American Religion: A History*. New York: New York University Press.

Fama, Eugene F. 1980. "Agency Problems and the Theory of the Firm." *Journal of Political Economy* 88: 288–301.

Fama, Eugene F., and Michael C. Jensen. 1983. "Separation of Ownership and Control." *Journal of Law and Economics* 26 (2): 301–25.

Farman, Joseph C., Brian G. Gardiner, and Jonathan D. Shanklin. 1985. "Large Losses of Total Ozone in Antarctica Reveal Seasonal ClOx/NOx Interaction." *Nature* 315 (6016): 207–10.

Fayol, Henri. 1949 [1916]. *General and Industrial Management*, translated by Constance Storrs. London: Pitman.

Federal Council of Churches. 1947. *Report of the National Study Conference on the Church and Economic Life, Pittsburgh, February 18–20, 1947*. Pittsburgh: Federal Council of Churches.

Ferrell, Odies C., Deebbie Torne LeClair, and Linda Ferrell. 1998. "The Federal Sentencing Guidelines for Organizations: A Framework for Ethical Compliance." *Journal of Business Ethics* 17 (4): 353–63.

Fetzer, Thomas. 2010. "Defending Mitbestimmung: German Trade Unions and European Company Law Regulation (1967–2000)." *Economic and Industrial Democracy* 31 (4), suppl.: 24–39.

Feuerbach, Ludwig. 1854 [1841]. *The Essence of Christianity*, translated by Mary Anne Evans. London: Chapman.

Fiedler, Fred E. 1967. *A Theory of Leadership Effectiveness*. New York: McGraw-Hill.

Fiedler-Winter, Rosemarie. 1977. *Die Moral der Manager: Dokumentation und Analyse*. Stuttgart: Seewald.

Filene, Edward A. 1922. "A Simple Code of Business Ethics." *Annals of the American Academy of Political and Social Science* 101: 223–8.

Filios, Vassilios P. 1985. "Assessment of Attitudes Toward Corporate Social Accountability in Britain." *Journal of Business Ethics* 4 (3): 155–73.

Fischel, Daniel R. 1982. "The Corporate Governance Movement." *Vanderbilt Law Review* 35: 1259–92.

Flume, Johannes W. 2014. "Law and Commerce: The Evolution of Codified Business Law in Europe." *Comparative Legal History* 2 (1): 45–83.

Foot, Philippa. 1958. "Moral Arguments." *Mind*, new ser., 67 (268): 502–13.

Foot, Phillipa. 1967. "The Problem of Abortion and the Doctrine of the Double Effect." *Oxford Review* 5: 5–15.

Foucault, Michel. 1972 [1969]. *The Archaeology of Knowledge and the Discourse on Language*, translated by A.M. Sheridan Smith. London: Tavistock.

Foucault, Michel. 1977. "Nietzsche, Genealogy, History." In *Language, Counter-Memory, and Practice*, edited by Donald F. Bouchard, 87–109. Ithaca: Cornell University Press.

Fox, Alan. 1985. *History and Heritage: The Social Origins of the British Industrial Relations System*. London: Allen & Unwin.

Francis. 2015. *Encyclical Letter* Laudatio si' *of the Holy Father Francis: On Care for Our Common Home*. Vatican City: Vatican Press.

Frankland, Gene E., and Donald Schoonmaker. 1992. *Between Protest & Power: The Green Party in Germany*. Boulder, CO: Westview Press.

Franklin, Benjamin. 1839 [1736]. "Necessary Hints to those that Would be Rich." In *The Life and Miscellaneous Writings of Benjamin Franklin*, 56. Edinburgh: William & Robert Chambers.

Frederick, William C. 1960. "The Growing Concern Over Business Responsibility." *California Management Review* 2 (4): 54–61.

Frederick, William C. 1981. "Free Market vs. Social Responsibility: Decision Time at the CED." *California Management Review* 23 (3): 20–8.

Frederick, William C. 2006. *Corporation, Be Good! The Story of Corporate Social Responsibility*. Indianapolis, IN: Dog Ear.

Freedley, Edwin T. 1853. *A Practical Treatise on Business: Or, How to Get, Save, Spend, Give, Lend, and Bequeath Money*. Philadelphia: Lippincott, Grambo & Co.

Freeman, Edward R. 1984. *Strategic Management: A Stakeholder Approach*. Boston: Pitman.

Freeman, Edward R., Jeffrey S. Harrison, Andrew C. Wicks, Bidhan Parmar, and Simone de Colle. 2010. *Stakeholder Theory: The State of the Art*. Cambridge: Cambridge University Press.

Freshfields Bruckhaus Deringer. 2005. *A Legal Framework for the Integration of Environmental, Social and Governance Issues Into International Investment*. Geneva: United Nations Environment Programme Finance Initiative.

Freud, Sigmund. 1961 [1925]. "Some Psychical Consequences of the Anatomical Distinction Between the Sexes." In *The Standard Edition of the Complete*

Psychological Works of Sigmund Freud, edited and translated by James Strachey, XIX, 241–58. 24 vols. London: Hogarth.

Frey, Michael. 2004. "Shifting to Confrontation. Herbert Marcuse and the Transformation of the American Student Movement." *Bulletin of the GHI Washington* 34: 99–111.

Friedman, Milton. 1962. *Capitalism and Freedom.* Chicago: University of Chicago Press.

Friedman, Milton. 1970. "The Social Responsibility of Business Is to Increase Its Profits." *New York Times Magazine*, September 13, pp. 33 & 122–6.

Fry, Simon, and Bernard Mees. 2017. "Two Discursive Frameworks Concerning Ideology in Australian Industrial Relations." *The Economic and Labor Relations Review* 28 (4): 483–99.

Fussler, Claude, Aron Cramer, and Sebastian van der Vegt, eds. 2004. *Raising the Bar: Creating Value With the UN Global Compact.* London: Greenleaf.

Galambos, Louis. 1975. *The Public Image of Big Business in America, 1880–1940: A Quantitative Study in Social Change.* Baltimore, MD: Johns Hopkins University Press.

Galbraith, J. Kenneth. 1952. *American Capitalism: The Concept of Countervailing Power.* Boston: Houghton Mifflin.

Galbraith, J. Kenneth. 1958. *The Affluent Society.* New York: Houghton Mifflin.

Gaultier, Paul. 1904. "La morale des affaires." *Revue politique et littéraire (Revue bleue)* 5th ser., 2: 157–60.

Geary, Daniel. 2009. *Radical Ambition: C. Wright Mills, the Left, and American Social Thought.* Berkeley: University of California Press.

Gehman, Joel, Lianne M. Lefsrud, and Stewart Fast. 2017. "Social License to Operate: Legitimacy by Another Name?" *Canadian Public Administration/ Administration publique du Canada* 60 (2): 293–317.

Gentile, Mary C. 2010. *Giving Voice to Values.* New Haven: Yale University Press.

Gerth, Jeff. 1981. "Wall St. Hails Williams's Record." *New York Times*, March 2.

Giddens, Anthony. 1999. *Runaway World: How Globalisation Is Reshaping Our Lives.* London: Profile.

Gilligan, Carol. 1982. *In a Different Voice.* Cambridge, MA: Harvard University Press.

Global Reporting Initiative (GRI). 1999. *Sustainability Reporting Guidelines: Exposure Draft for Public Comment and Pilot Testing.* Boston: CERES.

Gordon, Robert A., and James E. Howell. 1959. *Higher Education for Business.* New York: Columbia University Press.

Goyder, George A. 1951. *The Future of Private Enterprise: A Study in Responsibility.* Oxford: Blackwell.

Goyder, George A. 1961. *The Responsible Company.* Oxford: Blackwell.

Graham, Jesse, Brian A. Nosek, Jonathan Haidt, Ravi Iyer, Spassena Koleva, and Peter H. Ditto. 2011. "Mapping the Moral Domain." *Journal of Personality and Social Psychology* 101 (2): 366–85.

Gramsci, Antonio. 1991 [1948–51]. *Prison Notebooks*, translated by Joseph A. Buttigieg and Antonio Callari. New York: Columbia University Press.

Gray, Hillel. 1983. *New Directions in the Investment and Control of Pension Funds.* Washington, DC: Investor Responsibility Research Center.

Gray, John. 1986. *Liberalism.* Milton Keynes: Open University Press.

Gray, John. 2012. "The Knowns and the Unknowns." *The New Republic*, April 20.

Green, Mark J. 1980. "The Case for Corporate Democracy." *Regulation* 4 (3): 20–31.

Green, Mark J., Alice Tepper Marlin, Victor Kamber, and Jules Burnstein. 1979. *The Case for a Corporate Democracy Act of 1980*. Washington, DC: Americans Concerned About Corporate Power.

Green, Michael. 1983. "Marx, Utility, and Right." *Political Theory* 11 (3): 433–46.

Green, Thomas H. 1884. *Prolegomena to Ethics*. Oxford: Clarendon.

Greenslade, Roy. 1992. *Maxwell: The Rise and Fall of Robert Maxwell and His Empire*. New York: Carol.

Greer, Jed, and Kenny Bruno. 1996. *Greenwash: The Reality Behind Corporate Environmentalism*. New York: Apex.

Gremillion, Joseph B. 1961. *The Catholic Movement of Employers and Managers* (Studia socialia 5). Rome: Gregorian University Press.

Grey, Christopher, and Hugh C. Willmott, eds. 2005. *Critical Management Studies: A Reader*. Oxford: Oxford University Press.

Griffin, Mark, Frank Landy and Lisa Mayocchi. 2002. "Australian Influences on Elton Mayo: The Construct of Revery in Industrial Society." *History of Psychology* 5: 356–75.

Griffiths, Brian. 1982. *Morality and the Market Place: Christian Alternatives to Capitalism and Socialism*. London: Hodder and Stoughton.

Grosser, Kate and Jeremy Moon. 2019. "CSR and Feminist Organization Studies: Towards an Integrated Theorization for the Analysis of Gender Issues." *Journal of Business Ethics* 155 (2): 321–42.

Gueneau, Jean-Claude, Dominique Bertier, Jacques Bidault, and Claude Bijon. 1969. *Vers une morale des affaires? L'éthique du responsable commercial: cas concrets*. Paris: Spes.

Gunn, Jeremy T. 2009. *Spiritual Weapons: The Cold War and the Forging of an American National Religion*. Westport, CT: Praeger.

Gunningham, Neil, Robert A. Kagan, and Dorothy Thornton. 2004. "Social License and Environmental Protection: Why Businesses Go Beyond Compliance." *Law & Social Inquiry* 29: 307–41.

Hadley, Arthur T. 1907. *Standards of Public Morality*. New York: Palgrave Macmillan.

Hagedorn, Jonas. 2018. *Oswald von Nell-Breuning SJ: Aufbrüche der katholischen Soziallehre in der Weimarer Republik*. Paderborn: Schöningh.

Haidt, Jonathan. 2001. "The Emotional Dog and Its Rational Tail: A Social Intuitionist Approach to Moral Judgement." *Psychological Review* 108 (4): 814–34.

Haidt, Jonathan, and Craig Joseph. 2004. "Intuitive Ethics: How Innately Prepared Intuitions Generate Culturally Variable Virtues." *Dædalus* 133 (4): 55–67.

Hajduk, Thomas, and Thomas Beschorner. 2015. "Fünfundzwanzig Jahre Institut für Wirtschaftsethik der Universität St. Gallen—ein kurzer historischer Rückblick." In *St. Galler Wirtschaftsethik: Programmatik, Positionen, Perspektiven*, edited by Thomas Beschorner, Peter Ulrich, and Florian Wettstein, 19–25 (Ethik und Ökonomie 16). Marburg: Metropolis.

Hall, Patricia, and Henry William Locke. 1938. *Incentives and Contentment: A Study Made in a British Factory*. London: Pitman.

Hall, Peter A., and David Soskice, eds. 2001. *Varieties of Capitalism: The Institutional Foundations of Comparative Advantage*. Oxford: Oxford University Press.

Hallahan, Kirk. 2002. "Ivy Lee and the Rockefellers' Response to the 1913-1914 Colorado Coal Strike." *Journal of Public Relations Research* 14: 265–315.

Handlin, Oscar, and Mary F. Handlin. 1945. "Origins of the American Business Corporation." *Journal of Economic History* 5 (1): 1–23.

Hansmann, Henry, and Reinier Kraakman. 2001. "The End of History for Corporate Law." *Georgetown Law Journal* 89: 439–68.

Hargreaves, John, and Jan Dauman. 1975. *Business Survival and Social Change: A Practical Guide to Responsibility and Partnership*. London: Associated Business Programmes.

Hariman, Robert, ed. 2003. *Prudence: Classical Virtue, Postmodern Practice*. University Park, PA: Pennsylvania State University Press.

Harmel, Léon. 1877. *Manuel d'une corporation chrétienne*. Tours: Mame.

Harmel, Léon. 1889. *Catéchisme du patron: élaboré avec le concours d'un grand nombre de théologiens*. Paris: Aux bureaux du journal "la Corporation".

Harmon, Elizabeth A. 2017. *The Transformation of American Philanthropy: From Public Trust to Private Foundation, 1785–1917*. Dissertation, University of Michigan.

Harrington, John C. 1992. *Investing With Your Conscience: How to Achieve High Returns With Socially Responsible Investment*. New York: Wiley.

Hartley, William D. 1977. "Why Oppose 'Motherhood'?" *Wall Street Journal*, March 23, p. 1.

Havlovic, Stephen J. 1990. "German Works Councils: A Highly Evolved Institution of Industrial Democracy." *Labour Studies Journal* 15 (2): 62–71.

Hayek, Friedrich A. 1944. *The Road to Serfdom*. London: Routledge.

Heald, Morrell. 1970. *The Social Responsibilities of Business: Company and Community, 1900–1960*. Cleveland: Press of Case Western Reserve University.

Heath, Eugene, Byron Kaldis, and Alexei Marcoux, eds. 2018. *The Routledge Companion to Business Ethics*. London: Routledge.

Heermance, Edgar L. 1924. *Codes of Ethics: A Handbook*. Burlington, VT: Free Press.

Heermance, Edgar L. 1926. *The Ethics of Business: A Survey of Current Standards*. New York: Harper & Bros.

Heermance, Edgar L. 1935. *The Connecticut Guide: What to See and Where to Find It*. Hartford, CT: Emergency Relief Commission.

Hegel, Georg W.F. 1975 [1837]. *Lectures on the Philosophy of World History*, translated by Hugh B. Nisbet. Cambridge: Cambridge University Press.

Hegel, Georg W.F. 1991 [1820]. *Elements of the Philosophy of Right*, edited by Allen W. Wood, translated Hugh B. Nisbet. Cambridge: Cambridge University Press.

Hennesy, James. 1978. "Leo XIII's Thomistic Revival: A Political and Philosophical Event." *Journal of Religion* 58, suppl.: S185–97.

Herzberg, Frederick. 1966. *Work and the Nature of Man*. Cleveland: World Publishing.

Hodges, Luther H. 1963. *The Business Conscience*. Englewood Cliffs, NJ: Prentice-Hall.

Hoffman, Andrew J. 2001. *From Heresy to Dogma: An Institutional History of Corporate Environmentalism*. Stanford: Stanford University Press.

Hoffman, Michael W., ed. 1977. *Business Values and Social Justice: Compatibility or Contradiction? Proceedings of the First National Conference on Business*

Ethics, March 11 and 12, 1977. Waltham, MA: The Center for Business Ethics, Bentley College.

Hoffman, Michael W., and Jennifer Mills Moore. 1982a. "Results of a Business Ethics Curriculum Survey Conducted by the Center for Business Ethics." *Journal of Business Ethics* 1 (2): 81–3.

Hoffman, Michael W., and Jennifer Mills Moore. 1982b. "What Is Business Ethics? A Reply to Peter Drucker." *Journal of Business Ethics* 1 (4): 293–300.

Hope, Sarah, and Terry Dowling. 1975. "Business Studies and Business Ethics." *The Vocational Aspect of Education* 27 (67): 41–4.

Hopt, Klaus J. 2007. "Globalisation of Corporate Governance: The Difficult Process of Bringing About European Union Internal and External Corporate Governance Principles." In *Globalisation and Business Ethics*, edited by Karl Homann, Peter Koslowski, and Christoph Luetge, 81–100. Aldershot: Ashgate.

Hubbert, King M. 1956. "Nuclear Energy and the Fossil Fuels." *American Petroleum Institute, Drilling and Production Practice* 1956: 7–25.

Hunt, James G. 1999. "Transformational/Charismatic Leadership's Transformation of the Field: An Historical Essay." *The Leadership Quarterly* 10 (2): 129–44.

Intergovernmental Panel on Climate Change. 2007. *Climate Change 2007: Synthesis Report. Contribution of Working Groups I, II and III to the Fourth Assessment Report of the Intergovernmental Panel on Climate Change.* Geneva: IPCC.

Ireland, Paddy W. 2009. "Financialization and Corporate Governance." *Northern Ireland Legal Quarterly* 60 (1): 1–34.

Irwin, Terence. 2007–2009. *The Development of Ethics: A Historical and Critical Study.* 3 vols. Oxford: Oxford University Press.

Ivens, Michael. 1970. *Industry and Values: The Objectives and Responsibilities of Business.* London: Harrap.

Jacoby, Neil H. 1977. "Federal Charters: A Flawed Case." *Wall Street Journal*, January 19, p. 14.

James, Edmund J. 1891. *The Education of Business Men.* New York: W.B. Greene.

Jaroslaw, Benno. 1912. *Ideal und Geschäft.* Jena: Diederichs.

Jensen, Michael C. 2009. "Integrity: Without It Nothing Works." *Rotman Magazine* 6 (1): 16–20.

Jensen, Michael C. and William H. Meckling. 1976. "Theory of the Firm: Managerial Behavior, Agency Costs, and Ownership Structure." *Journal of Financial Economics* 3 (4): 305–60.

John Paul II. 1991. *Encyclical Letter Centesimus Annus of the Supreme Pontiff John Paul II in the Hundredth Anniversary of Rerum Novarum.* Homebush, NSW: St Pauls Publications.

Johnson, Harold L. 1957. "Can the Businessman Apply Christianity?" *Harvard Business Review* 35 (5): 68–76.

Johnson, Lyndon B. 1965 [1964]. "Remarks at the University of Michigan, May 22, 1964." In *Public Papers of the Presidents of the United States: Lyndon B. Johnson, 1963–1964*, I, 704–7. 2 vols. Washington, DC: National Archives and Records Service.

Johnston, Herbert. 1956. *Business Ethics.* New York: Pitman.

Jones, Campbell, Martin Parker, and René ten Bos. 2005. *For Business Ethics.* London: Routledge.

Jones, Geoffrey. 2017. *Profits and Sustainability: A History of Green Entrepreneurship.* Oxford: Oxford University Press.

Jones, Ian W., and Michael G. Pollitt. 2002. "Who Influences Debates in Business Ethics? An Investigation Into the Development of Corporate Governance in the UK Since 1990." In *Understanding How Issues in Business Ethics Develop*, edited by Ian W. Jones and Michael G. Pollitt, 14–68. Basingstoke: Palgrave Macmillan.

Jones, Thomas M. 1991. "Ethical Decision Making by Individuals in Organizations: An Issue-Contingent Model." *Academy of Management Review* 16: 366–95.

Jonsen, Albert R. 1988. *The Birth of Bioethics*. Oxford: Oxford University Press.

Josephson, Matthew. 1934. *The Robber Barons: The Great American Capitalists, 1861–1901*. New York: Harcourt, Brace.

Kaltenborn, Wilhelm. 2018. *Raffeisen: Beginning and End*, translated by Mark Thomas. Berlin: Zentralkonsum.

Kant, Immanuel. 1998 [1781]. *Critique of Pure Reason*, translated by Paul Guyer and Allen W. Wood. Cambridge: Cambridge University Press.

Kant, Immanuel. 1998 [1785]. *Groundwork of the Metaphysic of Morals*, translated by Mary Gregor. Cambridge: Cambridge University Press.

Katz, Eric. 1990. "Defending the Use of Animals by Business: Animal Liberation and Environmental Ethics." In *Business, Ethics, and the Global Environment: The Public Policy Debate*, edited by W. Michael Hoffman, Robert Frederick, and Edward S. Perry, 223–32. New York: Quorum.

Keidanren. 1997. *Urgent Recommendations Concerning Corporate Governance*. Tokyo: Keidanren.

Kell, Georg. 2005. "The Global Compact Selected Experiences and Reflections." *Journal of Business Ethics* 59 (1/2): 69–79.

Kell, Georg, and David Levin. 2003. "The Global Compact Network: An Historic Experiment in Learning and Action." *Business and Society Review* 108 (2): 151–81.

Kell, Georg, and John G. Ruggie. 1999. "Global Markets and Social Legitimacy: The Case of the 'Global Compact'." *Transnational Corporations* 8 (3): 101–20.

Kellner, Douglas. 1984. *Herbert Marcuse and the Crisis of Marxism*. Berkeley: University of California Press.

Kempner, Thomas, Keith McMillan, and Kevin Hawkins. 1974. *Business and Society: Tradition and Change*. London: Allen Lane.

Kennedy, John F. 1960. "We Must Climb to the Hilltop." *Life*, August 22, pp. 70–7.

Khurana, Rakesh. 2007. *From Higher Aims to Hired Hands: The Social Transformation of American Business Schools and the Unfulfilled Promise of Management as a Profession*. Princeton: Princeton University Press.

Kinderman, Daniel. 2012. "'Free Us Up So That We Can Be Responsible' The Co-evolution of Corporate Social Responsibility and Neo-Liberalism in the UK, 1977–2010." *Socio-Economic Review* 10: 29–57.

King, Mervyn E. 1994. *The King Report on Corporate Governance*. Johannesburg: Institute of Directors in Southern Africa.

Kirby, William C. 1995. "China Unincorporated: Company Law and Business Enterprise in Twentieth-Century China." *Journal of Asian Studies* 54 (1): 43–63.

Klein, Naomi. 1999. *No Logo: Taking Aim at the Brand Bullies*. Toronto: Knopf.

Klikauer, Thomas. 2015. "Critical Management Studies and Critical Theory: A Review." *Capital & Class* 39 (2): 197–220.

Knoepfel, Ivo. 2004. *Who Cares Wins: Connecting Financial Markets to a Changing World*. Geneva: United Nations Department of Public Information.

Kohlberg, Lawrence. 1958. *The Development of Modes of Thinking and Choices in Years 10 to 16*. Dissertation, University of Chicago.

Kohlberg, Lawrence. 1976. "Moral Stages and Moralization: The Cognitive-Development Approach." In *Moral Development and Behavior: Theory, Research, and Social Issues*, edited by Thomas Lickona, 31–53. New York: Holt, Rinehart & Winston.

Korn/Ferry International. 1973ff. *Board of Directors Annual Study*. New York: Korn/Ferry International.

Kramer, Samuel N. 1956. *History Begins at Sumer: Thirty-nine Firsts in Recorded History*. New York: Doubleday.

Kreps, Theodore. 1962. "Measurement of the Social Performance of Business." *The Annals of the American Academy of Political and Social Science* 343 (1): 20–31.

Krippner, Greta R. 2005. "The Financialization of the American Economy." *Socio-Economic Review* 3: 173–208.

Lambert, Ben. 2018. "Trail Dedicated to Celebrate Preservation of Rocky Top Property in Hamden." *New Haven Register*, September 28.

Laufer, William S., and Diana C. Robertson. 1997. "Corporate Ethics Initiatives as Social Control." *Journal of Business Ethics* 16 (10): 1029–48.

Leccese, Stephen R. 2017. "John D. Rockefeller, Standard Oil, and the Rise of Corporate Public Relations in Progressive America, 1902–1908." *Journal of the Gilded Age and Progressive Era* 16 (3): 245–63.

Lee, James Melvin. 1926. *Business Ethics: A Manual of Modern Morals*. New York: Ronald.

Lefebvre-Teillard, Anne. 1981. "L'intervention de l'État dans la constitution des sociétés anonymes (1807–1867)." *Revue historique de droit français et étranger*, Quatrième série 59 (3): 383–418.

Lemarié, Octave. 1928. *La morale des affaires: Précis d'une morale économique*. Paris: Alcan.

Leo XIII. 1983 [1891]. *Rerum Novarum: Encyclical Letter of Pope Leo XIII on the Condition of the Working Classes*, translated by Joseph Kirwan. London: Catholic Truth Society.

Lewin, Kurt, Ronald Lippit, and Ralph K. White. 1939. "Patterns of Aggressive Behavior in Experimentally Created Social Climates." *Journal of Social Psychology* 10: 271–99.

Lewin, Tamar. 1982. "The Corporate-Reform Furor." *New York Times*, June 10, p. D1.

Likens, Gene E., F. Herbert Bormann, and Noye M. Johnson. 1972. "Acid Rain." *Environment* 14 (2): 33–40.

Likert, Rensis. 1967. *The Human Organization: Its Management and Value*. New York: McGraw-Hill.

Literary Digest. 1894. "Revolt Against Bad Leadership." *The Literary Digest* 10 (2): 62.

Locke, John. 2003 [1690]. *Two Treatises of Government; and a Letter Concerning Toleration*. New Haven: Yale University Press.

Lopez, Tara Martin. 2014. *The Winter of Discontent: Myth, Memory and History*. Liverpool: Liverpool University Press.

Lord, Everett William. 1926. *The Fundamentals of Business Ethics*. New York: Ronald.

Louche, Céline, and Steven Lydenberg. 2010. "Responsible Investing." In *Finance Ethics: Critical Issues in Theory and Practice*, edited by John R. Boatright, 393–417. Hoboken, NJ: Wiley.

Lovelock, James E. 1972. "Gaia as Seen Through the Atmosphere." *Atmospheric Environment* 6 (8): 579–580.

Lowe, Robert. 1856. "Law of Partnership and Joint-Stock Companies." In *Hansard's Parliamentary Debates: Third Series, Vol. CXL, Jan.-Mar. 1856*, 110–38. London: Cornelius Buck.

Lowery, Daniel L. 1962. "Moral Problems in Business Practice." *Proceedings of the American Catholic Theological Association* 1962: 121–46.

Lund, Leonard. 1974. *Corporate Organization for Environmental Policy-Making*. New York: Conference Board.

Luther, Martin. 1518. *Decem Praecepta Wittembergensi Predicata Populo*. Wittemberg: Viridimontanu.

Luttwak, Edward. 1994. "Franco-German Reconciliation: The Overlooked Role of the Moral Re-Armament Movement." In *Religion, the Missing Dimension of Statecraft*, edited by Douglas Johnston and Cynthia Sampson, 37–57. Oxford: Oxford University Press.

MacIntyre, Alasdair. 1966. *A Short History of Ethics*. London: Routledge & Kegan Paul.

MacIntyre, Alasdair. 1977. "Why Are the Problems of Business Ethics Insoluble?" In *Business Values and Social Justice: Compatibility or Contradiction? Proceedings of the First National Conference on Business Ethics, March 11 and 12, 1977*, edited by Michael W. Hoffman, 99–110. Waltham, MA: The Center for Business Ethics, Bentley College.

MacIntyre, Alasdair. 1981. *After Virtue: A Study in Moral Theory*. Notre Dame, IN: University of Notre Dame Press.

Mahoney, Jack. 1990. *Teaching Business Ethics in the UK, Europe and the USA: A Comparative Study*. London: Athlone.

Marcello, Patricia Cronin. 2004. *Ralph Nader: A Biography*. Westport, CT: Greenwood.

March, Gary J. 1962. "The Business Firm as a Political Coalition." *Journal of Politics* 24: 662–78.

Marchand, Roland. 1998. *Creating the Corporate Soul: The Rise of Public Relations and Corporate Imagery in American Big Business*. Berkeley: University of California Press.

Marcuse, Herbert. 1964. *One-Dimensional Man: Studies in the Ideology of Advanced Industrial Society*. London: Routledge & Kegan Paul.

Marcuse, Herbert. 1969. "Revolution Out of Disgust." *Der Spiegel*, July 28, translated by Henry Zimmermann, *Australian Left Review*, December 1969: 36–47.

Marinetto, Michael. 1998. *Corporate Social Involvement: Social, Political and Environmental Issues in Britain and Italy*. London: Routledge.

Marinetto, Michael. 1999. "The Historical Development of Business Philanthropy: Social Responsibility in the New Corporate Economy." *Business History* 41 (4): 1–20.

Maritain, Jacques. 1951. *Man and the State*. Washington, DC: The Catholic University of America Press.

Markey, Raymond, Greg Patmore, and Nikola Balnave. 2010. "Worker Directors and Worker Ownership/Cooperatives." In *The Oxford Handbook of Participation in Organisations*, edited by Adrian Wilkinson, Paul J. Gollan, Mick Marchington, and David Lewin, 237–57. Oxford: Oxford University Press.

Marsh, David. 1991. "British Industrial Relations Policy Transformed: The Thatcher Legacy." *Journal of Public Policy* 11 (3): 291–313.

Marshall, Leon C. 1913. "The College of Commerce and Administration of the University of Chicago." *The Journal of Political Economy* 21 (2): 97–110.

Marx, Karl. 1992 [1867]. *Capital: A Critique of Political Economy*, translated by Ben Fowkes. 3 vols. London: Penguin.

Marx, Karl. 1938 [1875, 1891]. *Critique of the Gotha Programme*, edited by C.P. Dutt. New York: International Publishers.

Marx, Karl. 1955 [1847]. *The Poverty of Philosophy*, translated by the Institute of Marxism Leninism. Moscow: Progress.

Marx, Karl. 1970 [1844]. *Critique of Hegel's "Philosophy of Right"*, translated by Annette Jolin and Joseph O'Malley. Cambridge: Cambridge University Press.

Marx, Karl, and Friedrich Engels. 1888 [1848]. *Manifesto of the Communist Party*, translated by Samuel Moore. London: Reeves.

Maslow, Abraham H. 1943. "A Theory of Human Motivation." *Psychological Review* 50: 370–96.

Maslow, Abraham H. 1954. *Motivation and Personality*. New York: Harper.

Maslow, Abraham H. 1965. *Eupsychian Management: A Journal*. Homewood, IL: Irwin.

McCarthy, Kathleen D. 1982. *Noblesse Oblige: Charity and Cultural Philanthropy in Chicago, 1849–1929*. Chicago: University of Chicago Press.

McCartrin, Joseph A. 1998. *Labor's Great War: The Struggle for Industrial Democracy and the Origins of Modern American Labor Relations, 1912–1921*. Chapel Hill: University of North Carolina Press.

McCormick, Anne O'Hare. 1932. "Roosevelt's View of the Big Job." *New York Times Magazine*, September 11, p. 1.

McCormick, John. 1991. *British Politics and the Environment*. London: Earthscan.

McGaughey, Ewan. 2014. "British Codetermination and the Churchillian Circle." UCL Labour Rights On-line Working Papers—LRI WP 2/2014.

McGaughey, Ewan. 2015. "The Codetermination Bargains: The History of German Corporate and Labour Law." LSE Law, Society and Economy Working Papers 10/2015.

McGregor, Douglas. 1960. *The Human Side of Enterprise*. New York: McGraw-Hill.

McGuire, Joseph W. 1963. *Business and Society*. New York: McGraw-Hill.

McLean, Bethany, and Peter Elkind. 2003. *The Smartest Guys in the Room: The Amazing Rise and Scandalous Fall of Enron*. New York: Portfolio.

McMahon, Gary, ed. 1998. *Mining and the Community: Results of the Quito Conference*. Quito, Ecuador: World Bank.

McMahon, Thomas F. 1966. "Moral Problems of Middle Management." *Proceedings of the Catholic Theological Society of America* 20: 23–49.

McMahon, Thomas F. 1975a. *Report On The Teaching of Socio-Ethical Issues in Collegiate Schools of Business/Public Administration*. Charlottesville, WA: Center for the Study of Applied Ethics.

McMahon, Thomas F. 1975b. "Classroom Ethics: A Survey of Business School Courses." *Business and Society Review* 14: 21–4.

Meadows, Dennis L., ed. 1977. *Alternative to Growth I: A Search for Sustainable Futures*. Cambridge, MA: Ballinger.

Meadows, Donella H., Dennis L. Meadows, Jorgen Randers, and William W. Behrens, III. 1972. *The Limits to Growth*. New York: New American Library.

Mees, Bernard. 2015. "Corporate Governance as a Reform Movement." *Journal of Management History* 21: 194–209.

Mees, Bernard. 2017a. "Changing Approaches to Business Ethics." In *The Routledge Companion to Business History*, edited by John F. Wilson, Steven Toms, Abe de Jong, and Emily Buchnea, 373–82. London: Routledge.

Mees, Bernard. 2017b. "Industrial Democracy and Corporate Governance: Two Discourses of Reform in Liberal-Market Economies." *International Journal of Corporate Governance* 8 (1): 44–60.

Mees, Bernard. 2018. "The History of Business Ethics." In *The Routledge Companion to Business Ethics*, edited by Eugene Heath, Byron Kaldis, and Alexei Marcoux, 7–22. London: Routledge.

Melrose-Woodman, Jonquil E., and Ingrid Kverndal. 1976. *Towards Social Responsibility: Company Codes of Ethics and Practice* (Survey Report No. 28). London: British Institute of Management.

Merrill, Harwood F., ed. 1948. *The Responsibilities of Business Leadership*. Cambridge, MA: Harvard University Press.

Mertens, Hans-Joachim, and Erich Schanze. 1979. "The German Codetermination Act of 1976." *Journal of Comparative Corporate Law and Securities Legislation* 2: 75–88.

Messner, Johannes. 1968. *Das Unternehmerbild in der katholischen Soziallehre*. Cologne: Bund Katholischer Unternehmer.

Mill, John S. 1859. *On Liberty*. London: Parker & Son.

Mill, John S. 1861. *Utilitarianism*. London: Parker, Son & Bourn.

Miller, Arthur S., ed. 1962. *The Ethics of Business Enterprise* (Annals of the American Academy of Political and Social Science 343). Philadelphia: American Academy of Political and Social Science.

Mills, Geoffrey. 1981. *On the Board*. Aldershot: Gower.

Mills, C. Wright. 1951. *White Collar: The American Middle Classes*. New York: Oxford University Press.

Mills, C. Wright. 1956. *The Power Elite*. Oxford: Oxford University Press.

Mills, C. Wright. 1960. "Letter to the New Left." *New Left Review* 1 (5): 18–23.

Millstein, Ira M. 1998. *Corporate Governance: Improving Competitiveness and Access to Capital in Global Markets*. Paris: OECD.

Mirvis, Phillip H. 2000. "Transformation at Shell: Commerce and Citizenship." *Business and Society Review* 105 (1): 63–84.

Mitchell, Andrew D. 1998. "Industrial Democracy: Reconciling Theories of the Firm and State." *International Journal of Comparative Labour Law and Industrial Relations* 14: 3–40.

Mitnick, Barry M. 1975. "The Theory of Agency: The Policing 'Paradox' and Regulatory Behavior." *Public Choice* 24 (Winter): 27–42.

Montagnon, Peter. 2016. *The Institute of Business Ethics: The Next 30 Years*. London: IBE.

Morgan, Gareth. 1997. *Images of Organization*. 2nd ed. Thousand Oaks: Sage.

Münsterberg, Hugo. 1913 [1912]. *Psychology and Industrial Efficiency*. Boston: Houghton, Mifflin.

Murphy, Patrick E. 1978. "An Evolution: Corporate Social Responsiveness." *University of Michigan Business Review* 30 (6): 19–25.

Nader, Ralph. 1965. *Unsafe at Any Speed: The Designed-In Dangers of the American Automobile*. New York: Grossman.

Nader, Ralph. 1984. "Reforming Corporate Governance." In *Corporate Governance and Institutionalising Ethics: Proceedings of the Fifth National Conference on Business Ethics*, edited by W. Michael Hoffman, Jennifer Mills Moore, and David A. Fedo. Lexington, MD: Lexington Books.

Nader, Ralph, and Mark J. Green. 1977. "For Federal Charters." *Wall Street Journal*, February 9, p. 22.

Nader, Ralph, Mark J. Green, and Joel Seligman. 1976. *Taming the Giant Corporation*. New York: Norton.

Næss, Arne. 1973. "The Shallow and the Deep, Long-Range Ecology Movement." *Inquiry* 16: 95–100.

Nasaw, Davis. 2006. *Andrew Carnegie*. New York: Penguin.

Naszályi, Philippe. 2017. "Gouverner, c'est prévoir!" *La Revue des Sciences de Gestion* 283 (1): 1–2.

Nell-Breuning, Oswald von. 1928. *Grundzüge der Börsenmoral*. (Studien zur Katholischen Sozial- und Wirtschaftsethik 4) Freiburg i.Br.: Herder.

Neuloh, Otto. 1956. *Die deutsche Betriebsverfassung und ihr Sozialformen bis zur Mitbestimmung*. Tübingen: Mohr.

New York Times. 1976. "Shockwaves in Japan." *New York Times*, July 28, p. 23.

Newman, John Henry. 1873. *The Idea of a University, Defined and Illustrated*. London: Pickering.

Newman, William H. 1951. *Administrative Action*. Englewood Cliffs, NJ: Prentice-Hall (5th edition retitled *The Process of Management*. Englewood Cliffs, NJ: Prentice-Hall, 1982).

Niebuhr, Reinhold. 1932. *Moral Man and Immoral Society*. New York: Charles Scribner's Sons.

Nietzsche, Friedrich. 1967 [1886]. *Beyond Good and Evil: Prelude to a Philosophy of the Future*, translated by Helen Zimmern. London: Allen & Unwin.

Nietzsche, Friedrich. 1974 [1882]. *The Gay Science: With a Prelude in Rhymes and an Appendix of Songs*, translated by Walter Kaufmann. New York: Random House.

Nietzsche, Friedrich. 2013 [1887]. *On the Genealogy of Morals*, translated by Michael A. Scarpitti. London: Penguin.

Noble, Kenneth B. 1982. "The Dispute Over the S.E.C." *New York Times*, April 21.

Northcott, Clarence Hunter. 1958. *Christian Principles in Industry: Their Application in Practice*. London: Pitman.

Novak, Michael. 1982. *The Spirit of Democratic Capitalism*. New York: Simon & Schuster.

Nyland, Chris. 1998. "Taylorism and the Mutual-Gains Strategy." *Industrial Relations* 37 (4): 519–42.

Nyland, Chris, Kyle Bruce and Prue Burns. 2014. "Taylorism, the International Labour Organization, and the genesis and diffusion of codetermination." *Organization Studies* 35: 1149–69

O'Hara, James B. 1988. "The Modern Corporation Sole." *Dickinson Law Review* 93: 23–39.

O'Reilly, Charles A., III, Jennifer Chatman, and David F. Caldwell. 1991. "People and Organizational Culture: A Profile Comparison Approach to Person-Organization Fit." *Academy of Management Journal* 34 (3): 487–516.

OECD. 1999. *OECD Principles of Corporate Governance*. Paris: OECD.

Ohmann, Oliver A. 1955. "'Skyhooks': With Special Implications for Monday Through Friday." *Harvard Business Review* 33 (3): 33–41.

Otto, Berthold. 1931. *Moral und Wirtschaft*. Berlin-Lichterfelde: Verlag des Hauslehrers.

Otto, Rudolf. 1917. *Das Heilige: Über das Irrationale in der Idee des Göttlichen und sein Verhältnis zum Rationalen*. Breslau: Trewendt & Granier.

Owen, Robert. 1813. *A New View of Society; Or, Essays on the Principle of the Formation of the Human Character and the Application of the Principle to Practice*. London: Taylor & Co.

Page, Edward D. 1914. *Trade Morals: Their Origin, Growth and Province*. New Haven: Yale University Press.

Palmieri, Victor H. 1978. "Officers of the Board?" *Wall Street Journal*, August 14, p. 12.

Park, Chris C. 1989. *Chernobyl: The Long Shadow*. London: Routledge.

Parker, Edwin B. 1924. "The Fifteen Commandments of Business." *Nation's Business*, June 5, p. 16.

Parker, Martin. 2002. *Against Management: Organization in the Age of Managerialism*. Cambridge: Polity Press.

Parker, Martin. 2018. *Shut Down the Business School: What's Wrong with Management Education*. London: Pluto Press.

Patmore, Greg. 2016. *Worker Voice: Employee Representation in the Workplace in Australia, Canada, Germany, the UK and the US 1914–1939*. Liverpool: Liverpool University Press.

Payne, Peter L. 1967. "The Emergence of the Large-Scale Company in Great Britain, 1870–1914." *The Economic History Review* n.s. 20 (3): 519–42.

Percival, Thomas. 1803. *Medical Ethics Or, A Code of Institutes and Precepts Adapted to the Professional Conduct of Physicians and Surgeons*. Manchester: Johnson.

Peters, Jaap F. M. 1997. *Corporate Governance in the Netherlands: Forty Recommendations*. Amsterdam: Committee on Corporate Governance.

Pfeffer, Jeremy. 1981. "Management as Symbolic Action." In *Research in Organizational Behaviour, Volume III*, edited by Larry L. Cummings and Barry M. Staw, 1–52. Greenwich, CT: JAI Press.

Piaget, Jean. 1948 [1932]. *The Moral Judgment of the Child*, translated by Marjorie Gabain. Glencoe: Free Press.

Pieper, Josef. 1966. *The Four Cardinal Virtues: Prudence, Justice, Fortitude, Temperance*. Notre Dame, IN: University of Notre Dame Press.

Pierson, Frank C., and others. 1959. *The Education of American Businessmen: A Study of University-College Programmes in Business Administration*. New York: McGraw-Hill.

Pinderhughes, Raquel. 2006. "Green Collar Jobs: Work Force Opportunities in the Growing Green Economy." *Race, Poverty & the Environment* 13 (1): 62–3.

Piper, John F., Jr. 1969. "The Formation of the Social Policy of the Federal Council of Churches." *Journal of Church and State* 11: 63–5.

Pius XI. 1931. *Encyclical Letter (Quadragesimo anno) of His Holiness Pius XI, by Divine Providence Pope: On Reconstructing the Social Order and Perfecting It Conformably to the Precepts of the Gospel in Commemoration of the Fortieth Anniversary of the Encyclical Rerum Novarum*. Melbourne: Australian Catholic Truth Society.

Pius XII. 1949. "An Address to Catholic Employers." *Relations industrielles/Industrial Relations* 4 (9): 81–3.

Plato. 1992. *The Republic,* translated by George M.A. Grube. 2nd ed. Indianapolis, IA: Hackett.

Platt, James. 1875. *Business.* London: Simpkin, Marshall & Co.

Plesser, Ernst H. 1975. "Verhaltenskodizes für Unternehmensleiter." *Zeitschrift für Organisation* 44 (3): 121–5.

Plesser, Ernst H. 1977. "Leben zwischen Wille und Wirklichkeit." In *Leben zwischen Wille und Wirklichkeit: Unternehmer im Spannungsfeld von Gewinn und Ethik,* edited by Ernst H. Plesser, 9–67. Düsseldorf: Econ.

Pocock, Charles C. 1978. *More Jobs: A Small Cure for a Big Problem.* London: Ashridge.

Polanyi, Karl. 1957 [1944]. *The Great Transformation: The Political and Economic Origins of Our Time.* Boston: Beacon.

Pontifical Council for Justice and Peace. 2012. *The Vocation of the Business Leader: A Reflection.* Vatican City: Pontifical Council for Justice and Peace.

Porter, Michael E. 1991. "America's Green Strategy." *Scientific American,* April, p. 168.

Porter, Michael, and Mark R. Kramer. 2006. "Strategy and Society: The Link Between Competitive Advantage and Corporate Social Responsibility." *Harvard Business Review* 84 (12): 78–92.

Porter, Michael E., and Claas van der Linde. 1995. "Green and Competitive: Ending the Stalemate." *Harvard Business Review* 73 (5): 120–34.

Prichard, Alex. 2013. *Justice, Order and Anarchy: The International Political Theory of Pierre-Joseph Proudhon.* London: Routledge.

Proudhon, Pierre-Joseph. 1857 [1853]. *Manuel du spéculateur à la bourse.* 5th ed. Paris: Garnier.

Proudhon, Pierre-Joseph. 1993 [1840]. *What Is Property?,* edited and translated by Donald R. Kelley and Bonnie G. Smith. Cambridge: Cambridge University Press.

Pullen, Alison, and Carl Rhodes, eds. 2015. *The Routledge Companion to Ethics, Politics and Organizations.* London: Routledge.

Rafferty, Oliver P. 2014. "The Thomistic Revival and the Relationship Between the Jesuits and the Papacy, 1878–1914." *Theological Studies* 75 (4): 746–73.

Randall, Clarence B. 1952. *A Creed for Free Enterprise.* Boston: Little, Brown, and Co.

Rauschenbusch, Walter. 1907. *Christianity and the Social Crisis.* New York: Palgrave Macmillan.

Rawls, John. 1963. "The Sense of Justice." *Philosophical Review* 72 (3): 281–305.

Rawls, John. 1971. *A Theory of Justice.* Cambridge, MA: Belknap.

Read, Alfred. 1953. *The Company Director: His Functions, Powers and Duties.* London: Jordan.

Rest, James R. 1994. "Background: Theory and Research." In *Moral Development in the Professions: Psychology and Applied Ethics,* edited by James Rest and Darcia Narvaez, 1–26. Hillsdale, NJ: Erlbaum.

Rest, James R., Darcia Narvaez, Stephen J. Thoma, and Muriel J. Bebeau. 2000. "A Neo-Kohlbergian Approach to Morality Research." *Journal of Moral Education* 29 (4): 381–95.

Reynolds, Scott J., and Norman E. Bowie. 2004. "A Kantian Perspective on the Characteristics of Ethics Programs." *Business Ethics Quarterly* 14 (2): 275–92.

Rhoads, Charles. 1882. *Business Ethics in Relation to the Profession of the Religious Society of Friends: An Address Delivered Before the Friends' Institute for Young Men, of Philadelphia, Second Month 9th, 1882*. Philadelphia: n.p.

Rhodes, Carl. 2016. "Democratic Business Ethics: Volkswagen's Emissions Scandal and the Disruption of Corporate Sovereignty." *Organization Studies* 37 (10): 1501–18.

Rhodes, Carl, and Edward Wray-Bliss. 2013. "The Ethical Difference of Organization." *Organization* 20 (1): 39–50.

Robbins Lionel. 1952. *The Theory of Economic Policy in English Classical Political Economy*. London: Macmillan.

Robinson, Lynn D. 2002. "Doing Good and Doing Well: Shareholder Activism, Responsible Investment and Mainline Protestantism." In *The Quiet Hand of God: Faith-based Activism and the Public Role of Mainline Protestantism*, edited by Robert Wuthnow and John H. Evans, 343–63. Berkeley: University of California Press.

Rockefeller, John D., Sr. 1909. *Random Reminiscences of Men and Events*. New York: Doubleday, Page & Co.

Rockefeller, John D., Jr. 1924 [1917]. *The Personal Relation in Industry*. New York: Boni and Liveright.

Roethlisberger, Fritz J. 1942. *Management and Morale*. Cambridge, MA: Harvard University Press.

Rome, Adam. 2013. *The Genius of Earth Day: How a 1970 Teach-In Unexpectedly Made the First Green Generation*. New York: Hill and Wang.

Rosemberg, Anabella. 2010. "Building a Just Transition: The Linkages Between Climate Change and Employment." *International Journal of Labour Research* 2 (2): 125–62.

Ross, Stephen A. 1973. "The Economic Theory of Agency: The Principal's Problem." *American Economic Review* 62 (2): 134–9.

Rotary. 1918. *Proceedings of the Ninth Annual Convention of the International Association of Rotary Clubs*. Chicago: Rotary.

Roth, Günther. 1979. "Corporate Social Responsibility—European Models." *Hastings Law Journal* 30 (5): 1433–62.

Rothman, David J. 1971. *The Discovery of the Asylum: Social Order and Disorder in the New Republic*. Boston: Little, Brown and Co.

Rousseau, Jean-Jacques. 1986 [1762]. *The Social Contract; and, Discourses*, translated by George D.H. Cole. London: Dent.

Rowlinson, Michael, and John Hassard. 1993. "The Invention of Corporate Culture: A History of the Histories of Cadbury." *Human Relations* 46 (3): 299–326.

Royal Dutch/Shell. 1998. *Profit and Principles: Does There Have to Be a Choice?* London: Royal Dutch/Shell.

Ruder, David S. 1979. "Corporate Governance: An Analysis of Duties, Attacks and Responses." *Delaware Journal of Corporate Law* 4: 741–59.

Ruder, David S. 1981. "Current Issues Between Corporations and Shareholders: Private Sector Responses to Proposals for Federal Intervention Into Corporate Governance." *The Business Lawyer* 36: 71–82.

Ruggie, John Gerard. 2002. "The Theory and Practice of Learning Networks: Corporate Social Responsibility and the Global Compact." *Journal of Corporate Citizenship* 5 (Spring): 27–36.

Sacks, Daniel. 2009. *Moral Re-Armament: The Reinventions of an American Religious Movement*. New York: Palgrave Macmillan.

Saint-Simon, Henri de. 1821. *Du système industriel*. Paris: Renouard.

Saint-Simon, Henri de. 1834 [1825]. *New Christianity*, translated by J.E. Smith. London: Cousins & Wilson.

Sanderson, Michael. 1972. *The Universities and British Industry 1850–1970*. London: Routledge & Kegan Paul.

Santoro, Michael A., and Ronald J. Strauss. 2013. *Wall Street Values: Business Ethics and the Global Financial Crisis*. New York: Cambridge University Press.

Sauvant, Karl P. 2015. "The Negotiations of the United Nations Code of Conduct on Transnational Corporations: Experience and Lessons Learned." *Journal of World Investment and Trade* 16: 11–87.

Sawyer, James S. 1972. "Man-Made Carbon Dioxide and the 'Greenhouse' Effect." *Nature* 239: 23–6.

Schein, Edgar C. 1985. *Organizational Culture and Leadership*. San Francisco: Jossey Bass.

Schilling, Otto. 1933. *Katholische Wirtschaftethik: Nach den Richtlinien der Enzyklika Quadragesimo Anno des Papstes Pius XI*. Munich: Hueber.

Schmidheiny, Stephen. 1992. *Changing Course: A Global Business Perspective on Development and the Environment*. Cambridge, MA: MIT Press.

Schoen, Edward J. 2017. "The 2007–2009 Financial Crisis: An Erosion of Ethics: A Case Study." *Journal of Business Ethics* 146: 805–30.

Schrager, Laura Shill, and James F. Short. 1978. "Toward a Sociology of Organizational Crime." *Social Problems* 25 (4): 407–19.

Schroder, Klaus T. 1978. *Soziale Verantwortung in der Fuhrung der Unternehmung*. Berlin: Duncker & Humblot.

Schutte, Thomas F. 1965. "Executives' Perceptions of Business Ethics." *Journal of Purchasing* 1 (1): 38–52.

Schwab, Klaus. 1971. *Moderne Unternehmensführung im Maschinenbau*. Frankfurt a.M.: VDMA.

Schwab, Klaus. 2009. *The World Economic Forum: A Partner in Shaping History: The First 40 Years, 1971–2010*. Geneva: World Economic Forum.

Schwab, Stewart J., and Randall S. Thomas. 1998. "Realigning Corporate Governance: Shareholder Activism by Labor Unions." *University of Michigan Law Review* 96: 1018–94.

Schwartz, Donald E. 1976. "A Case for Federal Chartering of Corporations." *The Business Lawyer* 31: 1125–59.

Schwartz, Justin. 2001. "Rights of Inequality: Rawlsian Justice, Equal Opportunity, and the Status of the Family." *Legal Theory* 7 (1): 83–117.

Scott, Kenneth E. 1983. "Corporation Law and the American Law Institute Corporate Governance Project." *Stanford Law Review* 35: 927–48.

Scott, Walter D. 1912. *Increasing Human Efficiency in Business: A Contribution to the Psychology of Business*. New York: Palgrave Macmillan.

Securities and Exchange Commission. 1977. *43rd Annual Report*. Washington, DC: U.S. Govt. Printing Office.

Seipel, Ignaz. 1907. *Die wirtschaftsethischen Lehren der Kirchenväter*. Vienna: von Mayer.

Selekman, Benjamin M. 1959. *A Moral Philosophy for Business*. New York: McGraw-Hill.

Seligman, Joel. 1987. "A Sheep in Wolf's Clothing: The American Law Institute Principles of Corporate Governance Project." *George Washington Law Review* 55: 325–82.

Seligman, Joel. 2003. *The Transformation of Wall Street: A History of the Securities and Exchange Commission and Modern Corporate Finance*. 3rd ed. New York: Aspen.

Sethi, Prakash S. 1975. "Dimensions of Corporate Social Performance: An Analytic Framework." *California Management Review* 17: 58–64.

Shackleton, John Richard. 1998. "Industrial Relations Reform in Britain Since 1979." *Journal of Labor Research* 19 (3): 581–605.

Sharp, Frank Chapman, and Phillip D. Fox. 1937. *Business Ethics: Studies in Fair Competition*. New York: Appleton-Century.

Shaw, Albert. 1904. *The Business Career in Its Public Relations*. San Francisco: Elder.

Shepherd, Alice, and Steve Toms. 2019. "Entrepreneurship, Strategy and Business Philanthropy: Cotton Textile Factory Regulation in the British Industrial Revolution." *Business History Review*, 93 (3): 502–27.

Shields, Leo W. 1941. *The History and Meaning of the Term Social Justice*. Dissertation, Notre Dame, Indiana.

Shrivastava, Paul. 1992. *Bhopal: Anatomy of a Crisis*. 2nd ed. London: Chapman.

Simon, William E. 1976. "A Challenge to Free Enterprise." In *The Ethical Basis of Economic Freedom*, edited by Ivan Hill, 405–18. Chapel Hill, NC: American Viewpoint.

Small, Marshall L. 1979. "The Evolving Role of the Director in Corporate Governance." *Hastings Law Journal* 30: 1353–403.

Smith, Adam. 1904 [1776]. *An Inquiry Into the Nature and Causes of the Wealth of Nations*. London: Methuen.

Smith, Adam. 2002 [1759]. *The Theory of Moral Sentiments*. Cambridge: Cambridge University Press.

Smith, Andrew, Kevin Tennant, and Jason Russell. 2019. "Berle and Means's the Modern Corporation and Private Property: The Military Roots of a Stakeholder Model of Corporate Governance." *Seattle University Law Review* 42 (2): 535–64.

Smith, J. Andy, III. 1993. "The CERES Principles: A Voluntary Code for Corporate Environmental Responsibility." *Yale Journal of International Law* 18 (1): 307–17.

Smith, John William. 1843. *A Compendium of Mercantile Law*. 3rd ed. London: Saunders and Benning.

Sobel, Robert. 1977. *The Fallen Colossus: The Great Crash of the Penn Central*. New York: Weybright & Talley.

Sohm, Rudolf. 1888. *Kirchengeschichte im Grundriss*. Leipzig: Böhme.

Sokal, Michael M. 1984. "James McKeen Cattell and American Psychology in the 1920s." In *Explorations in the History of Psychology in the United States*, edited by Josef Brožek, 273–323. Lewisburg, PA: Bucknell University Press.

Solberg, Winton U., and Robert W. Tomlinson. 1997. "Academic McCarthyism and Keynesian. Economics: The Bowen Controversy at the University of Illinois." *History of Political Economy* 29 (1): 55–81.

Solomon, Lewis D., and Leslie G. Linville. 1976. "Transnational Conduct of American Multinational Corporations: Questionable Payments Abroad." *Boston College Law Review* 17: 303–44.

Soskis, Benjamin J. 2010. *The Problem of Charity in Industrial America, 1873–1915*. Dissertation, Columbia University.

Spencer, Herbert. 1893. *Negative Beneficence and Positive Beneficence*. New York: Appleton.

Spira, Laura F., and Judy Slinn. 2013. *The Cadbury Committee: A History*. Oxford: Oxford University Press.

Sporn, Philip, Leon E. Hickman, and Luther H. Hodges, eds. 1963. *The Ethics of Business: Corporate Behavior in the Market Place. A Symposium Conducted at the Columbia Graduate School of Business*. New York: Columbia Graduate School of Business.

Starkey, Ken. 1998. "Durkheim and the Limits of Corporate Culture." *Journal of Management* 35 (2): 125–36.

Staudiger, Franz. 1907. *Wirtschaftliche Grundlagen der Moral*. Darmstadt: Roether.

Steiner, George A. 1971. *Business and Society*. New York: Random House.

Steiner, George A. 1973. *Issues in Business and Society*. New York: Random House.

Steinmann, Horst. 1973. "Zur Lehre von der 'gesellschaftlichen Verantwortung der Unternehmensfuehrung'—zugleich eine Kritik des Davoser Manifest." *Wirtschaftswissenschaftliches Studium* 2 (10): 467–73.

Stern, Nicholas. 2007 [2006]. *The Economics of Climate Change*. Cambridge: Cambridge University Press.

Stevens, Betsy. 2008. "Corporate Ethical Codes: Effective Instruments for Influencing Behaviour." *Journal of Business Ethics* 78 (4): 601–9.

Stevens, Tina M.L. 2000. *Bioethics in America: Origins and Cultural Politics*. Baltimore, MD: Johns Hopkins University Press.

Stevens, William D., ed. 1962. *The Social Responsibilities of Marketing: Proceedings of the Winter Conference of the American Marketing Association*. Chicago: American Marketing Association.

Stiglitz, Joseph. 2010. *Freefall: Free Markets and the Sinking of the Global Economy*. New York: Penguin.

Stogdill, Ralph M., and Bernard Bass. 1981. *Stogdill's Handbook of Leadership: A Survey of Theory and Research*. New York: Free Press.

Stogdill, Ralph M., and Carroll L. Shartle. 1948. "Methods for Determining Patterns of Leadership Behavior in Relation to Organization Structure and Objectives." *Journal of Applied Psychology* 32: 286–91.

Stogdill, Ralph M., Robert J. Wherry, and William E. Jaynes. 1953. *Patterns of Leader Behavior: A Factorial Study of Navy Officer Performance*. Columbus: Ohio State University Research Foundation.

Stoner, Charles R. 1989. "The Foundation of Business Ethics: Exploring the Relationship Between Organization Culture, Moral Values, and Actions." *SAM Advanced Management Journal* 54 (3): 38–43.

Stradling, David. 1999. *Smokestacks and Progressives: Environmentalists, Engineers, and Air Quality in America, 1881–1951*. Baltimore, MD: Johns Hopkins University Press.

Strauss, David F. 1846 [1835]. *The Life of Jesus, Critically Examined*, translated by George Elliot. 3 vols. London: Chapman, Brothers.

Sutherland, Edwin. 1949. *White Collar Crime*. New York: Holt, Rinehart & Winston.

Sutton, Francis X., Seymour Edwin Harris, Carl Kaysen, and James Tobin. 1956. *The American Business Creed*. Cambridge, MA: Harvard University Press.

Sylla, Richard, and Robert E. Wright. 2013. "Corporation Formation in the Antebellum United States in Comparative Context." *Business History* 55 (4): 653–69.

Taeusch, Carl F. 1926. *Professional and Business Ethics*. New York: Holt.

Taeusch, Carl F. 1931. *Policy and Ethics in Business*. New York: McGraw-Hill.

Taeusch, Carl F. 1932. "Business Ethics." *International Journal of Ethics* 42 (3): 273–88.

Taeusch, Carl F. 1935. "The Relation Between Legal Ethics and Business Ethics." *California Law Review* 24: 79–95.

Tangley, Lord. 1961. *Standard Boardroom Practice*. London: Institute of Directors.

Tannenbaum, Jeffrey A. 1983. "Business Bulletin." *Wall Street Journal*, May 5, p. 1.

Taparelli d'Azeglio, Luigi. 1841–43. *Saggio teoretico di dritto naturale appoggiato sul fatto*. 5 vols. Palermo: Muratori.

Tarbell, Ida. 1904. *The History of the Standard Oil Company*. New York: McClure, Phillips & Co.

Tautscher, Anton. 1957. *Wirtschaftsethik* (Handbuch der Moraltheologie 11). Munich: Max Hueber.

Tawney, Richard H. 1921. *The Acquisitive Society*. London: Bell & Sons.

Tawney, Richard H. 1926. *Religion and the Rise of Capitalism: A Historical Study*. London: Murray.

Taylor, Frederick W. 1911. *The Principles of Scientific Management*. New York: Harper.

Thau, Theodore L. 1962. "The Business Ethics Advisory Council: An Organization for the Improvement of Ethical Performance." *Annals of the American Academy of Political and Social Science* 343: 128–41.

Thompson, Edward P. 1971. "The Moral Economy of the English Crowd in the Eighteenth Century." *Past & Present* 50: 76–136.

Thompson, Stewart. 1958. *Management Creeds and Philosophies*. New York: American Management Association.

Tönnies, Ferdinand. 1931. *Einführung in die Soziologie*. Stuttgart: Enke.

Toulmin, Stephen E. 1950. *An Examination of the Place of Reason in Ethics*. Cambridge: Cambridge University Press.

Towle, Joseph W. 1964. *Ethics in Standards in American Business*. Boston: Houghton Mifflin.

Treviño, Linda K. 1986. "Ethical Decision Making in Organizations: A Person-Situation Interactionist Model." *Academy of Management Review* 11 (3): 601–11.

Treviño, Linda K., Laura P. Hartman, and Michael Brown. 2000. "Moral Person and Moral Manager: How Executives Develop a Reputation for Ethical Leadership." *California Management Review* 42 (4): 128–42.

Treviño, Linda K., and Gary Weaver. 2003. *Managing Ethics in Business Organizations: Social Sciences Perspectives*. Stanford: Stanford University Press.

Treviño, Linda K., and Stuart A. Youngblood. 1990. "Bad Apples in Bad Barrels: A Causal Analysis of Ethical Decision-Making Behaviour." *Journal of Applied Psychology* 75 (4): 378–85.

Tricker, Robert I. 1984. *Corporate Governance: Practices, Procedures, and Powers in British Companies and Their Boards of Directors*. Aldershot: Gower.

Trompenaars, Fons. 1993. *Riding the Waves of Culture*. London: Brealey.

Truell, Peter, and Larry Gurwin. 1992. *False Profits: The Inside Story of BCCI, the World's Most Corrupt Financial Empire*. Boston: Houghton Mifflin.

Turner, John D. 2017. "The Development of English Company Law Before 1900." In *Research Handbook on the History of Corporate and Company Law*, edited by Harwell Wells, 121–41. Cheltenham: Elgar.

United Nations. 1972. *Declaration of the United Nations Conference on the Human Environment, Stockholm, 16 June 1972*. New York: United Nations.

United Nations Global Compact. 2007. *The Global Compact Leaders Summit 2007. Facing Realities: Getting Down to Business, Palais des Nations, Geneva, 5–6 July 2007*. New York: United Nations Global Compact.

United Nations Global Compact. 2008. *A Global Initiative, A Global Agenda, Principles for Responsible Management Education*. New York: United Nations Global Compact.

Van Dam, Cees, and Luud M. Stallaert, eds. 1978. *Trends in Business Ethics: Implications for Decision-making*. Leiden: Nijhoff.

Van Luick, Henk J.L. 1990. "Recent Developments in European Business Ethics." *Journal of Business Ethics* 9 (7): 537–44.

Vienot, Marc. 1995. *Le conseil d'administration des sociétés cotées*. Paris: Association française des entreprises privées and Conseil national du patronat français.

Viganò, Eleonora. 2017. "Not Just an Inferior Virtue, nor Self-Interest: Adam Smith on Prudence." *Journal of Scottish Philosophy* 15: 125–43.

Visser 'T Hooft, Willem A., ed. 1949. *The First Assembly of the World Council of Churches*. New York: Harper & Brothers.

Wall St Journal. 1980. "The Boardroom as Legislature." *Wall Street Journal*, May 12, p. 26.

Walton, Clarence. 1967. *Corporate Social Responsibilities*. Belmont, CA: Wadsworth.

Walton, Clarence, and Frederick W. Cleveland. 1963. *Corporations on Trial: The Electric Cases*. Belmont, CA: Wadsworth.

Ward, Harry F. 1914. *The Social Creed of the Churches*. New York: Abingdon Press.

Warren, Kenneth. 2001. *Big Steel: The First Century of the United States Steel Corporation, 1901–2001*. Pittsburgh: University of Pittsburgh Press.

Watson, John H., III. 1953. *The Corporate Directorship* (Studies in Business Policy 63). New York: National Industrial Conference Board.

Weatherburn, Michael. 2019. "Human Relations' Invented Traditions: Sociotechnical Research and Worker Motivation at the Interwar Rowntree Cocoa Works." *Human Relations*. https://doi.org/10.1177/0018726719846647

Weaver, Gary R. and Linda K. Treviño. 1999. "Compliance and Values Oriented Ethics Programs." *Business Ethics Quarterly* 9: 315–335.

Webb, Sidney, and Beatrice Webb. 1897. *Industrial Democracy*. 2 vols. London: Longmans, Green.

Webb, Sidney, and Beatrice Webb. 1920. *The History of Trade Unionism*. London: Longmans, Green.

Weber, Max. 1930 [1904/5]. *The Protestant Ethic and the Spirit of Capitalism*, translated by Talcott Parsons. New York: Scribner.

Weber, Max. 1978 [1922]. *Economy and Society*, translated by Ephraim Fischoff et al. Berkeley: University of California Press.

Weber, Max. 1993 [1920]. *Sociology of Religion*, translated by Ephraim Fischoff. Boston: Beacon Press.

Weber, Max. 2008 [1908]. "The Bernhard Case." In *Max Weber's Complete Writings on Academic and Political Vocations*, translated by Gordon C. Wells, 53–8. New York: Algora.

Webley, Simon. 1971. *British Businessman's Behaviour*. London: Industrial Educational and Research Foundation.

Webley, Simon. 1972. *Towards a Code of Business Ethics*. London: Christian Association of Business Executives.

Webley, Simon. 1973. "Business Policy and Business Ethics." *Journal of Business Policy* 3 (3): 3–10.

Webley, Simon. 1974. *Corporate Social Responsibility: Report on a Survey Conducted on Behalf of the Public Relations Consultants Association*. London: Public Relations Consultants Association.

Wedderburn of Charlton, Lord. 1984. "The Legal Development of Corporate Responsibility: For Whom Will Corporate Managers Be Trustees?" In *Corporate Governance and Directors' Liabilities: Legal, Economic, and Sociological Analyses on Corporate Social Responsibility*, edited by Klaus J. Hopt and Gunther Teubner, 3–54. Berlin: De Gruyter.

Weddigen, Walter. 1951. *Wirtschaftsethik: System humanitärer Wirtschaftsmoral*. Berlin: Duncker & Humblot.

Weitzig, Joachim K. 1979. *Gesellschaftsorientierte Unternehmenspolitik und Unternehmensverfassung*. Berlin: De Gruyter.

Welford, Richard. 1997. "Introduction: What Are We Doing to the World?" In *Hijacking Environmentalism: Corporate Responses to Sustainable Development*, edited by Richard Welford, 3–17. London: Earthscan.

Wells, C.A. Harwell. 2002. "The Cycles of Corporate Social Responsibility: An Historical Retrospective for the Twenty-First Century." *University of Kansas Law Review* 51 (1): 77–140.

Wesley, John. 1768. *The Good Steward*. London: n.p.

Whewell, William. 1872. "Introduction." In *On the Progress of Ethical Philosophy*, edited by James Mackintosh. 4th ed. Edinburgh: Black.

White, Lynn. 1967. "The Historical Roots of Our Ecological Crisis." *Science* 155: 1203–7.

Whyte, Max. 2008. "The Uses and Abuses of Nietzsche in the Third Reich: Alfred Baeumler's 'Heroic Realism'." *Journal of Contemporary History* 43 (2): 171–94.

Williamson, Adrian. 2016. "The Bullock Report on Industrial Democracy and the Post-war Consensus." *Contemporary British History* 30 (1): 119–49.

Willis, Alan. 2003. "The Role of the Global Reporting Initiative's Sustainability Reporting Guidelines in the Social Screening of Investments." *Journal of Business Ethics* 43 (3): 233–7.

Wilson, H. Hubert. 1951. "Techniques of Pressure-Anti-Nationalization Propaganda in Britain." *The Public Opinion Quarterly* 15: 225–42

Windolph, Sarah Elena, Dorli Harms, and Stefan Schaltegger. 2013. "Motivations for Corporate Sustainability Management: Contrasting Survey Results and Implementation." *Corporate Social Responsibility and Environmental Management* 21 (5): 272–85.

Winerman, Marc. 2003. "The Origins of the FTC: Concentration, Cooperation, Control, and Competition." *Antitrust Law Journal* 71 (1): 1–97.

Woermann, Minka. 2012. *On the (Im)Possibility of Business Ethics: Critical Complexity, Deconstruction, and Implications for Understanding the Ethics of Business*. Dordrecht: Springer.

Working Group on Corporate Governance. 1991. "New Compact for Owners and Directors." *Harvard Business Review* 69 (4): 141–3.

Wrege, Charles D., and Anne Marie Stotka. 1978. "Cooke Creates a Classic: The Story Behind F.W. Taylor's Principles of Scientific Management." *Academy of Management Review* 73 (4): 736–49.

Wren, Daniel A., and Arthur G. Bedeian. 2009. *The Evolution of Management Thought*. 6th ed. Hoboken, NJ: Wiley.

Wright, Christopher, Daniel Nyberg, and David Grant. 2012. "'Hippies on the Third Floor': Climate Change, Narrative Identity and the Micro-Politics of Corporate Environmentalism." *Organization Studies* 33 (11): 1451–75.

Wünsch, Georg. 1927. *Evangelische Wirtschaftsethik*. Tübingen: Mohr.

Young, Stephen B., and Frank Straub. 2006. "The Caux Round Table: Taking CSR From Aspiration to Action 385." In *The ICCA Handbook on Corporate Social Responsibility*, edited by Judith Hennigfeld, Manfred Pohl, and Nick Tolhurst, 385–99. Chichester: Wiley.

Zsolnai, Laszlo. 2011. "Environmental Ethics for Business Sustainability." *International Journal of Social Economics* 38 (11): 892–9.

Index